The Handbook of Coaching

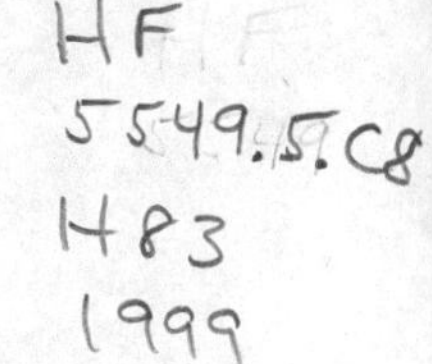

The Handbook of Coaching

A Comprehensive Resource Guide for Managers, Executives, Consultants, and Human Resource Professionals

Frederic M. Hudson, Ph.D.

Jossey-Bass Publishers
San Francisco

Jossey-Bass books and products are available through most bookstores. To contact Jossey-Bass directly, call (888) 378-2537, fax to (800) 605-2665, or visit our website at www.josseybass.com.

Manufactured in the United States of America on Lyons Falls Turin Book. This paper is acid-free and 100 percent totally chlorine-free.

Library of Congress Cataloging-in-Publication Data

Hudson, Frederic M., date.
The handbook of coaching: a comprehensive resource guide for managers, executives, consultants, and human resource professionals/Frederic M. Hudson.—1st ed.
p. cm.
Includes bibliographical references and index.
ISBN 0-7879-4795-4
1. Employees—Counseling of. 2. Personnel management. 3. Mentoring in business. I. Title.

HF5549.5.C8 H83 1999
658.3'124—dc21 99-6304

FIRST EDITION
HC Printing
10 9 8 7 6 5 4 3 2 1

CONTENTS

This book is dedicated to the coaches and mentors
who helped me find the paths ahead:

My grandfather, Marshall "Pop" Hudson
My nurse Susan, when I had polio
Human Kuffs, YMCA leader and trusted friend
George Earnshaw, camp counselor and guide
Miss Anderson, eleventh-grade English teacher
Dr. L. J. Hemmes, college philosophy teacher
T. William Hall, philosophy department chair
Gertrude Patch, college president
Robert Goulding, mentor and trainer
Larry Mousouris, tennis coach

PREFACE

I wrote this book about coaching because I see the new profession of adult coaching as a partial remedy for the cultural crisis we are undergoing today—a crisis due, in part, to our bewilderment over changes in the rules that govern our lives. Many rules we had counted on to keep us on a steady course in life no longer apply. Here are four:

- The *linear rule,* which promised progress if we were honest and worked hard. According to this rule, our lives, careers, economy, and culture would get better and better, year by year, generation by generation if we simply did our best.
- The *steady-state rule,* which said that if we worked hard, we would each arrive at a steady state, or plateau, of security and happiness, which would last for the rest of our lives.
- The *outside-in rule,* which said that our personal lives are defined and determined by the directives of the society around us. To be winners, we should simply follow the cues in our marriage, schools, religious organizations, careers, and laws of the land.
- The *learning rule,* which said that learning is for kids. They learn so they can get launched into adult careers, family life, and leadership roles. Adults shift from learning to working as their main activity and, for the rest of their lives, training outside the workplace plays a minor role.

Ever so gradually during the past forty years, the breakdown in the effectiveness of the old rules led us to a sense of decline and discouragement. Those rules could only work in a culture high in continuity, control, and agreed-upon authority. As the culture gradually changed and the rules stopped working, we began to feel that something was wrong with us. We felt frustrated and helpless. We still do.

THE NEW RULES

So how does coaching offer hope for people who labor under the old rules? It does so by teaching people new rules—to change their expectations, to free themselves and enjoy their own strength.

Four of the new rules are

- The *cyclical rule,* which better describes our lives today than the linear rule. We each live a chapter, then renew ourselves and move on to the next; we cycle through the chapters, followed by transitions. Coaches teach clients to manage change; they teach the art of cycling through, of practicing self-renewal.
- The *continuous change rule,* which will not let us rest. We can no longer expect to arrive at a steady state, a time when our lives become crystallized and predictable. Coaches show clients how to manage ongoing change and not be afraid or defeated by it.
- The *inside-out rule,* which says that, to stay on course, we must rely most deeply on our own inner beliefs. Coaches teach clients to be on-purpose people who shape their own actions in a rapidly changing world with the strength of their positive thoughts about how they want to be in the world.
- The *learning-is-for-everyone rule,* which says that learning is our primary activity, no matter how young or old we are. Coaches help adults acquire skills, change professions, and do well in a social milieu that often appears as blurry chaos.

THE COACHING FIELD

Adult coaching is a new career area. Whether it will become a stand-alone profession—as psychiatry, dentistry, and economics stand alone as professions—has yet to be decided. At the moment, coaching can be considered a skill set, based on the principles of developmental psychology (that facilitates renewal and resilience in adults of all ages), and of human systems thinking (that informs people how to manage roles, technological change, and social turbulence). It can also be a catalytic resource for freeing up organizations and community groups to manage change and performance with renewed optimism and enthusiasm. For now, coaching is a calling and a source of income for a great many people who often combine coaching with consulting, leading, managing, and other professional roles.

The term *coach* is used, in this book and in the profession, the way it's used in athletics. A coach both guides and mentors. In this new field, a coach helps a client see options for becoming a more effective human being. The appeal of the profession is in the satisfaction good coaches take in seeing their clients discard the old, fixed, constricting rules and begin to follow new rules that give them the strength to thrive in whatever situation they find themselves.

Coaching has been applied effectively to corporate settings, with such applications as executive coaching, team coaching, conflict management, training, and life-work balance coaching.

PURPOSE AND AUDIENCE

The purpose of this *Handbook* is to introduce aspiring and novice coaches to the full scope of the field and to provide seasoned coaches with in-depth information about the field and its theoretical underpinnings. The resources to be found here provide a basis for getting acquainted with the extant research and for making further contributions to the literature. Readers will also learn how they can make contact with practitioners in the field.

Specifically, the *Handbook* was written for

- Persons considering entering coaching training programs who want first to examine the field of coaching
- Personal and organizational coaches who need a reference book for their chosen field of work
- Professionals in allied fields who may want to add coaching skills to their portfolios: consultants, psychologists, human resource professionals, career professionals, leaders, managers, gerontologists, community leaders, teachers, parents, the clergy
- Libraries needing a reference guide to the field of coaching
- University professors who want to create academic courses on coaching
- Human resource directors and organization development professionals who want to train internal coaches
- Employers of coaches who may want to know more about the field in order to find and hire a qualified coach

ORGANIZATION OF THE BOOK

The contents are divided into four parts: Part One: Introduction to Coaching (Chapters One, Two, and Three), Part Two: Theoretical Roots of Coaching (Chapters Four and Five), Part Three: A Conceptual Model for Coaching (Chapters Six through Ten), and Part Four: Coaching for Mastery of the Adult Years (Chapters Eleven and Twelve). Special coaching tools—assessments and inventories—appear in Appendix A. A list of training programs for coaches appears in Appendix B.

In Part One, I begin by discussing how the field of coaching came into being, what coaches do, and who they are—that is, what kinds of people make good coaches. Next I show how to find clients and how to build a good coach-client relationship. And finally in that section, I describe the rapidly developing profession of coaching as it stands today—its professional organizations, business side, and ethical standards.

Part Two is devoted to explaining the intellectual underpinnings of coaching. The field is based on a solid academic foundation of psychological and social theory. Developmental psychology has been of particular benefit to coaches, who must understand adult development if they are to coach effectively. An acquaintance with social theory gives a coach the important background that is needed in order to work with clients within social systems such as families, work organizations, and communities.

In Part Three, beginning with Chapter Six, I present my conceptual model of coaching, which is based on the theory I mentioned earlier that adults develop in a series of change cycles, or life chapters and transitions, rather than along a straight, linear path. Figure 1 illustrates the theory.

Each cycle of change includes four phases that are distinctly different from each other. I call these Phase One: Go for It, Phase Two: The Doldrums, Phase Three: Cocooning, and Phase Four: Getting Ready for the Next Life Chapter. In between are Minitransitions. The names are almost self-explanatory, but I develop those ideas more fully in the chapter. Good coaching requires an understanding of these cycles.

Chapter Seven further elucidates the model. I describe a basic coaching task: articulating values. Values coaching represents a major difference between coaching and other professions. For example, personal values aren't a core part of a would-be dentist's curriculum, but values must be at the forefront of a coach-client relationship, the sole purpose of which is for the client to find ways of getting grounded in the moment and beginning to face the future with realism and optimism.

Chapter Eight is about systems coaching, that is, dealing with clients as part of systems (families, couples, work organizations, communities). Chapter Nine

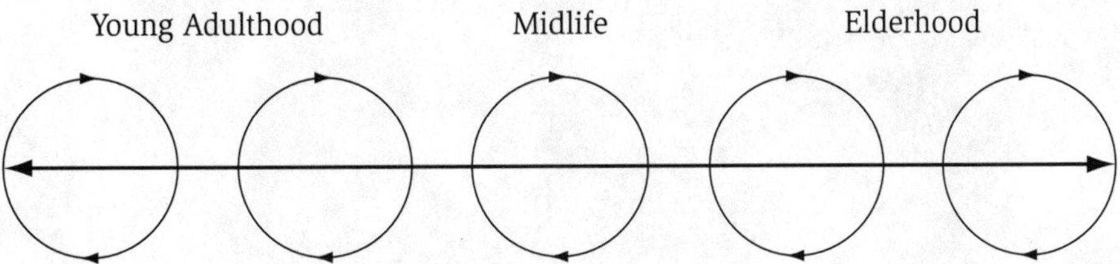

Figure 1. Cycles of Change in Adulthood.

illustrates another basic coaching task: coaching for visioning and purpose. If coaches are to help clients plan and equip themselves for the future, that future must first be imagined. A client's purposes must be clarified.

One basic premise is that, whatever happens, adults must continue to grow and to learn. Just as the live-happily-ever-after expectation no longer applies in marriage, lifetime tenure is no longer routine in the workplace. Change is inevitable—everywhere. Continuous learning is mandatory. Chapter Ten lays out a learning agenda, which ideally begins in early adulthood.

Chapters Eleven and Twelve address the issue of how to coach adults throughout their many years. The chapters outline the optimal human challenges from age twenty through elderhood.

HOW TO USE THIS BOOK

This is a reference work, as well as a guide for those who want to learn about coaching. The Table of Contents is a good place to look next. See which topics interest you and dip into those as you wish. If you already know what coaching is and are ready to begin research, you can see where the reference lists for various topics are located. If you simply want to know what's what in coaching, many topics will draw your attention. And have fun! This *Handbook* will both enlighten and empower you.

June 1999
Santa Barbara, California

Frederic M. Hudson

ABOUT THE AUTHOR

Frederic M. Hudson is president of the Hudson Institute of Santa Barbara, California. He earned a Ph.D. (1968) in the history of consciousness from Columbia University in New York City. Hudson was a Rockefeller Fellow and a Danforth Fellow. He is a recognized expert on adult change and development.

For more than twenty-five years Hudson has conducted seminars for adults who want to exercise creative choices in planning their lives and careers. Through consultation, leadership training, transition management, and life-design seminars in educational and corporate settings, he has worked with thousands of persons. Eight times a year he leads the well-known seminar he founded in 1986 called "The LifeLaunch Seminar," which facilitates future vision and planning with persons and work groups.

Hudson is a member of the Society for Values in Higher Education, the American Society for Training and Development, the Organization Development Network, the American Counseling Association, the Professional Coaches and Mentors Association, and the International Coach Federation (ICF). In 1999, he was designated a "master coach" by the ICF. He has served as president of the National Association of Free-Standing Graduate Schools and trustee of the California Family Studies Foundation and the San Francisco Consortium.

Hudson's publications include articles in *Innovations in Counseling Psychology* (1977), *Instant Relief: The Encyclopedia of Self-Help* (1979), *Rothman's World Symposium on Human Resources* (1983), *Meeting the New Demand for Standards* (1983), and *Career Transitions in Turbulent Times: Exploring Work,*

Learning and Careers (1996). His books include *Careers in World Affairs* (1960), *The Reign of the New Humanity* (1968), *Planning Your Life Through 2004: A Guide for College Graduates* (1979), *Poems from Midlife* (1982), *The Adult Years: Mastering the Art of Self-Renewal* (1991; second edition, 1999), *The Joy of Old: A Guide to Successful Elderhood* (1995), and *LifeLaunch: A Passionate Guide to the Rest of Your Life* (1996).

Hudson's career has been devoted to leadership roles in experiential education for adults. He has designed learning programs at several collegiate institutes to help students grow and develop as persons and as innovative change agents. After teaching and serving in administrative roles at Stephens College, Colby College, and the University of San Francisco, Hudson became the founding president (1974) of the Fielding Institute, a professional graduate school in psychology and organization development. At Fielding, Hudson applied his knowledge of adult development and social systems to the graduate training of midlife adults.

In 1986 Hudson began the Hudson Institute of Santa Barbara, which is devoted to the renewal of persons, careers, and organizations. Since then, over three hundred coaches have been trained and certified as professionals at the Institute, where programs include seminars for life planning, life transition management, retirement planning, outplacement, career renewal, and couples development, as well as long-term leadership programs for community leaders, corporate executives, and professionals who want mastery in the principles of the adult life cycle.

Hudson has consulted and coached with the World Bank, Motorola, IBM, Apple, Hewlett-Packard (HP), Quantum, Tandem, Sun Microsystems, Unisys, Sybase, Syntex, Pacific Bell, GE Medical Systems, Boeing, Lockheed, DuPont, Pepsi, Hallmark, 3M, Corning, AT&T, AMEX, Pritikin, AARP, Harvard, Stanford, Gemini Consulting, Pegasus Communications, Lee Hecht Harrison, Drake Beam Morin, Right Associates, the Young Presidents' Organization, and the American Nurses Association.

PART ONE

INTRODUCTION TO COACHING

Coaching: A Profession Born of Change

> **BASIC LIBRARY FOR COACHES**
>
> A valuable feature of this book is its *Basic Library for Coaches,* which contains references (many are annotated) that pertain to topics introduced in the text. The references provide a useful guide to in-depth study and research. *Basic Library for Coaches* appears at the end of each chapter and is broken into topical subsections that correspond to the chapter text. The most valuable introductory readings for coaches are marked with an asterisk. All Basic Library topics are listed in the Table of Contents for easy reference.

Very few professions have been born in a change-dominated world. Most professionals (teachers, physicians, lawyers, psychologists, and others) function with a set of basic skills and concepts that they use repeatedly throughout their careers. Coaching, however, emerged as a field that, as its central function, facilitates change and development.

A BRIEF HISTORY OF COACHING

In the 1960s and 1970s, government and large-organization planning was conducted from the top down. Upper management made the decisions; middle managers saw to it that decisions were carried out. But in the 1970s and 1980s, more flexibility was needed if organizations were to thrive, and the hierarchical control of employees began giving way to trust and collaboration with workers.

Widespread training was needed to help every worker think and behave like a leader. The emphasis was on business performance, as in TQM (total quality management). Then came seminars on teamwork and empowerment, which made the focus more personal, but training was still focused on immediate corporate issues.

The use of consultants added to the movement toward coaching; they worked with key corporate figures and system interventions. But these approaches to change had one common flaw: they came and went like waves hitting the beach. They didn't last. Then it occurred to many people that if organizations were going to make lasting changes, the individuals working in them must change first. Stephen Covey, author of *Seven Habits of Highly Effective People,* was a major figure in the shift from corporate talk to training highly effective persons.

In the late 1980s, corporate coaching came on the scene. The idea was for coaches to work over a period of time with both individuals and systems. They were to function like leaven in bread, to get the job done in a lasting way. Some of the new emphases that coaches contributed were visionary leadership training, executive coaching, renewal coaching, and transition management.

The field of leadership, particularly entrepreneurial leadership, has influenced and shaped the new profession of coaching as much as anything else. The trend toward coaching was accelerated by the need for human caring and daring during the corporate convulsions of downsizing, mergers, acquisitions, and outplacement.

Sometime in the late 1980s, the professional field of coaching was born—a field promoting continuous resilience and performance in persons and organizations. A major need was to help individuals and corporate entities formulate scenarios for the future, given the complexities and speed of change in today's world. Coaches were often asked about personal evolving, succession planning, career shifting, work performance, high-performance teams, outplacement, burn-out, scenario building, leadership training, work-home balance, and individual and organizational renewal.

CHANGES IN SOCIETY

We all know that change has become the most dependable reality in our lives and that people and organizations throughout the globe live with continuous uncertainty, tentativeness, and worry. Most have no long-term expectations and plans. They simply follow their intense daily and weekly schedules.

But this was not true for most of the twentieth century. The world we lived in seemed fairly dependable, uniform, and evolving. So our lives took on those dimensions. The professions or work fields we entered were organized around the assumptions of a stable culture of perpetual progress, central authority and control, and willingness to follow the rules. Today we are vividly aware, through media coverage of crises around the globe, that the world we live in is turbulent, unpredictable, and fragile. Our society—its workplaces and communities, its neighborhoods and its people—reflect those qualities.

Organizations have struggled against the forces of change, both in the United States and around the world. But the short-term interventions that have been tried, as a way of managing change in entrenched corporate cultures, have mainly failed. American work organizations have been forced to retrench and flatten, and to measure their financial success in the short term. The trend away from the long-term, human dimensions of work toward immediate financial issues has altered most work organizations in the United States. A great many people are working harder than ever and enjoying it less.

People are finding it more and more difficult to see how to face the future and to connect the chapters of their lives—from childhood, through the adult years, to elderhood. It is also more difficult to navigate through careers and marriages and community connections. Our adult lives used to be programmed according to the linear rule discussed in the Preface—more or less stable and continuous careers, families, neighborhoods, churches, community organizations carried us inexorably through our entire lives. Careers were also linear—they were progressions through the stages from apprenticeship to expertise. Organizations and communities seemed permanent. But today our lives and settings are increasingly unstable, tentative, discontinuous, and transitory. And we have considerable cynicism about the future.

As our perception of the world shifted from a stable, orderly, steady-state model to an unstable, disorderly, change-driven one, many of us failed to change accordingly. We went on living as if the steady-state model were fully operative. We raged or whined when we found it wasn't so. Most of us wanted—we still want and expect—some life plan, career, or work organization to lead us toward definite security, happiness, and financial prosperity. Instead of learning how to fulfill ourselves within the change process that now prevails, we tend to view our prospects as declining, as unfilled promises the generations before us lodged deeply in our minds.

MENTORING-COACHING: A RESPONSE TO CHANGE

In the wake of widespread confusion—sometimes panic—about change, I became increasingly interested in what I call mentoring-coaching. I began to see mentor-coaches as a readily available resource for promoting deep renewal and learning in most work organizations and communities.

The idea of mentoring is an old one. In Homer's *Odyssey,* the King of Ithaca, Odysseus, left his young son, Telemachus, in the care of Mentor, a wise and proven teacher who had agreed to raise the boy until Odysseus could return, which turned out to be twenty-one years later. Mentor modeled the manhood skills that Telemachus needed, and the young prince grew as a whole person, a leader, and man of integrity. When Odysseus arrived home, he immediately recognized the faithful, good work of Mentor. Since then, the word *mentor* has been used to describe someone who has the inner competence to pass on knowledge and skills through example, inner authority, and dialogue.

Mentoring is the model for coaching, but I find the word *mentor* too formal for purposes of this training model. I prefer the term *coach* here. Used in the athletic sense, *coach* is now widely applied to a person who facilitates experiential learning that results in future-oriented abilities. The term, as I use it, refers to a person who is a trusted role model, adviser, wise person, friend, mensch, steward, or guide—a person who works with emerging human and organizational forces to tap new energy and purpose, to shape new visions and plans, and to generate desired results. A coach is someone trained and devoted to guiding others into increased competence, commitment, and confidence. The most profound way to learn skills, culture, and values is directly from other human beings who already possess those qualities and who are available to offer guidance and counsel.

See (1) Basic Library: Mentoring and Coaching and (2) Basic Library: Sports Concepts in Coaching for references.

EXAMPLES OF COACHING TASKS

Many descriptions of specific coaching tasks and of how a coach would approach those tasks appear throughout the book. But two examples will indicate something of what a coach does. First, a coach who is working in an organization

- Models mastery in professional areas that others want to obtain
- Guides others to high performance in emerging scenarios
- Advocates, criticizes, and extends corporate culture and wisdom
- Endorses and sponsors others without using power or having control over them
- Facilitates professional development and organizational system development

Coaches play many roles within organizations to achieve future-oriented results: they help clients develop career paths and find personal and professional renewal; they train high-performance teams; and they provide informal leadership for transition management.

Another example is the use of coaching strategies by professionals (whether they are officially called coaches or not) to guide clients through career changes.

The typical college graduate today is expected to have six to eight careers in a lifetime. Coaching can help people learn to manage such changes, to move in and out of work settings with some degree of confidence and inner leadership, and to connect their inner skills to outer work.

WHY WE NEED COACHES NOW

Coaching is important today, not only in corporate America but throughout society. In the pages to follow, I'll discuss eight of the specific reasons that coaches are needed.

Coaches Help Adults Manage Change Effectively

The most probable scenario for the future is that the intensity of change will increase steadily in both pace and in the number of life dimensions affected. Although we are not the first human beings to face the dilemmas and opportunities of constant change, the technical and universal aspects of our global situation are unique, continuously altering human consciousness and priorities everywhere. Change diminishes our sense that we can depend on the world. Whenever change predominates over stability throughout a culture, many become angry that they have been abandoned by their society or by their work organizations. Others drop out because they see no future with a promise for them. Still others are paralyzed by fear or cynicism. Complex change often affects workers' abilities to sustain motivation and to commit to long-term projects.

In the new environment of perpetual change, workers who cannot manage the discontinuities of their own lives and work will not produce great results, no matter how good their technical skills or leadership abilities. But coaches help clients search for the advantages of change, not only in work settings but anywhere that people are struggling to cope with change. Coaches are positive change agents. They motivate people around them with new hope, purpose, and concrete steps for sustaining a cautious optimism.

The more the world around us is in flux, the more we must be certain about what matters in our lives: how we spend our time, who we are connected to, and where we are going. When the macrosystems of our lives are in considerable flux, as they are today, the microsystems rise in importance; they become anchors. A coach can show how this happens.

The highest calling of coaches today is to become guides to a transient culture, including a transient corporate culture. A coach helps to grow strong persons, committed work teams, dynamic work systems, and sustainable communities that function from the grass roots up. Effective coaches model the future because they are willing to invent it, design it, and insist on it. As for change, they see change as an asset for getting a job done rather than a reason to be afraid.

Coaches Model Mastery

Much is being written about the fragmentation of our culture today, with its many self-interest groups and much culturewide anger, violence, and cynicism. Coaches cannot solve this social problem, but they represent one mature resource that can make a difference. Coaches work in small but deep ways to anchor people and human systems in a public philosophy of trust, vision, strategic thinking, conflict management, and collaboration. Effective coaches inspire those they coach with a sense of self-reliance and deep-seated determination that is much needed in these uncommon times.

Coaches facilitate personal mastery through the development of *radar* and *gyroscopes* in people and in human systems. *Radar* is the ability to detect the best track to follow through a changing environment. A *gyroscope* is a perpetual balancing system that includes the ability to redefine identity, ego-strength, roles, and personal commitment. Coaches help their clients use these devices to master their own lives, careers, and the flow beyond.

If adults can develop dependable radar systems for guiding themselves in and out of the never-ending maze of daily life, they can sustain confidence, self-esteem, and hope. If adults can develop dependable gyroscopes for guiding themselves through the indefiniteness of their social experience, creating sufficient inner stability and outer constancy for living their beliefs, they will have surplus energy and courage for designing work and communities in our kind of world.

Coaches Provide Ongoing Training in Technology

We live in a technocratic age in which an effective person knows how to use and learn from evolving technological systems. Because technology changes so swiftly, people must remain in perpetual learning systems to be at their best. Some people pursue advanced degrees or certificates in new skill areas, but most need technical resources that are more tutorial, informal, and readily available. Coaches who specialize in technical competencies can perform these functions and transform the "technical consultant" model into that of an ongoing enabler or trainer. This is an important part of coaching in the new environment.

Coaches Elicit Core Values and Commitments

There is a great tendency today to think that technical prowess is the pioneering edge of our post-modern society. Truth is, as important as technological knowledge and skills are, they pale when compared to our need to be value-driven, bonded to others, and clear about the ultimate purpose of our lives. Technology fosters communication tools and media—but not meaning. Most people are searching for meaning, for the ultimate concerns of life, for beliefs and values.

Technological advancements are typically the province of young people whose mathematical and specialized skills are often superior to those of older folk. Values and purpose, however, are most often the province of mature people who have been around long enough to transcend their intellectual skills and immediate personal needs and acquire trust in the flow of things. Such persons are effective generalists reaching out to a younger society of specialists. Adults in midlife and beyond are the most likely bearers of values for a culture. For that reason, many coaches—but by no means all—are persons in the second half of life.

Coaches Renew Human Systems

In the past twenty years, corporate America has sought to transform its management styles, and one of the groups targeted for removal has been middle managers. Typically, a middle manager is a well-paid, long-term, loyal worker who is responsible for getting work done in some part of a business. The new management style is to train workers to manage themselves through teams, leadership training, and new rewards. This transformation has brought some astonishing improvements in the development of quality goods and services in an increasingly competitive world. However, the middle managers were often the invisible mentors or coaches of these organizations, and without them there are fewer long-term role models to foster advanced skills, management abilities, new career directions, and loyalty in younger workers.

Coaches can be found and trained in most every workforce. Because they are already being paid, it is primarily a matter of allocating their time to establish them as coaches who are available to promising, less-experienced workers who seek to grow within a work system.

Coaches Sponsor Future Generations

One link in the generational chain is weak and unsure: the post-baby-boomer Americans. This group ranges in age from sixteen to thirty-five; members are called a variety of names, including Busters, Beavis and Buttheaders, and GenXers. This cohort is known for its skepticism, minimalism, individualism, and social silence.

This generation challenges the assumptions of the importance of work and success. They doubt that they will have much of a future, no matter what they choose to do. Of course, not everyone in this age group thinks this way, but a large number do, and it challenges the rest of us to learn how to communicate and cooperate with those who are cynical and not easily motivated by money, advancement, or recognition.

Adult coaches may be more effective than corporate or government leaders for facilitating the paths of this generation within adult roles. Coaches look for inner values as the primary source of motivation. In quiet ways, coaches seek to provide cultural continuity as their fundamental legacy to the future. Coaches are committed to reaching out, bridging gaps, and finding new ways to build on what has come before. They stand and deliver. They advocate inclusion of all persons, cohorts, and identities.

Coaches Model Collaboration and Consensus Building

Another way fragmentation is obvious in society today is in the many niche groups, each of which has some legitimate way in which to define its identity. Many groups form around a single moral concern; others around gender issues, illnesses, product lines, religious issues, racial or ethnic identification, or sports activities. Although these groups perform many positive functions through their special interests, they tend to pull their members away from forum discussions of the corporate and cultural issues that affect everyone.

Where do people learn and practice collaboration in a fragmented society? The grand American rhythm of conflict and consensus has devolved into more and more conflict and less and less consensus. And in the process, responsibility for teaching collaboration and consensus building has shifted. That responsibility used to be borne by schools, churches, town meetings, voluntary associations, even corporations. Debates about human concerns are still going on in these settings, but in our technology- and media-driven world, these institutions have much less impact on public concerns and opinions. Grassroots forums are regularly upstaged by TV and radio talk shows that focus on alarming news and celebrity events. Coaches can help this situation by exerting an influence toward human connections, alliances, and open systems.

Coaches plant the seeds of democratic, collaborative processes in their clients by

- Emphasizing priorities, connectedness, balance, fairness, passion, purpose, vision, and planning. Coaches show that living with "us" is a necessary part of living with "me" and promoting a future for the whole as well as the parts.
- Training clients to honor their core values, to articulate preferences, to negotiate differences, to compromise, and to manage conflict when necessary. These basic human abilities promote self-responsible behavior within interdependent contexts.
- Encouraging debate about the wise decisions for challenging scenarios. Coaches are concerned about making the future a developmental continuum with the past, and they promote those qualities in the persons and systems they touch.
- "Coaching" the organizations and environments they are in, as well as key individuals. Coaches advocate a process of decision making in which everyone affected by a decision has some way to influence the shaping of that decision. Coaches emphasize both personal empower-

ment and social consensus, fostering an essential mind-set for personal, career, and organizational leadership.

Coaches Tap the Genius of Older Workers

We live at a time of wasted human assets. Americans have been deluded by the myth of youthism—that we decline in all respects as we get older, particularly after the age of forty or so. This is simply not true, but the myth contributes greatly to the waste of corporate human resources. Corporations typically begin to divest themselves of the human potential of their older workers long before the workers have lost their competence. The graying of America will reach its zenith in the years immediately ahead, and with it will come a redefinition of *old* that will emphasize a diversity of contributions from older workers. The smart work system will begin, in the early years of the twenty-first century, to redefine its policies and attitudes toward its older workers.

Another American myth is that of retirement. Retirement evolved as a concept in the twentieth century to force older people out of full-time work. It was the doing of corporate and labor leaders, in collusion with the federal government. It has nothing to do with optimal human development or the best use of elders as a social resource. As generation after generation of adults extend life expectancy to higher ranges—into the eighties, nineties, and even beyond—some kind of positive engagement and recognition of elders is called for.

Many if not most older workers want to leave a legacy, make a difference, and exert influence on the priorities of the environment around them. In future generations, older workers will launch new careers, assume leadership, engage in volunteer service, and serve as consultants and mentors.

Coaches can foster new employment challenges for older workers, both within corporate environments and outside of them. Coaches can promote challenges for older workers to find new meaning and purpose in their work. Many of these coaches will come from the elder ranks themselves. Their voices will come from deep reservoirs; their actions will spring from gratitude; their joy will rise from spirit. Older workers, if prized by their companies, can help immensely to provide stability and pride in the work culture.

Coaching will not cure the perennial ills of corporate life or the American culture but it can enrich their environments with sharing, caring, and daring. Coaches roll up their sleeves to make things happen. They have that old-fashioned American spirit that if we work hard and work together, we'll all benefit. Anyone who has abilities that others covet and the heart to share should make himself or herself available and see what happens! Coaches are an enormously valuable resource. The time has come to use them.

As the old rules continue to change, as predictability and stability give way to technological change, political upheavals, community crises, global monetary crises, and territorial disputes, people are scrambling to find professional help—some resource to help them get stabilized and recover their passion and purpose. Personal and organizational coaches fill some of the need. They work directly with individuals and organizations to find inner anchors for outer challenges; they look for shifting advantages within the change process itself; they are catalysts for facilitating self-responsible behaviors in their clients; they improve imagining, performance, teamwork, and risk taking. Most important, it is clear that coaches can help people work through transition experiences with resilience, elan, staying power, renewal, and hope.

 BASIC LIBRARY FOR COACHES

Mentoring and Coaching

*Bell, C. R. *Managers as Mentors: Building Partnerships for Learning.* San Francisco: Berrett-Koehler, 1998. A passionate plea for mentoring in a popular, straightforward presentation.

Bogat, G. A., and Redner, R. L. "How Mentoring Affects the Professional Development of Women in Psychology." *Professional Psychology: Research and Practice,* 1985, *16,* 851–859.

Carew, J. *The Mentor: 15 Keys to Success in Sales, Business & Life.* New York: Fine, 1998.

Caruso, R. E. *Mentoring and the Business Environment: Asset or Liability?* Newcastle upon Tyne: Athenaeum Press, 1992.

Douglas, C. A. *Formal Mentoring Programs in Organizations: An Annotated Bibliography.* Greensboro, N.C.: Center for Creative Leadership, 1997.

Fagenson, E. A. "Mentoring: Who Needs It? Perceived Career/Job Experiences of Proteges vs. Nonproteges' Needs for Power, Achievement Affiliation, and Autonomy." *Journal of Vocational Behavior,* 1992, *41,* 48–60.

Fritts, P. *The New Managerial Mentor.* Palo Alto, Calif.: Davies-Black, 1998. Presents mentoring as the art of collaboration.

*Galbraith, M. W., and Cohen, N. H. *Mentoring: New Strategies and Challenges.* San Francisco: Jossey-Bass, 1995.

Hendricks, W. (ed.). *Coaching, Mentoring and Managing.* New York: Career Press, 1996.

Huang, C., and Lynch, J. *Mentoring.* New York: HarperCollins, 1995.

Johnson, H. E. *Mentoring for Exceptional Performance.* Glendale, Calif.: Griffin,

1997. Corporate applications of mentoring, including launching a mentoring program, mentoring teams, and mentoring transitions.

Kram, K. E. "Phases of the Mentor Relationship." *Academy of Management Journal,* 1983, *26*(4), 608–625.

Kram, K. E. *Mentoring at Work.* Glenview, Ill.: Scott, Foresman, 1988.

Murray, M. *Beyond the Myths and Magic of Mentoring: How to Facilitate an Effective Mentoring Program.* San Francisco: Jossey-Bass, 1991. Has good examples.

Orth, C. D., Wilkinson, H. E., and Benfari, R. C. "The Manager's Role as Coach and Mentor." *Organizational Dynamics,* 1987, *15*(4), 66–74.

*Parsloe, E. *Coaching, Mentoring and Assessing: A Practical Guide to Developing Confidence.* London: Kogan Page Limited, 1995.

Rawles, B. A. *The Influence of a Mentor on the Level of Self-Actualization of American Scientists.* Ann Arbor, Mich.: Dissertation Abstracts International, University Microfilms, *41,* 134AA.

Scandura, T. A. "Mentorship and Career Mobility: An Empirical Investigation." *Journal of Organizational Behavior,* 1992, *13,* 169–174.

Shea, G. F. *How to Develop Successful Mentor Behavior.* Menlo Park, Calif.: Crisp, 1998. An elementary book on mentoring.

Stone, F. M. *Coaching, Counseling & Mentoring.* New York: AMACOM, 1998.

Woodlands Group. "Management Development Roles: Coach, Sponsor, and Mentor." *Personnel Journal,* 1980, *59,* 918–921.

Wunsch, M. *Mentoring Revisited: Making an Impact on Individuals and Institutions.* San Francisco: Jossey-Bass, 1994.

Sports Concepts in Coaching

*Chambers, D. *Coaching: Winning Strategies for Every Level of Play.* Buffalo, N.Y.: Firefly, 1998. A comprehensive overview; covers self-management, team management, physical preparation, and psychological preparation.

Cox, R. *Sport Psychology: Concepts and Applications.* Dubuque, Iowa: W. C. Brown, 1997.

Jackson, P. *Sacred Hoops: Spiritual Lessons of a Hardwood Warrior.* New York: Hyperion, 1995.

Martens, R. *Successful Coaching.* Champaign, Ill.: Leisure, 1996.

Shula, D., and Blanchard, K. *Everyone's a Coach: You Can Inspire Anyone to Be a Winner.* Grand Rapids, Mich.: Zondervan, 1995.

 CHAPTER TWO 

Coaches: What They Do, Who They Are

What is a coach of adults and human systems? I will outline some specific coaching tasks later on in this chapter. But more generally speaking, what coaches do is anchor people to their own internal strengths; they inspire organizations to dream beyond their plans. They apply emotional and intellectual intelligence to the long haul of life and work. Although some coaching is short term, most is conducted over a longer term and serves to facilitate the change that clients need as they prepare to face the future with strength and optimism.

To be able to anchor and inspire clients, coaches must be very special people. First of all, they must be gifted in subjects or practices that followers want to gain expertise or endorsement in. Then they must be able to transcend their own ego needs so they can help others in unselfish ways. Finally, coaches must be selected and trusted by clients as highly competent and reliable learning resources. The value-added part of the coach-client process grows out of the quality of the relationships more than anything else. A person who has been well coached has a memorable connection to someone who has profoundly influenced his or her life—with knowledge, values, wisdom, mastery, compassion, and motivation.

Coaches draw much inspiration and information from other professions. (See Basic Library: Drawing from Other Professions.)

FUNCTIONS OF A PERSONAL OR ORGANIZATIONAL COACH

In Chapter One, I listed some of the things a coach who is working in an organization might do. The following outline of the functions of a personal or organizational coach will help focus the discussion further. Some terms will seem vague, merely suggestive. That is intentional. The outline is fleshed out in my comments throughout the book.

Basically, a coach

- Works with individuals and organizations as clients
- Works from what is possible, using imagination, vision, and motivation as resources
- Finds bridges to the future, connecting what is to what might be
- Links inner purpose to outer work, with persons, groups, and organizations
- Inspires others to be more effective as leaders, teams, networkers, managers
- Models the way ahead
- Trains, trains, trains
- Guides clients to high performance
- Questions the status quo and seeks creative, transformative results
- Advocates, criticizes, and extends corporate culture and wisdom
- Fosters emerging scenarios with a long view and a short action plan
- Endorses and sponsors others without having power or control over them
- Facilitates professional development and organizational system development
- Guides clients and organizations through necessary transitions
- Encourages networking through alliances and linkages with common goals
- Is a catalyst for renewal and resilience
- Motivates, seeks deep results, explores new directions, innovates, invests in the future

The process of facilitating change in a person or organization includes clarifying values, beliefs, and purpose in the personal lives or in the organizations of clients. A coach also helps identify key social roles and promote successful performance within a balanced schedule. Another coaching task is to locate any emergent developmental challenges that might exist and to invent vital learning agendas for clients, when those seem appropriate.

WHO COACHES ARE

It's hard to separate a description of *what coaches do* from *who coaches are,* as the two topics are inextricably entwined. But I will show next what coaches must *be* to *do* good coaching. My descriptions should give newcomers to the field a sense of the qualities and skills a good coach should have.

Coaches Are Generalists

Coaches must be human generalists. Whereas most professionals are specialists in one aspect of adult behavior (psychological healing, careers, organization development work, leadership roles, and so forth), coaches function as generalists, drawing from their vast experience to motivate, facilitate, and guide their clients, whose issues may vary. Coaches work with clients on many kinds of issues, ranging from leadership roles to domestic concerns to financial planning to management issues. Many types of issues are possibilities for coaching.

Coaches Are Change Agents

Coaches, at their best, are not only change agents—*they are change masters.* They understand that change is here to stay and that the sooner we all learn how to be resilient and effective in a permanent change environment, the better off we will be. As I mentioned earlier, coaching is one of a very few professions to be born in a change paradigm, requiring it to function and be organized differently from the older professions that embrace permanence, linearity, and hierarchies. Coaches are committed to change, so they can stay aligned to challenging and believable futures that are in constant flux. They are committed to external performance when that can be attained and to internal renewal and resilience when that is necessary.

As a change agent, a coach

- Questions the status quo
- Feels challenged by the unknown
- Looks at things from new perspectives
- Takes risks
- Is willing to make mistakes and learn from them
- Is driven by personal integrity

- Inspires others to be at their best
- Is future-oriented and cautiously optimistic
- Looks for new opportunities in the change process
- Pursues useful alliances and networks that enhance cooperation and results
- Rehearses scenarios thoroughly before making decisions
- Guides persons and systems into new developmental growth
- Imagines new ways to look at things
- Presents ideas and makes them convincing
- Confronts behaviors that shut down human energy and hope
- Nurtures clients in transition
- Facilitates learning, training, and referrals

Coaches Are Good Communicators

Coaches must have well-developed communication skills. Specifically, an effective coach must be able to

- Speak clearly and effectively in one-on-one sessions, in small groups, and in public meetings
- Present ideas and make them convincing
- Conduct coaching groups when that modality is the most effective coaching style
- Use a vocabulary rich in metaphors and stories
- Create consensus through win-win strategies
- Say no when necessary

WHAT COACHES DO

In the following sections, I discuss some specifics of what good coaches do.

Coaches Work with a Whole Person or Organization

Coaches work with the whole person or organizational unit as a client, weaving together the client's variety of concerns into an integrated plan that has vitality and purpose. Good coaches know how to listen, find core values, empathize, reflect, probe, ask questions, relate issues, challenge, foster alternative scenarios, find network resources, foster alliances, sustain ongoing evaluation, and conduct strategic reviews.

Coaches Work from Core Values

Coaches are guided by the core values in themselves and in their clients. They are not problem solvers, trend finders, or pollsters. They tap the emotional and mental vitality of their clients and help to translate it into transformative directions and goals. They work from the inside out, discerning the power of purpose within a client, as well as the values from which vital passion is derived.

The following qualities and characteristics are part of a good coach's makeup. Following each characteristic are some tasks a coach undertakes that require the particular characteristic.

First, a good coach *is emotionally competent* and thus is able to

- Sustain intimate bonds and relationships
- Provide an environment of caring for the coaching work
- Maintain high levels of self-confidence and self-esteem
- Imagine, wonder, and envision
- Listen intently and objectively to others
- Empathize with and validate others
- Express feelings naturally and appropriately
- Display gratitude and appreciation
- Manage conflicts fairly and directly
- Seek and maintain friendships that are mutually rewarding

Second, a good coach *is mentally sharp.* Therefore, the coach

- Possesses legitimate personal authority
- Gives and receives criticism fairly
- Reflects on sense of self and its personal life course
- Possesses legitimate personal authority
- Negotiates useful and accurate coaching agreements
- Distinguishes between trivial and significant problems
- Distinguishes between situational and patterned distress
- Provides accurate feedback
- Observes and understands the conduct of self and others
- Knows how to conclude coaching relationships professionally

Third, a good coach *is action-oriented.* He or she

- Discerns and clarifies personal values in self and others

- Collaborates effectively and acts fairly as a team player
- Celebrates, has fun, and pursues affirmations and rituals
- Plans and feels responsible for making the future happen
- Lives his or her own beliefs and concerns
- Challenges, tests, and expects high performance from self and others
- Looks for ways clients can experience their strengths
- Looks for ways clients can learn to be self-directed
- Looks for social settings and activities that can enrich the coaching plan
- Validates and rewards the efforts of others
- Embraces diversity in men and women and in people from other cultures

Coaches Connect Short-Term Strategies to Longer-Term Plans

Coaches are not quick-fix agents; they are catalysts for the emerging goals and purposes of individuals and organizations. They remain as resources, advocates, sponsors, evaluators, and facilitators for connecting short-term plans to longer-term goals.

A good coach should be able to

- Evoke a sense of purpose with clients
- Facilitate compelling visions of the future with clients
- Convert planning into scenario building; design the future
- Conduct personal and professional strategic-planning and time-management sessions with clients
- Be effective at facilitating small group process, including emotional work
- Facilitate persons and human systems through times of transition
- Promote personal renewal and career resilience

Coaches Seek Balance

Coaches try to find balance and proportion in the lives and settings of their clients. They work to ensure that all the life areas of an individual client have support, time, and resources so the client can sustain high levels of resilience for the long haul.

Coaches should be able to

- Understand appropriate adult roles throughout the life cycle
- Model and teach the balance of roles and show how to be one person in all roles

Coaches Promote Workable Futures

Coaches are visionaries; they are pathfinders, catalysts for the not-yet. They promote vision and facilitate creative yet realistic plans to make the future a challenging possibility. Basic skills include the ability to convert future plans into the kind of scenario building that invents the future.

Coaches Remain Available

Coaches must be accessible throughout the coaching relationship. They should be available for short coaching sessions and exchanges by telephone, e-mail, fax, as well as for long-term, collegial stewardship. Examples of specific tasks are arranging meetings when necessary; relating naturally and easily by phone, fax, and e-mail; and translating raw data into useful information.

TWO KINDS OF COACHING: BEING AND PERFORMANCE

The two poles of coaching are (1) coaching for *being* and (2) coaching for *performance.* Neither is more or less important; the two are necessary parts of every human being and every coaching task.

Being Coaching—Inner Work

Inner work has to do with resilience, beliefs, values, self-esteem, courage, purpose, centering. Transformation of set limits and assumptions is the gift of inner work. (Inner coaching is often called *spiritual coaching.*) Outer work has to do with reaching goals, performing well, choosing the right actions, and executing those actions effectively. (Outer coaching is often called *performance coaching.*) Neither inner nor outer work is better than the other. They need each other for the long haul of life. When one changes, the other is affected. Many coaches are trained in performance coaching and nothing else, which greatly limits the depth and staying power of their work. Quite often, clients enter coaching around a performance issue and, as the coaching relationship matures, inner (ontological) issues arise; with proper coaching, transformational development takes place. Yet transformation of the inner self leads directly to some new outer quest, and the coach must know how to foster achievement.

Performance Coaching—Outer Work

Performance coaching begins with establishing clear goals that both the coach and the client believe to be reachable. A coach's job is to inspire and validate clients while providing consistently accurate feedback. Coaching work should be considered more like a learning environment than a playing field. Coaches should ask lots of questions. They should encourage clients to move out of their safety zones and dare to fail. Coaches should challenge clients with new ways to excel—and expect success—while keeping their own ego under wraps. Coaches must not over-identify with clients. It's the relationship of trust, empathy, and reliability that matters more than words in good coaching. Rituals, fun, and celebration help build that relationship.

SOME COACHING DOS AND DON'TS

The following tips summarize some of the things that experienced coaches know they should and should not do:

Dos	*Don'ts*
• Do direct the structure and process of the session (focus the conversation, the time constraints, the rules of the tribe) and the process issues of the session (the flow, sequence of events, what's appropriate when and where).	• Don't direct the content of a discussion or impose a prearranged agenda on your client.
• Do ask questions that explore ways your client might manage the future.	• Don't rescue or offer direct advice to your client.
• Do listen and reflect back what you hear to discover if your hearing is accurate.	• Don't dominate the conversation.
• Do ask your client questions about his or her experience that guide the conversation toward a preferred future.	• Don't compare the client's experience with anyone else's, including your own.
• Do stay with the coaching agenda, the topics at hand; stay within time constraints.	• Don't let your client make you captive.
• Do stay in the present and future tenses, always looking for options and possibilities. Use yourself as an instrument for the future.	• Don't try to repair the past or to solve unsolvable problems.

THE COACHING PROCESS

Coaching is the art of guiding another person, persons, or human systems toward fulfilling futures. The coaching process is fundamentally developmental and systems-oriented, which means that a good bit of time is needed to do it, but coaching goes along faster and more effectively when one-on-one meetings are used in combination with group meetings. In both, the work is future-oriented and task-driven. Coaches do not conduct therapy or encounter groups or T-groups or educational seminars. They help clients invent futures that are exciting, valuable, and intensely personal.

Coaching is more about being than doing. It comes from the abiding qualities of mature people and is offered more out of compassion and concern than from a need to perform or be rewarded. Most coaching is one-on-one coaching, based on a relationship of trust and shared values. The relationship works because the client wants to gain something from the coach, and the coach is available for the exchange, usually through intuitive, informal, and personal interactions. Coaches and their clients often view their relationship as a friendship that validates both parties—the learner through a gain in competence, the teacher by engendering competence in others. Nevertheless, there are explicit tasks that coaches often perform in various settings and conditions. Coaches should strive to

- Be an example for the successful management of life, professional roles, and social leadership
- Inspire, motivate, keep on track; help build confidence, self-esteem, personal leadership
- Provide a listening post where problems and issues can often be identified, solved, or redirected; offer friendship and counsel in agreed-upon areas and beyond
- Offer tough love—confrontation, blunt feedback, concern over negative attitudes and behaviors, insistence that certain habits be changed
- Coach toward more effective, natural performance as persons and as professionals

Three specific coaching strategies, which often work in combination, are *one-on-one coaching, group coaching,* and *systems coaching.* A fourth topic in this section is *gender coaching.*

One-on-One Coaching

This kind of coaching is working with individual clients in one- to two-hour sessions per week or month over a fairly long period of time. Meetings are devoted to pursuing ways that clients can be more effective as human beings and as professionals. A good example of this is the widely practiced executive coaching, that is, facilitating the development of an executive so that all parts of his or her life become more effective and enjoyable.

Group Coaching

This kind of coaching means working with several clients as a group, in two- to four-hour seminar-type sessions, once or twice a month; issues of shared interest are discussed. Examples are groups wanting to conduct life planning, professional groups wanting to renew or change their profession, or men's, women's, or parents' groups, and so on. Developmental groups work best when they (1) maintain a focus on the present and the future, not the past; (2) use the word *plan* as the focus word, so the group does not veer off into therapy, anger work, twelve-step material, EST, or the many other group formats that people are familiar with. By using the creation of a plan as the goal of group work, all kinds of unfinished business (therapy contracts, interview skill development, couples work, résumé writing) can go into the plan. They do not need to be carried out in the group.

Systems Coaching

This kind of coaching refers to working with some system (a couple, a family, a work organization or a subunit, a community group, a government agency) to move beyond strategic planning to visionary planning, morale building, and renewal of purpose. Systems coaching is a combination of working with key people, key departments, and key system changes that will promote alignment with the current mission of the system.

Gender Coaching

Coaches must take the differences between coaching men and coaching women into account. Good coaches know that individuals often experience their situation and react to it differently, depending on their gender. I offer a generous selection of references to guide coaches' reading in that area. (See Basic Library: Gender Coaching.)

Coaching Women. Possible coaching goals for women include moving beyond stereotypical female behaviors, designing one's own identity, developing boundary skills, finding life balance, designing a personal life, developing the leader within, expanding communication skills, improving mothering skills, sustaining friendships, physical maintenance, spiritual resilience, learning conflict management skills, developing one's masculine side, redefining career goals, developing a leisure life, assuming community leadership, and maturing as a person. (See Basic Library: Coaching Women.)

Coaching Women on Career Development. Possible coaching goals: learning what purposive work would be like, understanding career options and how to take advantage of them, exploring entrepreneurial options, considering part-time employment, developing a portfolio of work roles, training in networking skills. (See Basic Library: Coaching Women on Career Development.)

Menopause. Possible coaching goals in this area include seeing menopause as a rite of passage, getting facts in place of cultural myths, understanding the physical changes and wellness choices, connecting to other women around this natural process, developing friendships with older women, and moving ahead. (See Basic Library: Menopause.)

Coaching Men. Possible coaching goals for men include moving beyond male stereotypical behaviors, consciously choosing how to be a person, expanding communication skills, improving fathering skills, finding multiple acceptable ways to express intimacy, transcending ego needs, developing a feminine side, finding the inner leader, redefining career goals, developing a liesure life, learning conflict management, developing friendships, and taking on caring roles in the community. (See Basic Library: Coaching Men.)

Dealing with Resistance

Coaches sometimes reach a point in the coaching process when they can go no further. The client resists all coaching efforts. It is well to remember that some clients have enormous difficulties just maintaining their day-to-day lives. The coach's task is to help search for optimal ways to do that—not to deal directly with an identified problem. Coaches look for vision, human resources, networking, and hope. They motivate, look ahead, and side with their clients. They supply facts and look for ways to live with what is while searching for what might be.

Coaches shouldn't avoid dealing with the down side of their clients' lives, but they must be able to recognize the difference between normal distress and true dysfunction. Clients who have patterned dysfunctions must be referred to trained clinicians. Clients with "boulders" and "resistance" to future options belong in coaching relationships. Boulders are a way of talking about what obstructs us along our life paths. Sometimes these are *internal obstacles* (anxiety, fear, anger, old messages, habits). At other times they are *external threats* (loss of jobs, accidents, bankruptcies, diseases, catastrophes). Often, when we reach a boulder on our path, instead of finding ways to get beyond it we consume our energy dealing with it. The object of boulder work is to get a client to minimize the control that a boulder exerts and look at visionary possibilities that might serve to minimize the impact of the boulder. Clients typically resist the future because their internal obstacle or external threat is so overwhelming.

Coaches have to understand clients' resistance to the future and know how to facilitate alternative ways of imagining and planning with future options, even if the boulder remains intact.

Possible sources of threat include living with an unsolvable problem or degenerative disease, cult membership, homelessness, and other social problems such as racism, sexism, and ageism. (See these topics in the Basic Library for Coaches.)

At times, being skilled in negotiating is a coach's best hope of being helpful to a client who is feeling threatened and is, as a result, uncommunicative or hostile. (See Basic Library: Negotiating Skills.)

WHO CAN BE A CLIENT?

Coaches search for clients they believe they can coach effectively, usually persons in fields and situations in which the coaches have performed successfully. They seek to match their inner concerns and abilities with clients seeking clarity in those areas. They look for what is most important in the lives and human systems of their clients and how to make those values central in the life-work plans of their clients.

In general, clients should

- Want to change, to grow, to become more conscious and competent as persons
- Be willing to restructure their lives and schedules
- Want to be the best they can be
- Be capable of visioning preferred futures
- Be willing to think beyond their own assumptions, mind-sets, and preferences
- Value other people and be able to reach decisions through collaboration
- Be willing to engage in whatever training it takes to resolve the coachable issues
- Be capable of disciplined and responsible planning steps

THE NATURE OF THE COACH-CLIENT RELATIONSHIP

I'm addressing my remarks to aspiring coaches here: *coaching is not giving advice.* It is not fixing things or solving problems. Coaching is establishing a vital relationship over a period of time with clients who are searching for the clarity and skills needed for making changes in their lives and human systems (couples, families, work, communities) in the near future.

The "product" of coaching comes from the bond between a coach and a client. It is not contained by the words used; nor is it easy to explain. Many clients call it empowerment, or growth, or breakthroughs. Coaching works to connect two dimensions of a client: the inner being or self and some outer action(s) or performance. Evolving this connection usually takes time, although there are many occasions in which the client has done much of the inner work before coaching begins.

You may be wondering where you would meet with your clients. For the most part, people do not go to a coach's office to meet on his or her turf. Coaching is more like anthropology—the coach goes to clients' natural environments to observe them. Do as much work as possible from the sidelines of the settings in which clients want to improve their performance: homes or workplaces. You can walk in parks with clients or chat in restaurants. Even if much coaching is to be conducted by telephone and on the Internet, make the first few sessions face-to-face meetings if at all possible. Settings for coaching should serve as facilitative environments for the coaching process—places that are quiet, home-like, near nature, and free of phones, noise, and electronics.

The best locations for group work are at places off the beaten path: retreat centers, cottages at hotels, and such. Use comfortable chairs but not lounge chairs, and have beverages and healthy snacks available. Be sure rest rooms are conveniently located. The room you meet in should have walls on which to tape easel paper.

When conducting systems coaching, use space available within the normal environments of the system, or, if it's important to get away from those environments in order to get a perspective on them, use off-site retreat facilities or unique hotels with private meeting quarters. The physical settings of coaching sessions are the stages on which coaching takes place, whether it is for one client or a group.

THE PROCESS OF DEVELOPING A GOOD COACH-CLIENT RELATIONSHIP

A sound relationship with a client must be created in stages. I'll describe the eight steps that coaches should take in that process.

Stage One: Establish the Coach-Client Relationship

The focus is to form trust. Listen, empathize, mirror back to the client what you hear. Lead from behind. Through listening to a client's story, you learn the language, issues, and ranges of possibility for the coaching work.

The overt goal is to understand the scenario your client is in and how he or she wants it to be different.

The covert goal is to understand how your client's inner self is related to outer actions under discussion. Is the real coaching focused on inner deepening, outer goal attainment, or both?

Your first coaching task is to facilitate a coach-client bond and a commitment to the purposes of the coaching process. At the first few meetings, you should become established as a concerned, helpful, and available resource—one who is supportive, affirming, listening, and confident. A climate of safety and trust should be established. Coaching cannot proceed unless the relationship is sound. You are the gatekeeper of fairness, pace, and focus.

Don't give formal assessments until after the relationship is well formed around the natural language and concerns of the client. By the third or fourth session it is usually effective to use the *Life Review* (see Appendix A, Hudson) or its equivalent to gather information on (1) background issues, assets, and deficits; (2) behavioral patterns; (3) value system and spiritual dimensions; (4) areas of distress and concern; (5) relationship strengths, weaknesses, and concerns; (6) career satisfaction and sense of importance; (7) leisure preferences, and (8) sense of the future.

Stage Two: Formulate a Coaching Agreement

The focus is to establish what is inside and outside the agreement. This will evolve and be redefined throughout the relationship. The initial coaching agreement is the first edition of a living document. Give clients copies of any current agreements you have, along with any rules, codes of ethics, or other professional information that is important to the coaching relationship.

The overt goal is to establish mutual expectations for the coaching relationship.

The covert goal is to keep the relationship within agreed-upon boundaries, which can be renegotiated by either party.

Stage Three: Move from a Problem Orientation to a Vision Orientation

The focus is on the future the client would prefer. Do not focus on what's not working in the client's life right now.

The overt goal is to discover your client's sense of purpose and to discover the qualities of the future scenario the client wants you to facilitate.

The covert goal is to shift from problem orientation to future orientation. Clients invariably seek out coaching because they are stuck with something they are having trouble mastering alone. Once they shift from a problem orientation to a future orientation, you can question and coach with a minimum of resistance.

Get into the work, not by hearing client complaints or problems but by getting clients to explore future options. Position clients toward their best options for visionary planning. Stay in a facilitative role, behind the clients, asking questions most of the time, such as, "What is your way to get that done?," "If achievement is your number-one passion, what shape will it take in the next chapter of your life?," "Since the roles you want in your life are about community improvement, how will you rearrange your other roles to make that happen?" "Since your vision is to be vice president of the corporation within two years, what are three steps you might take now to make it happen?"

Probe by asking questions; provide mirroring feedback—telling the client what you've heard and how you hear it relating to the overall story you are hearing. Listen and contextualize, always with tentativeness, by asking, "Do I have it about right?" In three or four sessions, you will have a pretty good picture of the gap between the ideal future the client wants and the actual conditions of the present. If that gap is too wide, you have to ask yourself how to foster a short-term plan with a challenging but not impossible dream. Never tell clients that their desired future is unreachable; ask them what they think and how they would get there, and provide realistic feedback on those details. Let the client stay in charge of his or her plan. You get realistic plans when your clients can freely imagine the future they really want. But those visions must be planned carefully and responsibly. Your success as a coach is in being able to facilitate passionate dreams that truly are within the reach of your clients.

Stage Four: Construct a Change Scenario

The focus is to develop a future-oriented personal or organizational strategic plan (or plans).

The overt goal is to create client-centered goals and action steps within the time frame the client prefers.

The covert goal is to keep the client responsible for each move into the future he or she prefers.

A coach can help clients create realistic plans for their visions and goals for the next chapter of their lives. Here the coach becomes more of a mechanic for the process, letting clients lead themselves. Some possible techniques are to

Use story boards. Provide clients with foam boards or laminated white plastic sheets, about 35 × 30 inches. Use Post-it® Notes to stick on the boards identifying purpose, vision, goals, roles, and action steps. Have clients plan out the next year or two of their lives, with goals, action steps, and time lines. This becomes a visual, changeable, dynamic tool for getting coaching results.

Rehearse plans. Have your clients rehearse their plans, receiving feedback each time. Rehearsal has the effect of building commitment and initiating the plan itself. Each time clients rehearse their plans, they fine-tune them, get validation from others, and begin to feel their plans taking place.

Encourage anticipatory behaviors. By the time the main phase of your coaching is over, your coaching is primarily to reinforce anticipatory behaviors, so clients are "leaning into the wind," feeling the future as if it were present, rehearsing tomorrow's scenarios today.

Stage Five: Resist Resistance

The focus is on resistance. As the coaching goals become more reachable, the client is likely to begin resisting the coaching. Clients sense a boulder across the path, an obstacle to getting what they want.

The overt goal is for the client to experience you, as coach, struggling with him as he struggles with himself.

The covert goal is to keep the client acutely responsible for his own resistance, so he chooses how he wants to live with it.

Clients would not be coming to you if they could figure out how to launch their own futures and feel good about them. Something, out of their awareness, holds them back. I have discussed this kind of resistance—threats come either from within (and prevent them from changing) or from the world around them (and prevent them from changing).

Resistance appears most strongly in the middle phase of a coaching process, after clients have fairly clear pictures of how they want to evolve but are finding all kinds of reasons why they can't do it. *The secret to doing resistance work is to cooperate with it.* It is not your job to remove it. But by asking your clients about their goals, sense of purpose, and vision for the next chapter, you can help clients take courageous steps ahead that diminish their resistance.

As the old Chinese proverb goes, "Give a fish to the hungry and they get a meal; teach them how to fish and they move beyond hunger." Teach your clients how to live with their resistances. Don't try to rescue clients from their resistance. Don't give advice. Don't create a climate that puts pressure on them to resolve their issue "for you" or "for the group." When they go home they will revert to their powerful resistance. But let them stew and feel their stuck points, while you remind them of what they have said is their preferred path ahead. Leave the decision to them. They will eventually make the best, conscious decisions they can. It is better to evolve brief, small, doable plans than long, huge, impossible ones. In coaching you can't avoid dealing with resistance in your clients. Be prepared for it, and learn to wait for your client to find the clearest paths ahead.

In this middle and longest phase of coaching, where the major work is done, you have a number of roles to play in order to move beyond resistance as an impasse. You should

- Observe ways your clients stay stuck—their patterned behavior to stay the way they are, along with their preferred form of distress.
- Facilitate resistance as it arises, using silence, questions, and sometimes confrontations. Invite your clients to find ways to lessen their resistance.
- Listen to the word pictures of your clients and to the story they are telling. Concentrate on how the client perceives his or her world and how you can enrich that perception.
- Observe ways your clients reveal their growth side: their "becoming" and "expectant" and "vital" concerns, and the words they use to express their vision and dreams. Encouraging and reinforcing these items will help your clients get beyond their resistance.
- Talk mainly through questions or mirroring summaries to be sure you understand what they are saying.

Stay behind your clients, waiting for them to lead themselves and taking responsibility for their own future. While staying behind, look for possible pathways ahead, and explore these with your clients in the form of questions. You want to tap the vision and dreams of each client, and then help clients find realistic plans to move their lives in visionary directions. It is when their vision becomes more powerful than their resistance that clients have breakthroughs.

As the process evolves over several sessions, the coaching culture evolves with high trust, openness, and expectancy. You invite clients to identify their finest vision of how they want to be at the end of their coachable issue (career, home life, corporate concern, and so forth). Have them write down their vision. From this point on, your leadership of the coaching process moves into the shadows. You continue to monitor the process but say less than you did earlier in the coaching process. Your client or clients will begin to coach themselves.

Stage Six: Challenge, Probe, Confront

The focus is on connecting a sense of purpose with a vision of a coaching "result." Create a set of action steps to ensure success.

The overt goal is to brainstorm, searching for new opportunities and potential obstacles, helping the client challenge herself.

The covert goal is to explore possibilities outside the client's normal assumptions and safety zones and to identify skills that she needs to obtain and see how they can be acquired.

There comes a time in every coaching relationship when the coach explores with the client matters that are outside the client's awareness. The client usually experiences discomfort. This phase often begins with a challenge by the coach, such as by asking, "What if you did this?" Or "I think you can do better than you're proposing. Let's aim higher, OK?" Ultimately, if a coach does not stretch a client to see and do things in new ways, the client will not feel fully served.

The secret to challenging is being sure that you've completed forming the coaching relationship with trust, care, listening, and questioning. Then as you shift into a more assertive mode, the client will not abandon you or fire you as you turn on some heat. Back off, somewhat, if the client becomes too uncomfortable with your confrontations. Remember, you have to stay within the relationship to complete your work with the client.

Stage Seven: Coach the New Scenario While Deepening the Relationship

The focus is on details, timing, priorities, training, integration, revision.

The overt goal is to validate, review, revise, and extend a strategic plan. This is usually where the bulk of the coaching relationship will be spent.

The covert goals are (1) for the client, to find the courage to evolve as a person and to perform at a higher level in some area of life; (2) for you, to seek a holistic integration of the being and action forces in your client.

As a coach you have forged an alliance with your client, and you are now working as a team to support and reach the coaching goals the client has formulated with you. As the bond between the two of you deepens, you can suggest other coachable issues if you think they are important to the goals of the client at this time. For example, you can suggest further training in communication skills, conflict management skills, or collaboration skills. The coaching agreement may be broadened and deepened at this point.

Stage Eight: Conclude the Formal Relationship; Begin Follow-Up Coaching

The focus is on celebrating the results of the coaching.

The overt goal is to validate and empower the client.

The covert goal is to provide a ritual for "graduating" the client, while you remain available if the client needs to return to the relationship for some reason.

In the last phase of a coaching process, the client or clients are energized, confident, and have many plausible planning steps in writing. They "coach" each other, informally. You shift to (1) facilitating the rehearsing of their visions and plans, (2) soliciting feedback regarding the integrity and realism of the plans, (3) celebrating the coaching outcomes with a meal, party, awards, and so on, and (4) establishing follow-up coaching contracts, which should provide personal or telephone support weekly or biweekly for four to eight weeks.

The termination of the formal coaching relationship requires some talk about the contract, its fulfillment or lack thereof, its transmutations, feelings in general, and any unfinished business. It is wise to say thank you and good-bye to the shared experience up to this point. Now the relationship will change, and the clients will be in an action mode, trying to invent the future, and you will be a coach on the sidelines offering encouragement, support, network suggestions, and evaluation of the plans.

During the follow-up phase, coaching often involves becoming an advocate and sponsor for your clients. Pick up the phone to help them make contact with experts they want to meet; suggest training programs where they can obtain skills; help them write a résumé or an important letter.

Follow-up coaching is devoted to keeping clients on course with their plans. Each time you contact a client after the intensive coaching relationship has ended, you ask—in one way or another—four questions:

1. What is working in your plan? (Identify the triumphs, the good stuff, the positives.)

2. What isn't working in your plan? (Identify concerns, disappointments, areas for revising the plan.)

3. What new conditions (internal and external to the client) suggest changes in your plan? (Identify new information that impedes the plan or opens it up to new opportunities. Identify whether these conditions are psychological issues or social-reality issues, or both.)

4. What do you want to accomplish from this brief coaching contact? Establish a contract for the telecoaching or in-person session you are in. Write down the agreement and have your client confirm that you've stated the proposed agenda for your time together correctly, and begin coaching. At the end of the session return to the agreement, read it, and see if you fulfilled the contract. If not, make a "homework" assignment of some sort—learning something, gathering data, visiting a specialist, writing something—and write it down so you can begin the next session asking how the homework came out.

After three months, six months, or a year or more—depending on your client's need for support and networking—you will want to conclude the coaching relationship with dignity and style. When you think the coaching is over, check it out with your client, and if there is general agreement, suggest that you have a special occasion—meal, glass of wine or sparkling water, walk together on a familiar path, or whatever—to appreciate each other and say good-bye.

 BASIC LIBRARY FOR COACHES

Drawing from Other Professions

*Argyris, C. *Knowledge for Action.* San Francisco: Jossey-Bass, 1993.
A portrayal of coaches as practical theorists, or thinkers, connected to action plans.

Barkow, J. H., Cosmides, L., and Tooby, J. (eds.). *The Adapted Mind: Evolutionary Psychology and the Generation of Culture.* New York: Oxford University Press, 1995. An original essay on the reciprocity between cultural change and personal adaptation.

Bateson, M. C. *Peripheral Visions: Learning Along the Way.* New York: HarperCollins, 1995. An exercise in getting comfortable with finding patterns and significance in the unfamiliar.

Beckhard, R., and Pritchard, W. *Changing the Essence: The Art of Creating and Leading Fundamental Change in Organizations.* San Francisco: Jossey-Bass, 1992. Outlines the fundamental tasks and foci coaches attend to when working with leaders.

Block, P. *Stewardship: Choosing Service Over Self-Interest.* San Francisco: Berrett-Koehler, 1993. A passionate call for putting service as the highest meaning of work and careers.

Carter, S. L. *Integrity.* New York: Basic Books, 1997. A blunt discussion by a professor at Yale Law School about the nature and importance of integrity.

*Csikszentmihalyi, M. *Finding Flow: The Psychology of Engagement with Everyday Life.* New York: Basic Books, 1998. A powerful argument that human life is an evolving process and that choosing optimal experiences for our growth is always available in the flow of our daily lives.

*Egan, G. *The Skilled Helper: A Problem-management Approach to Helping.* (6th ed.) Pacific Grove, Calif.: Brooks/Cole, 1998. A good beginning for learning coaching skills; used in graduate courses in the helping professions.

Egan, G. *Exercises in Helping Skills: A Manual to Accompany the Skilled Helper.* Pacific Grove, Calif.: Brooks/Cole, 1998. Useful exercises for coaching training.

Elgin, D. *Voluntary Simplicity.* (rev. ed.) New York: Quill, 1993. Originally published in 1981; a trumpet for personal downsizing.

*Goleman, D. *Emotional Intelligence: Why It Can Matter More than IQ.* New York: Bantam, 1995. One of the most important books for coaches, as all deep work begins and ends with emotions.

Goleman, D. *Working with Emotional Intelligence.* New York: Bantam, 1998. An organizational application of a previous book; identifies the skills of top performers.

Gozdz, K. *Community Building: Renewing Spirit and Learning in Business.* San Francisco: Sterling and Stone, 1996. A book of essays, including chapters by John Gardner, Peter Senge, Amitai Etzioni, Beth Jarman and George Land, Marvin Weisbord, and John Nirenberg.

Hammond, S. A. *Appreciative Inquiry.* Plano, Tex.: Kodiak Consulting, 1998. Looks for what is working and for ways to build the future on that information.

*Handy, C. *The Age of Paradox.* Cambridge, Mass.: Harvard Business School Press, 1995. A book about the paradoxes of our time and how we can find meaning and continuity in our lives.

*Hargrove, R. *Masterful Coaching.* San Francisco: Pfeiffer, 1995. The very best book on coaching, so far; combines "being" coaching with "performance" coaching and promotes both individual coaching and organizational coaching.

Herman, S. M. *A Force of Ones: Reclaiming Individual Power in a Time of Teams, Work Groups, and Other Crowds.* San Francisco: Jossey-Bass, 1994. Promotes ways to keep clear about your own strengths and priorities as the basis for how to connect with others.

*Hudson, F. M. *The Adult Years: Mastering the Art of Self-Renewal.* San Francisco: Jossey-Bass, 1999. (rev. ed.) Provides a framework for understanding the coaching process throughout the adult life cycle in the context of twenty-first-century realities.

*Hudson, F. M., and McLean, P. *LifeLaunch: A Passionate Guide to the Rest of Your Life.* Santa Barbara, Calif.: Hudson Institute Press, 1996. A workbook for helping a client find a sense of purpose, along with a visionary plan and action steps.

Hutchins, D. E., and Cole, C. G. *Helping Relationships and Strategies.* Monterey, Calif: Brooks/Cole, 1996. Describes how to establish a professional relationship through an interview process, how to establish a working relationship through active learning and questioning, how to reach agreed-upon goals, and how to conclude the relationship.

Jaques, E., and Cason, K. *Human Capability.* Falls Church, Va.: Cason Hall, 1994.

Kegan, R. *In Over Our Heads: The Mental Demands of Modern Life.* Cambridge, Mass.: Harvard University Press, 1995. A daring effort at what most of us simply refuse to face: how to make sound decisions that are teachable and defensible, in our kind of world; difficult reading.

Kennedy, P. *Preparing for the Twenty-First Century.* New York: Random House, 1994. An overview of the twenty-first century.

Knoke, W. *Bold New World: The Essential Road Map to the Twenty-First Century.* New York: Kodansha, 1997. A daring prospectus on how the next twenty-five years may evolve.

Kotter, J. P. *The New Rules: How to Succeed in Today's Post-Corporate World.* New York: Free Press, 1995. A book to help you stay focused on strategic issues leading to optimal choices with clients.

Langer, E. *Mindfulness.* Reading, Mass.: Addison-Wesley, 1990. A different way to think about being conscious and awake.

*Leider, R. J. *Life Skills: Taking Charge of Your Personal and Professional Growth.* Paramus, N.J.: Prentice Hall, 1993. A practical guide to coaching yourself.

*Leider, R. J. *The Power of Purpose.* (rev. ed.) San Francisco: Berrett-Koehler, 1997. A simple and powerful book by a visionary on the meaning of purpose.

Mahoney, M. J. *Human Change Processes.* New York: Basic Books, 1991.

Mandela, N. *Long Walk to Freedom.* Boston: Little, Brown, 1995. The most important autobiography of the twentieth century.

McNally, D. *Even Eagles Need a Push: Learning to Soar in a Changing World.* New York: Delecorte, 1994. A popular book about the need for leaders to be constantly renewing their motivation and vision—two important functions of coaches.

Miller, W. R., and Rollnick, S. *Motivational Interviewing.* New York: Guilford Press, 1991. Written for workers dealing with serious dysfunctions but describes the coaching skill-set remarkably well.

Pedler, M., Burgoyne, J., and Boydell, T. *The Learning Company.* New York: McGraw-Hill, 1998.

Prost, A., and Vincent, G. (eds.). *A History of Private Life: Riddles of Identity in Modern Times.* Cambridge, Mass.: Harvard University Press, 1991. A detailed, historical analysis of the change in how individuals experience their lives since the nineteenth century.

*Quinn, R. E. *Deep Change: Discovering the Leader Within.* San Francisco: Jossey-Bass, 1996. A corporate renewal book that begins with profound personal change.

Rusk, T. *Instead of Therapy: Help Yourself Change and Change the Help You're Getting.* Carson, Calif.: Hay House, 1993. Includes topics like "create your life," "face the awkwardness of change," and "find a guide to help you change."

Samples, R. *The Metaphoric Mind: A Celebration of Creative Consciousness.* Reading, Mass.: Addison-Wesley, 1993. Shows use of word pictures, stories, and even daydreams as vehicles for helping clients design for themselves the paths ahead.

Schein, E. H. *Organizational Culture and Leadership.* San Francisco: Jossey-Bass, 1992.

*Schön, D. *The Reflective Practitioner: How Professionals Think in Action.* New York: Basic Books, 1984.

Seligman, M. *Learned Optimism.* New York: Knopf, 1998. Easy to read and powerful information about how both helplessness and optimism are learned behaviors, as is optimism.

Weisbord, M. *Discovering Common Ground.* San Francisco: Berrett-Koehler, 1993.

Wheelis, A. *How People Change.* New York: Harper & Row, 1985. A classic by a profound thinker.

*Whyte, D. *The Heart Aroused.* New York: Doubleday, 1994. An inspiring book by a poet about the meaning of work.

Wilber, K. *The Spectrum of Consciousness.* Wheaton, Ill.: Theosophical Publishing, 1993. A philosophical and theological excursion into the history of consciousness.

Zeldin, T. *An Intimate History of Humanity.* New York: HarperPerennial, 1996. Cultural essays on the indefatigable spirit of humans.

Gender Coaching

*Arber, S., and Ginn, J. (eds.). *Connecting Gender and Aging.* Buckingham, England: Open University Press, 1995.

*Beall, A. E., and Steinberg, R. (eds.). *Psychology of Gender.* New York: Guilford Press, 1993. A book of readings on the topic, providing theories, life-span and cultural variations, and the integration of gender polarities.

Blumenfeld, W. J., and Raymond, D. *Looking at Gay and Lesbian Life.* (rev. ed.) Boston: Beacon, 1993.

Bly, R. (ed.). *Iron John: A Book about Men.* New York: Vintage Books, 1992.

Fox, M., Gibbs, M., and Auerbach, D. "Age and Gender Dimensions of Friendship." *Psychology of Women Quarterly,* 1985, *9,* 489–502.

Gonsiorek, J. C., and Weinrich, J. D. (eds.). *Homosexuality: Research Implications for Public Policy.* Newbury Park, Calif.: Sage, 1991.

Gray, J. *Men are from Mars, Women are from Venus.* New York: HarperCollins, 1992.

Nicholson, J. *Men and Women: How Different Are They?* New York: Oxford, 1993. A well-researched, scholarly book with reliable information.

Thompson, M. *Gay Soul: Finding the Heart of Gay Spirit and Nature.* San Francisco: Harper, 1994. Creative Education Foundation, 1050 Union

Road, Buffalo, NY 14224, 800-447-2774. Excellent resource for materials on and training opportunities in creative problem solving, using group techniques.

Women

*Bateson, M. C. *Composing a Life.* New York: Plume, 1990. A useful book with chapters by well-known women who show how they composed their lives.

*Belenky, M. F., Clinchy, B. M., Goldberger, N. R., and Tarule, J. M. *Women's Ways of Knowing: The Development of Self, Voice, and Mind.* New York: Basic Books, 1997. An important book about women's styles of perceiving, validating, and processing knowledge.

Betz, E., and Fitzgerald, L. F. *The Career Psychology of Women.* Orlando, Fla.: Academic Press, 1987. Although dated, one of the best guides in print.

*Brown, L. M., and Gilligan, C. *Meeting at the Crossroads: The Landmark Book About the Turning Points in Girls' and Women's Lives.* New York: Ballantine, 1992. A beautifully written book on female development, using many case studies and excellent research.

Carlson, K. J., Eisenstat, S. A., and Ziporyn, T. *The Harvard Guide to Women's Health.* Cambridge, Mass.: Harvard University Press, 1995.

Freudenberger, H. J., and North, G. *Women's Burnout: How to Spot It, How to Reverse It, and How to Prevent It.* New York: Doubleday, 1985.

*Gilligan, C. *In a Different Voice,* Cambridge, Mass.: Harvard University Press, 1979. A provocative and prophetic book that initiated a major drive to differentiate women's development from men's.

*Helgesen, S. *The Female Advantage: Women's Ways of Leadership.* New York: Doubleday, 1995. An original book on female leadership, stressing inclusion, finding vision and voice, and reconciling the efficient with the humane.

Helson, R. "Personality Change in Women from the Early 40s to the Early 50s." *Psychology and Aging,* 1992, *7,* 46–55.

Helson, R. "Women's Difficult Times and the Rewriting of the Life Story." *Psychology of Women Quarterly,* 1995, *16,* 331–347.

Helson, R., and Moane, G. "Personality Change in Women from College to Midlife." *Journal of Personality and Social Psychology,* 1987, *53,* 176–186.

HotFlash: A Newsletter for Midlife and Older Women. c/o National Action Forum for Midlife and Older Women, Box 816, Stony Brook, NY 11790. Contains articles and news about health and social issues.

Hulbert, K. D., and Schuster, D. T. (eds.). *Women's Lives Through Time: Educated American Women of the Twentieth Century.* San Francisco:

Jossey-Bass, 1993. A longitudinal study of American college women from 1930 on, examining role changes and adult life patterns.

*Josselson, R. *Finding Herself.* San Francisco: Jossey-Bass, 1990. An excellent introduction to understanding adult, female development.

*Lerner, H. G. *The Dance of Anger.* New York: Harper & Row, 1989.

*Levinson, D. J. *The Seasons of a Woman's Life.* New York: Knopf, 1996. Shows that women adhere closely to gender issues—family, work relationships, emotional states—making their development different from that of men.

Manson, J. E., Willett, W. C., and Associates. "Body Weight and Mortality Among Women." *New England Journal of Medicine,* 1995, *333,* 677–685.

Midlife Wellness Center for Climacteric Studies. University of Florida, 901 NW 8th Ave., Ste. B1, Gainesville, FL 32601. A quarterly journal on menopause and aging.

*Miller, J. B. *Toward a New Psychology of Women.* Boston: Beacon Press, 1986. Contrasts women's relationship orientation with women's subordinate group status. See *The Stone Center Working Papers* on women (The Stone Center, Wellesley College, Wellesley, MA 02181).

New Directions for Women, 108 West Palisade Ave., Englewood, NJ 07631. A good periodical for keeping track of new research and concepts for women's lives.

Photoflash: A Newsletter for Midlife and Older Women. c/o National Action Forum for Midlife and Older Women, Box 816, Stony Brook, NY 11790. Contains articles and news about health and social issues.

Reinke, B. J., Holmes, D. S., and Harris, R. L. "The Timing of Psychological Changes in Women's Lives: The Years 25–45." *Journal of Personality and Social Psychology,* 1985, *48,* 1,353–1,364.

Rogers, N. *Emerging Woman: A Decade of Midlife Transitions.* Santa Rosa, Calif.: Personal Press, 1980. A personal and sensitive book on how one woman sees women's development.

Rountree, C. *On Women Turning 50: Celebrating Midlife Discoveries.* New York: Three Rivers Press, 1996.

Rountree, C. *On Women Turning 60: Embracing the Age of Fulfillment.* New York: Three Rivers Press, 1997.

Rubin, B. M. *Fifty on Fifty: Wisdom, Inspiration, and Reflection on Women's Lives Well Lived.* New York: Warner, 1998.

Scott, L., with Schremp, K., Soldz, B., and Weiss, B. *Wise Choices Beyond Midlife: Women Mapping the Journey Ahead.* Watsonville, Calif.: Papier-Mache Press, 1997. A practical book for women over sixty who want to plan their lives proactively—relationships, money, health, and more. A handbook for life planning.

Scott-Maxwell, F. *The Measure of My Days: One Woman's Vivid, Enduring Celebration of Life and Aging.* New York: Penguin, 1979. A moving story by an American woman born in 1883 who died in 1979.

Sicherman, B., and Green, C. H. (eds.). *Notable American Women: The Modern Period.* Cambridge, Mass.: Belknap Press, 1980.

Troll, L. E., and others. *Looking Ahead: A Woman's Guide to the Problems and Joys of Growing Older.* Englewood Cliffs, N.J.: Prentice Hall, 1977. A little-known gem on the trade-offs women can make in their elder years.

*Turner, B. F., and Troll, L. E. (eds.). *Women Growing Older: Psychological Perspectives.* Thousand Oaks: Sage Press, 1994. Examines the realistic and optimal developmental paths for women, as well as the realistic deficits to expect.

Viorst, J. *Imperfect Control: Our Lifelong Struggles with Power and Surrender.* New York: Simon and Schuster, 1998.

Walker, B. G. *The Crone: Woman of Age, Wisdom, and Power.* New York: HarperCollins, 1988.

*Walker, B. G. *Women's Rituals: A Sourcebook.* New York: Harper & Row, 1990. Provides advice and information on how and when to conduct rituals, how to make mandalas, how to link rituals to rites of passage, and chantmaking.

Wesman, J. *Dive Right In, The Sharks Won't Bite: The Entrepreneurial Woman's Guide to Success.* New York: Dearborn Financial, 1995. A street-smart guide for women who want to run their own business and succeed.

Williams, J. H. *Psychology of Women.* (rev. ed.) New York: Norton, 1985. A standard reference.

Coaching Women

*Bateson, M. C. *Composing a Life.* New York: Plume, 1990. A very nice look at the introspective reports by several women on how their lives were shaped.

*Belenky, M. F., Clinchy, B. M., Goldberger, N. R., and Tarule, J. M. *Women's Ways of Knowing: The Development of Self, Voice, and Mind.* New York: Basic Books, 1997. An important book about women's styles of perceiving, validating, and processing knowledge.

Bernay, T., and Cantor, D. W. (eds.). *The Psychology of Today's Woman.* Hillsdale, N.J.: The Analytic Press, 1986. A report of psychoanalytic theories of women's relationships with family of origin and current family.

Bilson, J. M. *Keepers of the Culture: The Power of Tradition in Women's Lives.* San Francisco: Jossey-Bass, 1996. Presents new voices in the feminist debate: women of color, native women, and rural and immigrant women.

*Borysenko, J. *A Woman's Book of Life: The Biology, Psychology, and Spirituality of the Feminine Life Cycle.* New York: Riverhead, 1998.

Brown, L. M., and Gilligan, C. *Meeting at the Crossroads: The Landmark Book About the Turning Points in Girls' and Women's Lives.* New York: Ballantine, 1992. A beautifully written book on female development, using case studies and excellent research.

*Gilligan, C. *In a Different Voice.* Cambridge, Mass.: Harvard University Press, 1993. A provocative and prophetic book that initiated a major drive to differentiate women's development from men's.

Fitzgerald, L. F., and Nutt, R. "Division 17 Principles Concerning the Counseling/Psychotherapy of Women: Rationale and Implementation." *The Counseling Psychologist,* 1986, *14,* 180–216.

Helgesen, S. *The Female Advantage: Women's Ways of Leadership.* New York: Doubleday, 1995. An original book on female leadership, stressing inclusion, finding vision and voice, and reconciling the efficient with the humane.

Hulbert, K. D., and Schuster, D. T. *Women's Lives Through Time.* San Francisco: Jossey-Bass, 1997. A longitudinal examination of how education, gender, societal forces, and personal values affect the choices and achievements of educated American women in the twentieth century.

Jordan, J. V., Kaplan, A. G., Miller, J. B., Stiver, I. P., and Surrey, J. L. *Women's Growth in Connection: Writings from the Stone Center.* New York: Guilford Press, 1991. A useful collection of well-crafted essays.

*Josselson, R. *Finding Herself.* San Francisco: Jossey-Bass, 1990. An excellent introduction to understanding adult, female development.

Lerner, H. G. *The Dance of Anger.* New York: Harper & Row, 1989.

Lerner, H. G. *The Dance of Intimacy: Woman's Guide to Courageous Acts of Change in Key Relationships.* New York: Perennial, 1989.

McElroy, W. *The Reasonable Woman: A Guide to Intellectual Survival.* New York: Prometheus, 1998.

McFarland, B., and Watson-Rouslin, V. *My Mother Was Right: How Today's Women Reconcile with Their Mothers.* San Francisco: Jossey-Bass, 1998. Shows how baby-boomer women make peace with their mothers.

*Miller, J. B. *Toward a New Psychology of Women.* Boston: Beacon Press, 1986. Contrasts women's relationship orientation with women's subordinate group status. See *The Stone Center Working Papers* on women (The Stone Center, Wellesley College, Wellesley, MA 02181).

*Polster, M. F. *Eve's Daughters: The Forbidden Heroism of Women.* San Francisco: Jossey-Bass, 1996. Supplements the societal view of male heroism as aggressive and achieving with a reaffirmation of what women have done heroically for centuries: rely on their own innate and unique strengths and qualities in multiple settings.

Rawlings, E. I., and Carter, D. K. *Psychotherapy for Women: Treatment Toward Equality.* Springfield, Ill.: Thomas, 1977. Encourages women to develop as complete human beings; sets the stage for coaching principles.

Rogers, N. *Emerging Woman: A Decade of Midlife Transitions.* Santa Rosa, Calif.: Personal Press, 1980. A personal and sensitive book on how one woman sees women's development.

Rosoff, I. *The Woman Source Catalog and Review: Tools for Connecting the Community of Women.* Berkeley, Calif.: Celestial Arts, 1997. Practical information for finding resources for composing your life.

*Steenhouse, A. V. *A Woman's Guide to a Simpler Life.* New York: Harmony, 1996.

Coaching Women on Career Development

Davidson, C. *Staying Home Instead: Alternatives to the Two-Paycheck Family.* San Francisco: Jossey-Bass, 1995.

*Lonier, T. *Working Solo: The Real Guide to Freedom and Financial Success with Your Own Business.* New York: Wiley, 1998.

Rose, S., and Larwood, L. (eds.). *Women's Careers: Pathways and Pitfalls.* New York: Praeger, 1988.

*Sitterly, C. *The Female Entrepreneur: Overcoming Challenges in the Business World.* Menlo Park, Calif.: Crisp, 1994. A workbook for implementing a business plan.

*Walker, B. G. *Women's Rituals: A Sourcebook.* San Francisco: HarperCollins, 1990. A delightful excursion through the ways women can embroider their lives with, for example, play, silence, weaving, dancing.

Menopause

Bellantoni, M. F., and Blackman, M. R. "Menopause and Its Consequences." In E. L. Schneider and J. W. Rowe (eds.), *Handbook of the Biology of Aging.* San Diego, Calif.: Academic Press, 1996.

*Cutler, W. B., and Garcia, C. *Menopause: A Guide for Women and Those Who Love Them.* New York: Norton, 1993. A basic reference book.

*Greenwood, S. *Menopause, Naturally: Preparing for the Second Half of Life.* Volcano, Calif.: Volcano Press, 1996.

Landau, C., Cyr, M. G., and Moulton, A. W. *The Complete Book of Menopause.* New York: Peregrine, 1995. A good, overall guide to menopause, from physicians with traditional orientations.

*Love, S. M. *Dr. Susan Love's Hormone Book: Making Informed Choices About Menopause.* New York: Random House, 1997. A practical guide to menopause and alternative health considerations.

Midlife Wellness Center for Climacteric Studies. University of Florida, 901 NW 8th Ave., Ste B1, Gainesville, FL 32601. A quarterly journal on menopause and aging.

Myers, L. *Menopause and Beyond: A Fitness Plan for Life.* San Francisco: Adelaide, 1995.

Notelovitz, M., and Tonnessen, D. *Menopause & Midlife Health.* New York: St. Martin's, 1993.

*Riley, R., Bark, L., with Howard, T. A. *Compass: Your Roadmap Through Menopause.* San Francisco: LifeLines Institute, 1998. A workbook for women to understand their own experience of menopause.

Sheehy, G. *The Silent Passage: Menopause.* New York: Pocket Books, 1998.

Coaching Men

Brooks, G. R. *A New Psychotherapy for Traditional Men.* San Francisco: Jossey-Bass, 1998. Recommends a dialogical relationship between clinician and client about the culture and stresses of masculinity.

Clatterbaugh, K. *Contemporary Perspectives on Masculinity.* Boulder, Colo.: Westview Press, 1997. Traces the men's movement(s) through many iterations, orientations, and definitions.

Creative Education Foundation, 1050 Union Road, Buffalo, NY 14224, 800-447-2774. Excellent resource for materials on and training opportunities in creative problem solving, using group techniques.

Doyle, J. A. *The Male Experience.* Dubuque, Iowa: Wm. C. Brown, 1994. A comprehensive review of the male experience: historical, cultural, biological, sex roles, sexual experience, male heroes, homosexuality, power issues, and where we go from here.

Friedman, R. M., and Lerner, L. *Toward a New Psychology of Men.* New York: Guilford Press, 1986.

Gilmore, D. D. *Manhood in the Making: Cultural Concepts of Masculinity.* New Haven, Conn.: Yale University Press, 1989. Report by a cultural anthropologist on the great variety of male models throughout the world.

Hart, D. A. *Becoming Men. The Development of Aspirations, Values, and Adaptational Styles.* New York: Plenum, 1992.

*Hudson, L., and Jacot, B. *The Way Men Think: Intellect, Intimacy, and the Erotic Imagination.* New Haven, Conn.: Yale University Press, 1991. A brilliant book on why men are the way they are.

*Keen, S. *Fire in the Belly: On Being a Man.* New York: Bantam, 1991. A well-informed treatise on an array of male issues.

*Moore, R., and Gillette, D. *King, Warrior, Magician, Lover: Rediscovering the Archetypes of the Mature Masculine.* New York: HarperCollins, 1990. A clear and concise, Jungian interpretation of manhood.

*Osherson, S. *Wrestling with Love: How Men Struggle with Intimacy.* New York: Ballantine, 1992. Brilliant treatment of the male difficulty to attach to love objects.

Osherson, S., and Krugman, S. "Men, Shame, and Psychotherapy." *Psychotherapy, Journal of the Division of Psychotherapy,* American Psychological Association. Fall 1990, *27*(3), 327–339. An issue devoted to "Men's Roles and Psychotherapy."

Real, T. *I Don't Want to Talk About It: Overcoming the Secret Legacy of Male Depression.* New York: Scribner, 1997. Describes how men can unearth their pain, heal themselves, restore relationships, and break the legacy of abuse.

Schleisinger, L. *Ten Stupid Things Men Do to Mess Up Their Lives.* New York: HarperPerennial, 1997. Blunt and petulant advice for the downside of male life.

Sheehy, G. *Understanding Men's Passages.* New York: Random House, 1998.

*Thompson, K. (ed.). *To Be a Man: In Search of the Deep Masculine.* Los Angeles: Tarcher, 1991.

Dealing with Resistance

Alberti, R. E. (ed.). *Assertiveness: Innovations, Applications, Issues.* San Luis Obispo, Calif.: Impact, 1977. A book of readings on assertiveness, distinguishing assertiveness from aggression, and relating it to many issues and settings of relevance to coaches.

*Baumeister, R. F. *Escaping the Self: Alcoholism, Spirituality, Masochism, and Other Flights from the Burden of Selfhood.* New York: Basic Books, 1991. A great introduction of some heavy boulders.

Diagnostic and Statistical Manual of Mental Disorders. (4th ed.) Washington, D.C.: American Psychiatric Association, 1994. A reference work of mental disorders; can help coaches recognize symptoms and behaviors so they can make proper referrals.

Fromm, E. *The Anatomy of Human Destructiveness.* Austin, Tex.: Holt, Rinehart and Winston, 1973. A study of how instincts and human passions often lead to destructive forms of aggression.

*Hardy, R. E., and Schwartz, R. *The Self-Defeating Organization.* Reading, Mass.: Addison-Wesley, 1996. Compares low-performance loops with high-performance loops and describes how to transform the former to the latter.

*Kanter, D. L., and Mirvis, P. H. *The Cynical Americans: Living and Working in an Age of Discontent and Disillusion.* San Francisco: Jossey-Bass, 1989. An important book for coaches.

Loehr, J. E., and McLaughlin, P. J. *Mentally Tough: The Principles of Winning at Sports Applied to Winning in Business.* New York: Evans, 1986. This book aims to prevent boulders from forming by stressing positive energy, visualization, physical exercise, proper eating, performance rituals, problem solving skills, and the myth of stress.

*Maurer, R. *Beyond the Wall of Resistance: Unconventional Strategies that Build Support for Change.* Austin, Tex.: Bard Books, 1995. Examines the limits of "reengineering" in corporate systems and makes a convincing case that change requires managers who know how to transform their power of resistance into a positive force.

Miller, W. R., and Rollnick, S. *Motivational Interviewing.* New York: Guilford Press, 1991. A good book on coaching skills with several chapters on resistance.

Millman, H. L., and Associates. *Therapies for Adults: Depressive, Anxiety, and Personality Disorders.* San Francisco: Jossey-Bass, 1982. Contains concise descriptions of adult dysfunctions, extending from normal maladies to psychopathology.

Peck, M. S. *People of the Lie: The Hope for Healing Human Evil.* New York: Simon and Schuster, 1983.

*Robinson, B. E. *Chained to the Desk: A Guidebook for Workaholics.* New York: New York University Press, 1998. A thorough description of work addiction and how it affects marriages, families, and friendships.

*Seligman, M. *Helplessness: On Development, Depression, and Death.* New York: Freeman, 1992. Views helplessness as a learned behavior that can be unlearned.

Seuss, Dr. *Thidwick, The Big-Hearted Moose.* New York: Random House, 1948. A great story of a do-gooder who helped everyone else except himself until he got rid of his boulder.

Shapiro, D. *Neurotic Styles.* New York: Basic Books, 1965. Simple descriptions of the obsessive-compulsive, paranoid, hysterical, and impulsive styles, along with interpretations.

**Skills for Success: The Experts Show the Way.* Bristol, Vt.: Soundview, 1989.

Another book on preempting boulders in your life—by being successful, creative, organized, communicative; avoiding burnout; and leading and motivating others.

Negotiating Skills

Alberti, R. E. (ed.). *Assertiveness: Innovations, Applications, Issues.* San Luis Obispo, Calif.: Impact, 1977. A book of readings on assertiveness, distinguishing assertiveness from aggression, and relating it to many issues and settings of relevance to coaches.

Fisher, R., and Brown, S. *Getting Together: Building Relationships as We Negotiate.* New York: Penguin, 1988. Teaches how to deal well with differences and being unconditionally constructive, working with trust and persuasion (not coercion).

*Fisher, R., and Ury, W. *Getting to Yes: Negotiating Agreement Without Giving In.* (2nd ed.) New York: Penguin, 1991. A standard reference.

Heitler, S. M. *From Conflict to Resolution: Skills and Strategies for Individual, Couple, and Family Therapy.* New York: Norton, 1990.

*Tannen, D. *You Just Don't Understand: Women and Men in Conversation.* New York: Ballantine, 1990. Excellent for skill development in understanding the similarities and difference in communication styles of men and women.

Tannen, D. *Talking from Nine to Five.* New York: Morrow, 1994. Corporate applications of male-female communication and miscommunication.

Living with Unsolvable Problems

Adamec, C. *How to Live with a Mentally Ill Person: A Handbook of Day-to-Day Strategies.* New York: Wiley, 1996.

Allen, R. F., and Kraft, C. *The Organizational Unconscious.* Englewood Cliffs, N.J.: Prentice Hall, 1982. An early description of irrational, organizational turmoil that takes its toll.

*Johnson, B. *Polarity Management: Identifying and Managing Unsolvable Problems.* Amherst, Mass.: HRD Press, 1992. An original treatise on how to live creatively with unsolvable problems.

Kreilkamp, T. *The Corrosion of the Self: Society's Effects on People.* San Francisco: Jossey-Bass, 1976. Explores ways social scientists have described the harm that society often inflicts on individual lives.

Morris, E. K., and Braukmann, C. J. (eds.). *Behavioral Approaches to Crime and Delinquency: A Handbook of Applications, Research, and Concepts.* New York: Plenum, 1987.

Cults

*Lewis, J. R. *The Encyclopedia of Cults, Sects, and New Religions.* New York: Prometheus, 1998.

Singer, M. T., and Lalich, J. *Cults in Our Midst: The Hidden Menace in Our Everyday Lives.* San Francisco: Jossey-Bass, 1996. A definitive description of what cults are and how they work; explains how to escape cult entrapments and recover from the experience.

Other Social Issues

Antonucci, T. C. "Attachment, Social Support, and Coping with Negative Life Events." In E. M. Cummings, A. L. Greene, and H. H. Karracker (eds.), *Life-Span Developmental Psychology: Vol. 11. Stress and Coping Across the Life-Span.* Hillsdale, N.J.: Erlbaum, 1990.

Bassuk, E. L. "Homelessness: A Growing American Tragedy." *Division of Child, Youth, and Family Services Newsletter,* 1989, *12,* 1–13.

Bell, D. *Faces at the Bottom of the Well: The Permanence of Racism.* New York: Basic Books, 1992.

Bergler, E. *The Psychology of Gambling.* Madison, Conn.: International Universities Press, 1984.

Kieffer, G. H. *Bioethics: A Textbook of Issues.* Reading, Mass.: Addison-Wesley, 1979. Examines ethical decision making in relation to genetic tampering, reproductive techniques, euthanasia, medicine, obligations to future generations, and population control.

Matsakis, A. *I Can't Get Over It: A Handbook for Trauma Survivors.* Oakland, Calif.: New Harbinger, 1996. Explains how to get over traumatic crises throughout adult life.

Walsh, R. *Staying Alive: The Psychology of Human Survival.* Boulder, Colo.: New Science, 1984. Shows how to live with global threats and fears and put energy into healing.

Wenberg, J., and Associates. *Psychosocial Aspects of Nuclear Developments.* Report of the Task Force of the American Psychiatric Association. Washington, D.C.: APA, 1981.

White, R. K. (ed.). *Psychology and the Prevention of Nuclear War.* New York: New York University Press, 1986. A remarkable book on strategies that people in the helping professions can take to prevent nuclear war.

CHAPTER THREE 

Coaching as a Profession

As I mentioned earlier in the book, the status of coaching as a profession is unclear at this time. Certainly many good coaches are going about their duties in a professional manner. But, for example, coaching is not a college major. Nor is it a program in professional schools. There could well be such majors and programs in the near future. For the moment, though, *coaching* refers to a set of skills that are practiced in a professional manner and accompanied by a future-oriented point of view. (See Basic Library: Coaching as a Professional Field for references to guide further study of this topic.)

PROFESSIONAL ORGANIZATIONS FOR COACHES

One indicator of where coaching is going is that professional organizations are forming. Four of these are

International Coach Federation, PO Box 1393, Angel Fire, NM 87710. 888-423-3131; e-mail: audrey@newmex.com

Website: www/coachfederation.org

International Coaching Society, 4750 Vista Street, San Diego, CA 92116. 619-282-5760.

Professional Coaches and Mentors Association, PO Box 2907, Seal Beach, CA 90740. 800-979-7262.

Professional and Personal Coaches Association, 849 Independence Ave., Suite B, Mountain View, CA 94043. 650-903-8305.

Tampa Bay Professional Coaching Association, 21629 Teal Court, Lutz, FL 33549. 813-949-0718.

OTHER ASSOCIATIONS AS RESOURCES

Several other organizations, though not specifically for coaches, can be useful resources for coaches:

American Council on Exercise, 5820 Oberlin Drive, Suite 102, San Diego, CA 92121-3787. 800-825-3636.

Website: www.acefitness.org

American Counseling Association, 5999 Stevenson Ave., Alexandria, VA 22304. 703-823-9800.

American Society for Training & Development, 1640 King Street, Box 1443, Alexandria, VA 22313. 703-683-8100.

Website: www.astd.org

American Society on Aging, 833 Market Street, Suite 511, San Francisco, CA 94103. 415-974-9600.

Website: www.asaging.org

Creative Education Foundation, 1050 Union Road, Buffalo, NY 14224. 800-447-2774. Excellent resource for materials on and training opportunities in creative problem solving, using group techniques.

Future Search Training, c/o Sally Lord, Resources for Human Development, Inc., 4333 Kelly Drive, Philadelphia, PA 19129.

International Association of Facilitators, 7630 West 145th Street, Suite 202, St. Paul, MN 55124. 612-891-3541.

Website: www.1AF-world.com

National Council on Aging, 409 Third Street SW, 2nd fl., Washington, DC, 20024. 202-479-1200.

NTL Institute, 300 N. Lee Street, Suite 300, Alexandria, VA 22314. 800-777-5227.

Website: www.ntl.org

Organization Development Network, 76 Orange Ave., Suite 101, South Orange, NJ 07079. 973-763-7337.

Another indicator of the changing status of coaching as a profession is the number of training programs in existence. These are listed in Appendix B. The fact is, no matter what the activity of coaching is called, it's a business for many. And good business practices must be followed by individual coaches if coaching is to become a full-fledged profession.

THE BUSINESS SIDE OF COACHING

There is no universal way that coaches manage payment for their services. Some coaches work within organizations and are paid a salary; most are external coaches and are paid either by organizations or by individual clients.

Some coaches charge by the hour, but I recommend charging in such a way that the duration of the coaching relationship is reinforced. It works well to charge by the quarter (every three months); if possible, charge in advance of services. That way both coach and client develop a commitment to the work. If a client will agree to a six-month or one-year coaching agreement, the coach can bill by the quarter.

To formulate how much a fee should be, no matter how it is billed, the total time of service (in person, by phone, by e-mail) should be calculated and value established accordingly. In building a practice, most new coaches discover they need to begin at a low fee and gradually establish a reputation that will justify higher fees. Many coaches integrate coaching with their other professional functions, the most common of which are consulting, managing, training, and administering.

ETHICAL GUIDELINES FOR COACHES

The International Coach Federation (ICF) is seeking to coordinate the coaching community and has established these ethical guidelines for coaches:

> [Preamble] A coach believes in the dignity and integrity of every human being and is committed to eliciting the inherent capability and resourcefulness of every individual. A coach pursues, through an interactive process, the development of client-designed strategies and solutions which move the client toward the rapid attainment of his goals. A coach is respectful and protective of the vulnerability of each client, while constructively holding the client to a high standard of self-responsibility and accountability. The coach maintains an objectivity and competence where he claims it and practices in the best interests of the client, the community, and society.
>
> *Coaching Relationship and Contract:* At the beginning of any coaching relationship, ICF coaches will articulate the terms of the client-coach relationship in a clear, written communication or agreement. (Such an agreement may be recordable by Web site, brochure, e-mail, or a signed paper agreement.) Terms

of the coach-client agreement will include the qualifications of the coach; the nature of the services available; limitations, boundaries, and perspectives of the coach or the services offered; a Statement of Client's Rights; and terms of the contract, that is, times, frequency, and methods of communication, and fees for the coaching service.

Client Protection: The client's well-being is the central focus of a coaching relationship and thereby obligates the coach to maintain a high level of integrity and trustworthiness throughout the contract. Therefore, coaches are respectful of the client's needs and requests; constructive in their feedback; attentive to the boundaries and limitations of each party; mindful of confidentiality issues and conflicts of interest; forthright and authentic in addressing any such issues as they emerge. The coach will, under no circumstances, take advantage of a client personally, socially, sexually, or financially. The coach will disclose any and all personal gain accrued by the client-coach relationship, including but not limited to, useful knowledge, personal growth, fees received for referrals or recommendations made to and/or pursued by the client. The coach will not only communicate, but will continuously demonstrate that the intended outcome of an exchange of information, discussion, referral, or recommendation is the client's growth and well-being, not the promotion of the coach's self-interest.

Confidentiality: The coach will make every effort to honor the client's confidence, although the coach cannot provide an *a priori* guarantee. The coach will advise the client of circumstances that might influence the coach's objectivity or judgment and any decision or factors relating to a decision to reveal the client's confidential information to a higher authority. Clients will be apprised that their confidence is not privileged under law and could be subpoenaed via the coach. To the extent that a coach is uncomfortable holding a client's confidence, the coach is advised to consult a mentor coach in an effort to jointly determine how best to handle the situation. In rare cases, if the confidential information is of an "outrageous," "illegal," or "dangerous-to-the-client-or-others" nature, the coach is obligated to consult a mentor coach, and/or an attorney, in order to determine whether to notify authorities, with or without the client's consent. The client is apprised and agrees that any materials provided by the coach may not be resold, published, or used outside the coaching relationship with the explicit permission of the coach.

Conflicts of Interest: Any conflict of interest is to be discussed and resolved with the client's best interest in mind. Whenever a conflict becomes apparent, the coach is ethically obligated to identify it and attempt to resolve it. If, during the coaching relationship, the coach cannot serve the client objectively, respectfully, or without internal or external conflict, the coach is ethically obligated to terminate the coaching agreement/contract. Such a termination provides reasonable advance notice and a reasonable explanation of the conflict at the center of the termination decision.

Referrals and Terminations: Whenever internal or external conditions arise that seem "uncoachable" or unworkable, the coach is ethically committed to reveal his observations and opinion to the client. The coach will suggest a viable solution(s) to the problem, making every effort to avoid injury to the dignity of the client. If the solution includes a referral to another coach, the referring coach is ethically committed to refer to three (3) more suitable coaches, one (1) of which may be the ICF Referral Service. If the coach's suggested solution includes termination without referral, or postponement of the coaching contract until a more suitable time, the coach is ethically committed to a clear explanation of the rationale underlying the recommendation.

Ethical Violations: If a coach knowingly, consistently, or outrageously breaches the *Ethical Guidelines of the ICF,* the coach will be asked to work with a mentor coach and/or be expelled from the ICF association. A coach who receives a reprimand by the ICF is encouraged to train with a mentor coach for a period of months (length of time to be determined by the ICF Board), until the essence of the complaint is corrected. Expulsion from ICF will mean that the coach will no longer be authorized to claim or use membership in the ICF, nor represent forfeiture of any pre-paid dues to the organization by the coach being expelled.

SPECIALIZED COACHING AREAS

Most coaches are generalists first and foremost. But they often have a specialty as well, working with specific populations or areas of expertise. Coaches usually have had long and rich careers that have provided them with expert knowledge about areas in which they want to coach. Examples of such areas are executive development, transition management, outplacement, couples development, financial planning, strategic planning, team performance, entrepreneurism, and community development.

Other specializations of adult coaches are

Organizational Coaching	Elderhood Renewal
Team Performance Coaching	Coaching Professionals
Strategic Planning	Community Coaching
Career Resilience	Training Through Workshops
Corporate Training	Leading Coaching Groups
Executive Coaching	Motivational Speaking
Sales Coaching	Spiritual Renewal
Renewal for Men (or Women)	Couples Renewal

Please see the Basic Library for references on two coaching specialties: (1) Wellness Coaching; Nutrition and Exercise and (2) Financial Coaching.

THE FUTURE OF COACHING

The coaching world is busy weaving together its many successes as it moves beyond its first honeymoon phase into the blunt realities of professional practice. It is now well established that coaching is a skill set that is useful to many professionals, not only in corporate settings but in medical and law practices, community development, and life and career planning. Many coaching skills are shared with professionals of other fields.

Characteristics of the Profession

Some characteristics of the profession that are essential to its future include

- *Being facilitative.* Although coaching requires structure and boundaries, it is mostly process. Facilitation skills make the most difference. Coaching is a catalyst for change; coaches identify future choices and are able to coach leadership.
- *Being entrepreneurial.* The entrepreneurial characteristic in coaching keeps the field from becoming a traditional helping profession. The entrepreneurial drive is linked to vision, to the imagination, and to global thinking.
- *Mentoring.* Mentoring is the mode of delivery of coaches, who lead by example, through ongoing relationships. Coaches model the way, and no matter what the content of the particular coaching issue, the maturation of the person being mentored is the primary product. Mentoring, which takes time and perseverance, deepens consciousness and caring in the recipient.
- *Being focused on deep work.* Because so many of the tools of coaching come from psychology, organizational development, and the lives of mature people, coaches focus not on a quick fix but on profound human and organizational transformation. Coaches use tools that engage emotional as well as mental intelligence. In the end, coaches look for actions that are both value-based and possible.
- *Incorporating team and group work.* Coaching teams or working with coaching groups leverages the impact of a coach. It generally produces results faster than one-on-one work, but more important, it teaches interdependence and collaboration—two qualities essential for future leadership.
- *Fostering a broad range of specializations.* Coaches can be effective in a wide range of settings, dealing with a great variety of populations and concerns. This *Handbook* is an introduction to what is taking place in the field of coaching, but coaching skills can be empowering in any human setting.
- *Blending easily with other professions.* Because of its wide effectiveness, coaching appeals to leaders, managers, government workers, educators, medical professionals, lawyers, to name a few professionals. Many people who are coaching in part to make a living combine their coaching skills with other skills such as consulting, training, public speaking, future visioning, or managing conflict.

Hurdles to Jump

Remaining alive and well as a professional field will take staying power. Here are some of the hurdles that coaching faces in the next few years:

- *Self-regulation.* By and large, the certified coaches of the various training institutes are working together with due diligence to develop standards for the coaching profession, including training standards, a code of ethics, and continuing education requirements. This is an essential step if the field is to mature as a profession.
- *Recognition of essential knowledge and skills for all coaches.* Until those who certify coaches are using the same standards for education and evaluation, the public will rightfully question the consistency and substance of the coaching field. A careful bridge needs to be constructed between the internal definition of the field (how coaches think and act) and how the public can access reliable coaches for their specific needs. Otherwise, state licensing boards are likely to take over the task of defining the field and enforcing educational and practice standards.
- *Connections to other professional groups.* Several established professional groups have succeeded at what coaching organizations are struggling with in terms of standards, training, and professional ethics. The leaders in the coaching world could collaborate to form informal or formal alliances with the American Counseling Association, the Organizational Development Network, the American Society for Training and Development, The American Society on Aging, the Creative Education Foundation, International Association of Facilitators, and The National Training Laboratory Institute.

I have to believe that the sheer relevance of coaching for our global village will motivate the leaders and followers of coaching organizations to work rapidly toward unity, professionalism, and recognized standards for training and practice. It is no accident that coaching appeared in the last ten years and gained rapid momentum as a field. Coaching is a sound resource for making a difference to human and organizational development, and it will remain so for the indefinite future.

BASIC LIBRARY FOR COACHES

Wellness Coaching; Nutrition and Exercise

Balch, J. F, and Balch, P. A. *Prescription for Nutritional Healing: An A-Z Reference to Drug-Free Remedies Using Vitamins, Minerals, Herbs and Food Supplements.* (2nd ed.) Garden City Park, N.Y.: Avery, 1997.

Butler, K., and Rayner, L. *The New Handbook of Health and Preventive Medicine.* New York: Prometheus, 1992.

Carlson, K. J., Eisenstat, S. A., and Ziporyn, T. *The Harvard Guide to Women's Health.* Cambridge, Mass.: Harvard University Press, 1997.

*Editors of the University of California, Berkeley. *The New Wellness Encyclopedia.* Boston: Houghton Mifflin, 1995. A guide to nutrition, exercise, self-care, and coping with environmental problems.

Fisher, P. (ed.). *Age Erasers for Women: Actions You Can Take Right Now to Look Younger and Feel Great.* Emmaus, Penn.: Rodale, 1994. Practical steps for health and cosmetic care.

*Golan, R. *Optimal Wellness.* New York: Ballantine, 1995. A practical guide to wellness, written by a physician.

Hill, R. D., Storandt, M., and Malley, M. "The Impact of Long-term Exercise Training on Psychological Function in Older Adults." *Journal of Gerontology: Psychological Sciences,* 1993, *48,* 12–17.

Horwitz, A., Macfadyen, D. M., Nunro, H., Scrimshaw, N. S., Steen, B., and Williams, T. F. (eds.). *Nutrition in the Elderly.* Oxford, England: Oxford University Press, 1989.

Journal of Counseling and Development. Special Issue: Wellness Throughout the Life Span. Nov./Dec. 1992, *71*(2), American Counseling Association.

*Judelson, D. R., and Dell, D. L. *The Woman's Complete Wellness Book.* New York: Golden, 1998. A compilation of the latest information on women's health.

Kirshman, G. J., and Kirshman, J. D. *Nutrition Almanac.* (4th ed.) New York: McGraw-Hill, 1996. A reliable guide to eating and health.

Longfellow, L. *Healthy, Wealthy, and Wise. Who Says You Can't Have It All?* Videotape: Lecture Theatre Inc., PO Box 4317, Prescott, AZ 86302. 602-778-6629.

Moore, R. D. *The High Blood Pressure Solution.* Rochester, Vt.: Healing Arts Press, 1993.

Moyers, W. *Healing and the Mind.* New York: Doubleday, 1995. Bill Moyers' book of dialogue with healers of our time, concentrating on health and wholeness.

*Murray, M. M., and Pizzorno, J. (2nd ed.) *Encyclopedia of Natural Medicine.* Rocklin, Calif.: Prima, 1998. An outstanding compendium for understanding adult health issues and how to promote longevity.

*Ornish, D. *Everyday Cooking with Dr. Dean Ornish: 150 Easy, Low-Fat, High-Flavor Recipes.* New York: HarperCollins, 1997. Good recipes, along with his general approach to longevity.

Pritikin, R. *The New Pritikin Program.* New York: Pocket Books, 1991. Wise information, from the son of Nathan Pritikin, who began the Pritikin Programs.

Raso, J., and Barrett, S. *"Alternative" Healthcare: A Comprehensive Guide.* New York: Prometheus, 1994. A reliable reference book.

Salmon, H. E. *Fitness After Fifty.* 1992. Reprints of NIA publications on this topic. Obtain from 314-391-6258. $3.50.

Shealy, C. N. (ed.). *The Complete Family Guide to Alternative Medicine.* Rockport, Mass.: Element Books, 1996. A presentation of many available natural therapies and how they work, including a section on physical ailments.

Siegel, B. S. *Peace, Love and Healing: BodyMind Communication, and the Path to Self Healing.* New York: Harper & Row, 1990. A book about balance, wholeness, healing, and finding one's true self.

*Slupik, R. I. (ed.). *Complete Guide to Women's Health.* New York: Random House, 1996. The most complete single volume on this topic.

Stalker, D., and Glymour, C. *Examining Holistic Medicine.* New York: Prometheus, 1997. A thorough overview.

Stare, F. J., Aronson, V., and Barrett, S. *Your Guide to Good Nutrition.* New York: Prometheus, 1993.

*Weil, A. *Spontaneous Healing.* New York: Fawcett, 1995. Shows how to keep healthy.

**The Wellness Encyclopedia: The Comprehensive Family Resource for Safeguarding Health and Preventing Illness.* Boston: Houghton Mifflin, 1995. A thorough resource that is practical and useful.

*Williams, M. E. *The American Geriatrics Society's Complete Guide to Aging and Health.* New York: Harmony, 1995.

Financial Coaching

Bork, D., Jaffe, D. T., Lane, J. H., Dashen, L., and Heisler, Q. G. *Working with Family Businesses,* San Francisco: Jossey-Bass, 1996.

*Casey, J. C. *Estate Planning for Middle and Large Income Earners.* JC Publishing, PO Box 611, Solana Beach, CA 92075. 800-808-2112.

Chilton, D. *The Wealthy Barber.* Financial Awareness Corporation, c/o Prima Publishing, PO Box 1260BK, Rocklin CA 95677. 800-665-3913.

*Crumbley, D. L., and Smith, L. M. *Keys to Personal Financial Planning.* (2nd ed.) New York: Barrons, 1994. A short nuts-and-bolts paperback.

*Edelman, R. *The Truth About Money.* Washington, D.C.: Georgetown University Press, 1996. Widely recognized source of sound information.

Hughes, J. E., Jr. *Family Wealth: Keeping It in the Family.* Princeton Junction, N.J.: NetWrx, Inc., 1997. A unique book on financial planning, based on the concept of family wealth residing in the individual family members.

Loeb, M. *Marshall Loeb's Lifetime Financial Strategies: Your Ultimate Guide to Future Wealth and Security.* Boston: Little, Brown, 1996.

*Madanes, C., and Claudio. *The Secret Meaning of Money: How It Binds Together Families in Love, Envy, Compassion, or Anger.* San Francisco: Jossey-Bass, 1998. Introduces a problem-solving method that uses money to restore and heal family relationships.

National Association of Personal Financial Advisors, 1130 Lake Cook Road, Ste. 150, Buffalo Grove, IL 60089. 708-537-7722.

*Needleman, J. *Money and the Meaning of Life.* New York: Currency Doubleday, 1994. An outstanding philosophical exploration of the many meanings money has for human beings.

Registry of Financial Planning Practitioners, Two Concourse Pkwy., Ste. 800, Atlanta, GA 30328.

Tracy, J. A. *How to Read a Financial Report.* New York: John Wiley, 1993.

*Tyson, E. *Personal Finance for Dummie$: A Reference for the Rest of Us.* Foster City, Calif.: IDG Books, 1996. Highly detailed but simple to follow.

Wilson, R. *How to Insure Your Life: A Guide to Buying the Coverage You Need.* Santa Monica, Calif.: Merritt, 1996. A simple guide to audit life insurance planning.

Coaching as a Professional Field

"A Coach May Be the Guardian Angel You Need to Rev Up Your Career." *Money,* Dec. 1996.

Allenbaugh. G. E. "Coaching: A Management Tool for a More Effective Work Performance." *Performance Improvement Quarterly,* 1992, *5*(2), 2–12.

Aurelio, S., and Kennedy, J. K., Jr. "Performance Coaching: A Key to Effectiveness." *Supervisory Management,* 1991, *36,* 1–2.

Banning, L. K. "Executive Counsel." *Human Resource Executive,* Jan. 1997.

Barrett, F. J., "Creating Appreciative Learning Cultures." *Organizational Dynamics,* Feb. 1992, 36–49.

Barrett, F. J., Thomas, G. F., and Hocevar, S. P. "The Central Role of Discourse in Large-Scale Change: A Social Construction Perspective." *Journal of Applied Behavioral Science,* Sept. 1995, *31*(3), 352–372.

Bassi, C. S., and Lewis, E. "Trends in Workplace Learning: Supply and Demand in Interesting Times." *Training & Development,* Nov. 1998, *52*(11), 51 ff.

Bell, C. R. "Coaching for High Performance." *Advanced Management Journal,* 1987, *52,* 26–29.

*Bergquist, W., Merritt, K., and Phillips, S. *Executive Coaching: An Appreciative Approach.* Sacramento, Calif.: Pacific Soundings Press, 1999.

Bernstein, B. J., and Kaye, B. L. "Teacher, Tutor, Colleague, Coach." *Personnel Journal,* Nov. 1986.

Bielous, G. A. "Effective Coaching: Improving Marginal Performers." *Supervision,* 1994, *55,* 3–5.

Buckley, T. "Coaching Is Tough Medicine: Are You Your Company's Biggest Problem?" *The Costco Connection,* Feb./Mar. 1998, 24–25.

Bushe, G. R. "Advances in Appreciative Inquiry as an Organization Development Intervention." *Organization Development Journal,* Fall 1995, *13*(3), 14–22.

Bushe, G. R. "Appreciative Inquiry as a Team Development Intervention: A Controlled Experiment." *Journal of Applied Behavioral Science,* Mar. 1995, *31*(1), 13–30.

Bushe, G. R., and Pitman, T. "Appreciative Process: A Method for Transformational Change." *OD Practitioner,* Sept. 1991, *23*(3), 1–4.

Caudron, S. "Hire a Coach?" *Industry Week,* Oct. 21, 1996, *245*(19).

Chiaramonte, P., and Higgins, A. "Coaching for High Performance." *Business Quarterly,* 1993, *58,* 1–7.

Coggins, M. F. *Facilitating Change Through Peer Coaching.* (Doctoral dissertation, University of Georgia, 1991.)

Cohen, S. L., and Jaffe, C. L. "Managing Human Performance for Productivity." *Training and Development Journal,* 1982, *36*(12), 94–100.

Cook, M. J. *Effective Coaching.* New York: McGraw-Hill, 1999.

Consulting Psychology Journal, Special Issue on "Executive Coaching." Richard R. Kilburg, Guest Editor, Spring 1996, *48*(2), 57–152.

"Corporate Coaches May Help You Get Ahead." *The Seattle Post-Intelligencer,* Mar. 15, 1996.

"Could Your Career Use a Coach?" *Executive Female,* Sept./Oct. 1995.

Crane, T. G. *The Heart of Coaching: Using Transformational Coaching to Create a High-Performance Culture.* San Diego, Calif.: FTA Press, 1998.

Cunningham, S. "Coaching Today's Executive." *Public Utilities Fortnightly,* 1991, *128,* 22–25.

Darling, M. J. "Coaching People Through Difficult Times." *Human Resources Magazine,* Nov. 1994, *39,* 70–73.

Deeprose, D. *The Team Coach: Vital New Skills for Supervisors and Managers in a Team Environment.* New York: AMACOM, 1995.

Diedrich, R. C. "An Iterative Approach to Executive Coaching." *Consulting Psychology Journal: Practice and Research.* Spring 1996, *42*(2), 61–66.

Douge, B. "Coach Effectiveness." *Sport Science Review,* 1993, *2*(2), 14–29.

Dougherty, D. C. *Peer Coaching: Creating a Collaborative Environment for Change.* (Doctoral dissertation, University of Oregon, 1993). Dissertation Abstracts International, 1993, *54*(1–A), 71.

Duffy, E. M. *A Feedback-Coaching Intervention and Selected Predictors in Out Placement.* (Doctoral dissertation, Hofstra University, 1984.) Dissertation Abstracts International, 1984, *45*(5–B), 1.611–1.612.

Dutton, G. "Executive Coaches Call the Plays." *Management Review,* Feb. 1997, 39–43.

Evered, R. D., and Selman, J. C. "Coaching and the Art of Management." *Organizational Development Journal,* 1989, *18,* 16–32.

Filipczak, R. "The Executive Coach: Helper or Healer?" *Training,* Mar. 1998, *35*(3).

Flaherty, J. "Coaching and the New Biology." *Vision/Action, The Journal of the Bay Area OD Network,* Summer 1997, 11–14.

*Flaherty, J. *Coaching: Evoking Excellence.* Boston: Butterworth-Heinemann, 1998.

Fournies, F. F. *Coaching for Improved Work Performance.* New York: Liberty Hall, 1987. A substantial, helpful book on performance coaching from a behavioral point of view.

Freedman, L. D. "Coaching for the Game of Business." *Anchor Point,* May 1992, 38–42.

Frick, R. "Hire a Coach to Shape Up Your Life?" *Managing Money,* 1997, 119.

Fritts, P. J. *The New Managerial Mentor: Becoming a Learning Leader to Build Communities of Purpose.* Palo Alto, Calif.: Davies-Black, 1998. Views mentoring as a collaborative learning experience.

Gallup, B. "Professional Coaching: Changing the Corporate Game. One Player at a Time." *Vision/Action, The Journal of the Bay Area OD Network,* Fall 1994, 16–18.

*Gardner, J. W. "Renewal." *San Jose Mercury News,* Dec. 15, 1996, 1P, 4P.

Gathright, A. "Personal Zest: Hiring Coaches to Help Cope with Life's Stresses." *San Jose Mercury News,* Apr. 19, 1995.

Gilley, J. W., and Boughton, N. W. *Stop Managing, Start Coaching!: How Performance Coaching Can Enhance Commitment and Improve Productivity.* Chicago: Irwin, 1996. Two professors of Human Resource Development have a compelling application of coaching to corporate performance issues.

Glabman, M. "What Now, Coach?" *American Medical News,* Jan. 5, 1998, 17–19.

Good, D. J. "Coaching Practice in the Business-to-Business Environment." *Journal of Business and Industrial Marketing.* 1993, *8*(2), 53–60.

Graham, S., Wedman, J. F., and Garvin-Kester, B. "Manager Coaching Skills: Development and Application." *Performance Improvement Quarterly, 6*(1), 2–13.

"Growing Numbers of People Seeking Coaches for Careers." *The Seattle Times,* May 5, 1996.

Hamilton, K. "Need a Life? Get a Coach." *Newsweek,* Feb. 5, 1996.

Hammond, S. A. *Appreciative Inquiry.* Plano, Tex.: Kodiak Consulting, 1998.

*Hargrove, R. *Masterful Coaching: Extraordinary Results by Impacting People and the Way They Think and Work Together.* San Francisco: Jossey-Bass, 1995. The best overall book on all the dimensions of coaching.

*Hargrove, R. *Mastering the Art of Creative Collaboration.* New York: McGraw-Hill, 1998. The ultimate coaching goal: facilitating collaboration.

Hein, H. R. *Psychological Type, Coaching Activities and Coaching Effectiveness in Corporate Middle Managers.* (Doctoral dissertation, University of Bridgeport, 1990.) Dissertation Abstracts International *50*(10–A), 3293.

Hekelman, F. P. "Peer Coaching in Clinical Teaching: Formative Assessment of a Case." *Evaluation and the Health Professions,* 1994, *17,* 366–381.

"Help! You Need Somebody! A Coach Just Might Make Your Career." *BusinessWeek,* Oct. 13, 1997, 70E4–70E6.

Herring, K. "Coaches for the Bottom Line." *Personnel Administrator,* 1989, *34,* 22.

Himes, G. K. "Coaching: Turning a Group Into a Team." *Supervision,* 1984, *46,* 14–16.

Howe, B. "Psychological Skills and Coaching." *Sport Science Review,* 1993, *2*(2), 30–47.

Huang, C., and Lynch, J. *Mentoring.* New York: HarperCollins, 1995.

Hube, K. "A Coach May Be the Guardian Angel You Need to Rev Up Your Career." *Money,* Dec. 1996.

Hyatt, J. "The Zero-Defect CEO," *Inc.,* June 1997, 46–57.

Katz, J. H., and Miller, F. A. "Coaching Leaders Through Culture Change." *Consulting Psychology Journal: Practice and Research,* Spring 1996, *42*(2), 104–114.

Keeys, G. "Effective Leaders Need to Be Good Coaches." *Personnel Management,* 1994, *26,* 52–54.

Kelly, P. J. "Coach the Coach." *Training and Development Journal,* 1985, *39*(11), 54–55.

Kiechel, W., III. "The Boss as Coach." *Fortune,* 1991, 201.

Kiel, F., Rimmer, E., Williams, K., and Doyle, M. "Coaching at the Top." *Consulting Psychology Journal: Practice and Research,* Spring 1996, *42*(2), 67–77.

Kilburg, R. R. "Integrating Psychodynamic and Systems Theories in Organization Development Practice." *Consulting Psychology Journal: Practice and Research,* 1995, *47,* 28–55.

Kilburg, R. R. "Executive Coaching as an Emerging Competency in the Practice of Consultation." *Consulting Psychology Journal: Practice and Research,* Spring 1996, *42*(2), 59–60.

Kilburg, R. R. "Toward a Conceptual Understanding and Definition of Executive Coaching." *Consulting Psychology Journal: Practice and Research,* Spring 1996, *42*(2), 134–144.

Kinlaw, D. C. *Coaching for Commitment: Managerial Strategies for Obtaining Superior Performance.* San Diego: Pfeiffer, 1989. Good advice but thin on models and strategies.

Kinlaw, D. *The ASTD Trainer's Guide: Create Your Own Training Program.* New York: McGraw-Hill, 1999. A practical, highly detailed guide, with overheads and planning steps.

Koonce, R. "One on One." *Training & Development,* Feb. 1994.

Lamb, L. "From Couches to Coaches." *Minnesota Monthly,* Nov. 1998, *32*(11), 45ff.

LaMountain, D. *Executive Coaching: Cost-effective, One-on-One Guided Development Strategies* (audiotape). Alexandria, Va.: American Society for Training & Development.

Larry, B. K. "Executive Counsel." *Training,* Jan. 1997, 46–49.

Lee, R. J. "Send Me a Coach." *Issues and Observations,* 1997, *17.*

Leibowitz, Z., Kaye, B., and Farren, C. "Overcoming Management Resistance to Career Development Programs." [Special Issue: Communications]. *Training and Development Journal,* 1986, *40*(1), 10–15.

Levinson, H. "Counseling With Top Management." *Consulting Psychology Bulletin,* 1991, *43*(10), 10–15.

Levinson, H. "Executive Coaching." *Consulting Psychology Journal: Practice and Research.* Spring 1996, *42*(2), 115–123.

"Living Your Dreams." *New Age Journal,* Dec. 1996.

Lucas, R. W. *Coaching Skills: A Guide for Supervisors.* New York: McGraw-Hill, 1994. An elementary, straightforward guide for supervisors.

Lucas, R. W. "Performance Coaching Now and for the Future." *HR Focus,* 1994, *71,* 13ff.

Lukaszewski, J. E. "Behind the Throne: How to Coach and Counsel Executives." *Training and Development Journal,* 1988, *42*(10), 32–35.

Marsh, B. "Families Hire Mentors to Ease Succession." *Wall Street Journal,* July 23, 1991, B1–2.

McCall, M. W., Jr. *High Flyers: Developing the Next Generation of Leaders.* Cambridge, Mass.: Harvard Business School, 1998.

Miller, D. J. *The Effect of Managerial Coaching on Transfer of Training.* (Doctoral dissertation, United States International University, 1990.) Dissertation Abstracts International, 1990, *50*(8–A), 24–35.

Miller, J. B., and Brown, P. B. *The Corporate Coach.* New York: HarperBusiness, 1994.

Miller, W. C. "The Value of Non-Supervisory Feedback in Coaching Sessions." *Supervisory Management,* 1984, *29,* 2–8.

Mohr, D. C. "Negative Outcome in Psychotherapy: A Critical Review." *Clinical Psychology: Science and Practice,* 1995, *2*(1), 1–27.

Morgan, R. L. "Effects of Peer Coaching on the Acquisition of Direct Instruction Skills by Low-performing Preservice Teachers." *Journal of Special Education,* 1994, *28*(1), 59–76.

Murphy, K. "Coaching Socially Rejected Early Adolescents Regarding Behaviors Used by Peers to Infer Liking: A Dyad Specific Intervention." *Journal of Early Adolescence,* 1994, *14*(1), 83–95.

Murphy, K. "Generative Coaching: A Surprising Learning Odyssey." In S. Chawla and J. Renesch, *Learning Organizations,* Portland, Ore.: Productivity Press, 1995.

"Need a Life? Get a Coach." *Newsweek,* February 5, 1996.

O'Connell, J. J. "Process Consultation in a Content Field: Socrates in Strategy." *Consultation: An International Journal,* 1990, *9,* 199–208.

Olesen, M. "Coaching Today's Executive." *Training and Development,* 1996, *50,* 22–27.

*Orth, C. D., Wilkinson, H. E., and Benfari, R. C. "The Manager's Role as Coach and Mentor." *Organizational Dynamics,* 1987, *15*(4), 66–74.

Peters, H. "Peer Coaching for Executives." *Training & Development,* Mar. 1996.

Peters, T. *The Tom Peters Seminar: Crazy Times Call for Crazy Organizations.* New York: Vintage, 1994. A good description of what organizational coaches do.

*Peters, T., and Austin, N. *A Passion for Excellence: The Leadership Difference.* New York: Warner, 1989. One chapter (18) especially valuable for coaches.

Peterson, D. B. "Executive Coaching at Work: The Art of One-on-One Change." *Consulting Psychology Journal: Practice and Research,* Spring 1996, *42*(2), 78–86.

Peterson, D. B., and Associates. "Management Coaching at Work: Survey of Current Practices in Fortune 250 Organizations." Paper presented at the 104th Annual Conference of the American Psychological Association, Toronto, Ontario, Canada, Aug. 1996.

*Peterson, D. B., and Hicks, M. D. *The Leader as Coach: Strategies for Coaching and Developing Others.* Minneapolis, Minn.: Personnel Decisions, 1995.

Peterson, D. B., and Hicks, M. D. *Development FIRST: Strategies for Self-Development.* Minneapolis, Minn.: Personnel Decisions, 1996.

Pond, P., and Pendleton, M. "Professional Mentoring: An Asset to Business in the '90s." *Professional Review,* Winter 1993–94, 39–40.

Popper, M., and Lipshitz, R. "Coaching on Leadership." *Leadership and Organization Development Journal,* 1992, *13*(7), 15–18.

Pratt, S. R., and Eitzen, D. S. "Contrasting Leadership Styles and Organizational Effectiveness: The Case of Athletic Teams." *Social Science Quarterly,* 1989, *70,* 311–322.

Rancourt, K. L. "Real-time Coaching Boosts Performance." *Training and Development Journal,* 1995, *49,* 53–56.

Richardson, L. *Sales Coaching: Making the Great Leap from Sales Manager to Sales Coach.* New York: McGraw-Hill, 1996.

Rigoglioso, M. "Living Your Dreams." *New Age Journal,* Nov./Dec. 1996.

Roe, R. (ed.). *Coaching: The ASTD Trainer's Guide Sourcebook Series.* New York: McGraw-Hill, 1996.

Salisbury, F. *Developing Managers as Coaches. A Trainer's Guide.* New York: McGraw-Hill, 1994.

Sawczuk, M. P. *Transfer-of-Training: Reported Perceptions of Participants in a Coaching Study in Six Organizations.* (Doctoral dissertation, University of Minnesota, 1991). Dissertation Abstracts International, 1991, *51*(12–A), 4195.

Scandura, T. A. "Mentorship and Career Mobility: An Empirical Investigation." *Journal of Organizational Behavior,* 1992, *13,* 169–174.

Shore, L. M., and Bloom, A. J. "Developing Employees Through Coaching and Career Management." *Personnel,* 1986, *63,* 34–38.

Shula, D., and Blanchard, K. *Everyone's a Coach.* Grand Rapids, Mich.: Zondervan, 1995.

Smith, L. E. "The Executive's New Coach." *Fortune,* Dec. 1993, *203*(12), 126–134.

Smith, R. E., and Smoll, F. L. "Coaching the Coaches: Youth Sports as a Scientific and Applied Behavioral Setting." *Current Directions in Psychological Science, 6*(1), 16–21.

Snyder, A. "Executive Coaching: The New Solution." *Management Review.* New York: American Management Association, 1995.

Sperry, L. "Working with Executives: Consulting, Counseling, and Coaching." *Individual Psychology: Journal of Adlerian Theory, Research, and Practice,* 1993, *49,* 257–266.

Spinner, E. M. *The Relationship Between Selected Prescribed Leadership Behavior Variables and Self-Reported Measures of Coaching Leadership Behavior.* (Doctoral dissertation, Temple University, 1988). Dissertation Abstracts International, 1987, *48*(2–B), 589.

Stamps, D. "Communities of Practice." *Training,* Feb. 1997, 35–42.

Stone, F. M. *Coaching, Counseling & Mentoring.* New York: AMACOM, 1998.

Stowell, S. J. *Leadership and the Coaching Process in Organizations.* (Doctoral dissertation, University of Utah, 1987.) Dissertation Abstracts International, *48*(2–B), 589.

Stowell, S. J. "Coaching: A Commitment to Leadership." *Training and Development Journal,* 1988, *42,* 34–38.

*Stowell, S. J., and Starcevich, M. M. *The Coach.* Salt Lake City: Center for Management and Organization Effectiveness, 1998. About coaching within work organizations.

Sturman, G. M. "The Supervisor as Career Coach." *Supervisory Management.* Nov. 1990, 100–101.

Thompson, A. D. *A Formative Evaluation of an Individualized Coaching Program for Business Managers and Professionals.* (Doctoral dissertation, University of Minnesota, 1986.) Dissertation Abstracts International, 1987, *47*(12–A. Pt. 1), 4339.

*Tice, L. *Personal Coaching for Results: How to Mentor and Inspire Others to Amazing Growth.* Nashville, Tenn.: Nelson, 1997. A solid, basic book on coaching today.

Tichy, N., and Charan, R. "The CEO as Coach: An Interview with Allied Signal's Lawrence A. Bossidy." *Harvard Business Review,* Mar./Apr. 1995, 68–78.

Tobias, L. L. "Coaching Executives." *Consulting Psychology Journal: Practice and Research.* Spring 1996, *42*(2), 87–95.

Toomey, P. J. "Grace Under Fire: Time to Get a Coach." *Wall Street Journal,* July 4, 1994, B2–B3.

Tyson, L. L. "Coaching: A Tool for Success." *Training and Development Journal,* Sept. 1983, *28,* 19–22.

"University Trains Coaches for the Game of Life." *USA Today,* June 3, 1996.

Waldroof, J., and Butler, T. "The Executive as Coach." *Harvard Business Review,* Nov./Dec. 1996, 111–117.

Wallach, E. J. "Performance Coaching: Hitting the Bull's Eye." *Supervisory Management,* 1983, *28,* 19–22.

"Wanna Be a Player? Get a Coach!" *Fast Company.* Oct./Nov. 1996.

Wheeler, C. "Could Your Career Use a Coach?" *Executive Female,* Sept./Oct. 1995.

*Whitmore, J. *Coaching for Performance.* (2nd ed.) New York: Atrium, 1996. An introduction to performance coaching.

*Whitworth, L., Kimsey-House, H., and Sandahl, P. *Co-Active Coaching: New Skills for Coaching People Toward Success in Work and Life.* Palo Alto, Calif.: Davies-Black, 1998. Describes basic coaching skills, tools, and references.

Witherspoon, R., and White, R. P. *Four Essential Ways that Coaching Can Help Executives.* Greensboro, N.C.: Center for Creative Leadership, 1997. Coaching for skills, performance, development, and the executive's agenda.

Wolff, M. F. "Become a Better Coach." *Research Technology Management,* 1993, *36,* 10–11.

Woodlands Group. "Management Development Roles: Coach, Sponsor, and Mentor." *Personnel Journal,* 1980, *59,* 918–921.

Yalom, I. D., and Yalom, B. "It's Lonely at the Top." *Inc.,* April 1998.

Zemke, R. "The Corporate Coach." *Training,* Dec. 1996, *33*(12), 24–29.

Zemke, R., and Anderson, K. *Coaching Knock-Your-Socks-Off Service.* New York: AMACOM, 1996.

Zwillich, T. "Life Coaches Provide Motivational Consulting." *Clinical Psychiatry News,* July 1997, *24.*

 PART TWO 

THEORETICAL ROOTS OF COACHING

CHAPTER FOUR 

Psychological Theories of Adult Development

Coaching, as it is practiced today, has many conceptual and professional roots. Two major antecedents from which the coaching field has emerged are (1) psychological theories of adult development, including psychosocial stage theories, and (2) social theories of adult development. I will discuss the first type in this chapter and the second in Chapter Five.

PSYCHOANALYTICAL THEORIES

Even though coaches do not apply psychoanalytical theories directly in their practice, the theories have served to inform coaches' thinking. I'll show how that works, as I describe briefly what the major theorists have contributed to the coaching field.

Sigmund Freud

Freud's psychoanalytic interpretation of personal life became a benchmark for interpretation for all psychotherapy from about 1900 on. Freud believed that the driving forces in people's lives were not conscious (ego-driven) but were driven by the unconscious—the id (libido) and the superego (social conscience). Freud thought that these unconscious forces must be considered as symbols and studied indirectly, through the clinical interpretation of dreams, free associations, and similar approaches. Freud taught that people mask, in their everyday language, such ego defenses as repression and denial. Therapists still subscribe to the idea that it's important to try to understand the symbolic structure of the patient's mind—a structure that is formed in early childhood experience.

Even though little of the content of Freud's theory pertains to the coaching field, his emphasis on symbolic thinking is important. The language used in coaching often reveals more than the actual words denote. Coaches must read body language, silence, and the connotations of words, with the aim of bringing to clients' awareness any unconscious ideas they might have that can facilitate the coaching process.

Alfred Adler

After about ten years of collaboration with Sigmund Freud, Adler left the Vienna Psychoanalytic Society in 1911 and founded the Society for Individual Psychology. Adler preferred to understand human nature as psychosocial rather than as merely biological and deterministic, as Freud had proposed. According to Adler, humans are motivated by social urges. Adult behavior is purposeful and goal-directed, meaning that consciousness rather than the unconscious is the center of the personality. Adler's was a growth model, stressing what humans do with the possibilities in their lives and environment. His theory focused on personal values, beliefs, attitudes, goals, and interests.

The goal of Adlerian therapy is to reeducate adults to live in society as an equal with others. Although Adler believed that much of the therapeutic process was reworking the early childhood formation of personality, he engaged adults directly in goal setting and in reinventing their future, using techniques such as a paradoxical intention, acting "as if," role playing various options, and task setting.

Adler is important as a resource for understanding the conceptual model of coaching. Although his ideas are cloaked in the language of psychiatry, he is really talking about the power of purpose, visioning, and personal accountability.

Carl Gustav Jung

The father of modern stage theory is Carl Jung, a brilliant Swiss psychiatrist who wrote in the first half of the twentieth century. Jung thought of life as a progression in consciousness or self-awareness, so he viewed the second half of life as an acquisition of deeper human qualities. Like Adler, who was his friend and colleague for several years, Jung began as a Freudian and then departed into his own way of thinking.

Unlike Sigmund Freud, who thought of psychology as the study of symbolism, grounded in the psychosexual stages of the early childhood years, and Alfred Adler, who thought of psychology as social growth and development, Jung took psychology to be the study of universal symbolism in adult life—revealing lasting values, relationships, and meaning.

Jung's writings concentrate on life after forty. He addresses many of the issues expressed by people in midlife crisis or in midcareer development—issues of spirituality, male-female balance, young-old balance, individuation, and the deeper adventures of the self. He viewed the second half of life as a time when a major progression takes place—from ego to self, from body issues to spirit issues, from differentiation to inclusion. It is during this mature period in life that a person's true identity emerges, through a process he called individuation—the spiritual maturation of the self. Our self-centered ego needs become balanced by our self-connecting spiritual feelings; our feminine and masculine qualities find their balance; our love of young finds a balance with a love of old; and our will to kill finds a balance with a will to live and let live.

It is in the second half of life that Jung believed most of us have our full capacities available for recalibrating these polarities to claim our full human imprint. Through the conduct of a life review, we alter our basic commitments to how we will live and be in the balance of each polarity, and we normally choose to increase our self-individuation and our self-connectedness in the context of universal themes.

Jung makes several contributions to the coaching field. First, he proposes that adults experience a profound spiritual awakening in the second half of life, and coaches often experience this themselves and with their clients; they need to know how to facilitate the process. Second, he writes about the importance of myths. Coaches need to discern in their clients what the compelling stories of their lives are about and what they are drawn to in their lives. Third, Jung finds significant meaning in rituals, and coaching often includes ritual-making events that help clients experience their power and rites of passage.

Erik H. Erikson

Next to Carl Jung, no one is more seminal to developmental theory than Erik Erikson, the psychoanalytic (Freudian) child psychologist who expanded that field to include adult phases of development. Viewing development as a lifelong process, he hypothesized that a person must successfully resolve a series of eight polarities, in a prescribed developmental order, in order to develop as a normal and happy person throughout life. Failure to adequately resolve any polarity in favor of the positive developmental task at hand is to keep the person regressed and arrested at that stage. However, each polarity may reappear later in life—stimulated by "crises," by which Erikson means turning points for either maturation or regression.

Do Erikson's ideas help coaches understand the underlying concerns of clients and to anticipate their issues? Possibly so. Although coaches do not use psychological language as their main means of communication, they are in the business of growing people and organizations from one phase to another. The principles of growth and development are critical to successful coaching, and Erikson is the beginning place for this learning. Erikson also conveys the different developmental focus of each phase of human development, and whether coaches use his language or not, they need to grasp the different focus of people of different ages. Finally, Erikson writes about the "generativity" of elders, and this is a major theme in our society today, as the number of older adults increases at a rapid rate during the next thirty years.

Roger Gould

Coming from a psychoanalytic orientation, Gould, who wrote primarily in the late 1970s and early 1980s, emphasizes the change in personal perspective that people take from birth to death. That progression is a gradual reduction in the myth of absolute safety—a major source of delusion and disenchantment in adult life. At different points in life we think that someone or something will keep us absolutely safe: parents, muscles, good looks, a spouse, children, money, a career, an employer, possessions, a sport, a hobby, spiritual beliefs, and so on. As we grow and age, we gradually give up the myth of absolute safety and embrace the legitimate risks of life, including the inevitability of death. This process is mostly an unconscious one, in which we gradually disarm our false assumptions about the world.

A considerable amount of coaching deals with reframing clients' thought processes. That's what Gould proposes around the myth of absolute safety. Coaches experience various myths in their clients that need to be informed by facts and reframed to make actions significant and successful. (See Basic Library: Psychoanalytical Theories for references.)

PSYCHOSOCIAL THEORIES OF ADULT DEVELOPMENT

A major focus of coaching is on "the person" as client, so knowing how people evolve throughout the life cycle is critical information. Even if the client is a whole organization, the development of that organization relies heavily on the human performance and imagination of key people within the organization. A coach knows how to think developmentally within many contexts.

The field of adult development arose in the late 1950s as an outgrowth of developmental psychology. In contrast to clinical psychology, which has both theoretical and applied fields for understanding and treating people with mental health problems, developmental psychology began first as the study of children and adolescents and only half-way through the twentieth century expanded to include adult development—the study of normal and extraordinary growth and development of adults. For years it lacked an applied side; it thrived as a research field. Then people like Vivian McCoy (University of Kansas), Lillian Troll and Nancy Schlossberg (University of Maryland), Alan Entine (Empire State University), Arthur Chickering (University of Memphis), Malcolm Knowles (The Fielding Institute), Morris Keeton (CAEL), myself (founding president of The Fielding Institute), and many others began to apply adult developmental research to the lives and organizations of adults. Today there are thousands of professionals applying this body of knowledge: career centers, retreat programs, adult education institutes, applied research projects, longevity and health applications, and retirement programs.

Here are some of the relevant theorists:

Arnold Van Gennep

In 1908, Arnold Van Gennep, an anthropologist, published his monograph, "The Rites of Passage," in which he emphasized the importance of life events and rituals throughout the life cycle. He identified three major phases in all rites of passage: *separation* from the group or society; *transition,* an intermediate stage of learning; and *incorporation,* or a merger with the group in a new role or status. Rites of passage serve to help individuals take on new social roles and become reintegrated with the group. Pregnancy and childbirth are universal experiences that command a rite of passage in many if not most cultures, although those rites differ widely. Other rites include initiation rites into adulthood, betrothal and marriage, and death.

The importance of Van Gennep's work is in the identification of the components in human events going through major change: separation from the status quo, transition into a learning state, and incorporation into a new way of being and living. He also identified the importance of rites of passage, and many coaches work with clients experiencing a rite of passage from one phase of life to the next.

Bernice Neugarten

No one has contributed more to the study of adult development than Bernice Neugarten. She linked theory to empirical testing and added "adult study" to the already thriving study of children. Unlike Jung and Erikson, Neugarten looks at adult life less from a psychological perspective and more from a social-developmental point of view.

Neugarten's writings on human development form the foundation of that field. Her writings are basic to our understanding of how men and women develop throughout the adult years. She discerned important differences in the lives of men and women. Coaches can learn much from her long years of diligent research.

Daniel Levinson

Daniel Levinson wrote a major work on male development during the adult years entitled *The Seasons of a Man's Life* (1978). Levinson saw male development as proceeding from life structures (periods of stability) to transitions (periods of change) throughout the life cycle. He believed that adult development is age-specific and therefore chronologically predictable.

Perhaps the most important feature of Levinson's theory is the role of the midlife crisis in a man's life. To Levinson, the midlife transition is not just another transition. It is qualitatively different. Like Jung and Neugarten, Levinson sees life in two parts: (1) the first half, when a man is achieving, accumulating, procreating, obtaining approval, and gaining security, and (2) the second half, when a person is seeking quality (rather than quantity), internal meaning (more than external approval or acquisitions), leaving a contribution, and finding a universal, human perspective on the human journey.

Levinson's concepts of *life structure* and *transition* are useful for coaches to understand the ups and downs of their clients. He also stresses that transitions are times of major growing and learning. Because many coaching clients are in transition from one chapter of their lives to another, coaches can learn from Levinson the inner workings of transitions. Transitions, he says, are normal and inevitable, so we need coaches who understand how to guide people through meaningful and successful transitions. Levinson's book, *The Seasons of a Woman's Life,* reports the same general sequence of life structures and transitions, along with more complex themes and patterns. (See Basic Library: Psychosocial Theories of Adult Development for references.)

MORAL DEVELOPMENT THEORIES

Anchored in Piaget's theory of cognitive development is Lawrence Kohlberg. Piaget was the Swiss psychologist (1996–1980) who influenced the field of cognitive development more than any other person; his theory, in simple form, was that children grow mentally as they develop and move through stages that are qualitatively different from each other.

Lawrence Kohlberg

Kohlberg formulated a theory of the development of moral reasoning—a stage theory that presumed that each stage grows out of but supersedes the one that comes before. Kohlberg's theory has three levels and six stages (two stages per level). The levels are (1) Preconventional Moral Reasoning, (2) Conventional Moral Reasoning, and (3) Postconventional Moral Reasoning. The six stages, within the levels, range from Stage 1 (thinking in terms of obedience and punishment) to Stage 6 (thinking in terms of what conscience and principle dictate). According to Kohlberg, the movement through the levels is gradual; not everyone completes the journey.

Coaches often have clients who are struggling with moral issues, and understanding moral reasoning is important in coaching training. Much of coaching aims at helping clients "live their own integrity" in all that they do.

Robert Kegan

In a brilliant book, *The Evolving Self,* Kegan provides a neo-Piagetian model of human development. It is a theory of ongoing interpersonal and intrapsychic reconstruction. The model suggests that all development is in relationship to two fundamental poles: independence and inclusion. Kegan suggests that there are six levels or developmental stages (incorporative, impulsive, imperial, interpersonal, institutional, and interindividual) which move from independence (differentiation, distinctness, decentration) to inclusion (embeddedness, connectedness) and on to a new independence and a new inclusion, and on and on, like a rising spiral, or a helix of evolutionary truces throughout the adult years.

Kegan (1982) summarizes his idea this way: "We move from the overincluded, fantasy-embedded impulsive balance to the sealed-up self-sufficiency of the imperial balance; from the over differentiated imperial balance to overincluded interpersonalism; from interpersonalism to the autonomous, self-regulating institutional balance; from the institutional to a new form of openness in the interindividual" (p. 108). When a person enters the interindividual balance, the self senses itself apart from institutions. One no longer is one's career; one has a career. The self is located in one's interiority and has the capacity for intimacy that stems from self-caring. Interdependence, self-surrender, and interdependent self-definition become possible, and maturation reaches its zenith.

Kegan's writings are difficult to understand, but his concept of the spiral is much like Levinson's life transitions, only Kegan's concern is with what goes on in a person's mind as the transitions—growth and development—take place. Much of coaching has to do with clarifying a client's thinking so that it's congruent with how the person wants to evolve and perform in the future.

Carol Gilligan

Carol Gilligan provides an alternative developmental pattern for females in her book, *In a Different Voice* (1982); she challenges the theories of Erikson, Levinson, Gould, and Kohlberg. Whereas Erikson hypothesized that intimacy was a stage of development, Gilligan proposed that for women, intimacy is the context of female development. Women grow through their relationships; they measure themselves through their inclusion. Men grow through their individuation or autonomy; they push away from inclusion to measure themselves by their personally unique characteristics. Whereas Kohlberg had his final, sixth stage, at the level of principled reasoning, Gilligan suggests that there may be a higher stage: working things out through caring relationships. Gilligan's work is underscored by other theorists who've suggested that women construct their identities through connections and spirituality. This is not to suggest that women cannot succeed, achieve, wield power, or govern nations as well as men. They can and do. They just do these things differently than men.

Coaches work with both men and women and need conceptual tools for understanding how to promote human excellence in both genders. The debate that Gilligan raised in the eighties is ongoing and is worth coaches' attention. (See Basic Library: Moral Development Theories for references.)

ADULT DEVELOPMENT THEORIES

Developmental psychology referred to the study of children until after World War II when the study of adults was added. Today's field of adult development includes researchers, teachers, and practitioners, all concerned with various aspects of adult growth and development from about age eighteen to one hundred. How do the continuities and changes take place during adult life? What are the "convoys" or institutions through which adults grow or don't grow? Do the two genders manage the aging process in the same way, or differently? What are the developmental challenges and dilemmas of each age group throughout the life cycle? These are some of the critical questions. Because clients in the coaching field are typically adults, it is important to look at ways the adult development profession can inform the practice of coaching. (See the Basic Library: Adult Development Theories for references.)

THERAPIES

Even though coaches are not therapists—I must emphasize that point—much of their interaction with clients takes on characteristics of therapy. Therefore, coaches have much to learn by becoming acquainted with the various types of therapeutic interaction.

Psychotherapy

A trend today in psychotherapy is to move away from the idea of *treatment* to that of *learning*, using profound techniques that produce integrated persons with high levels of self-directed motivation. This trend connects to the coaching model. I believe there is much that coaches can pull out of the psychopathological framework and put to work for effective coaching relationships with individual and organizational clients. Both psychotherapy and coaching rely on the relationship of professional and client as the basis for the anticipated results. Coaching is often deep work that results in transformation. Understanding how to guide people toward the fullness of their promise requires acquiring the tools and abilities for understanding, facilitating, and supporting the transformation.

Solution-Focused Brief Therapy

Perhaps the type of psychotherapy that informs the field of coaching the most is solution-focused brief therapy. Instead of treating pathology, the therapist develops the competence of the client. In this modality the therapist becomes a personal consultant, pursuing with the client what the client would be like beyond whatever the presenting clinical problem might be. By asking questions in a mutual, collaborative language, the therapist seeks ways for the client to understand him- or herself "beyond the problem."

The role of the client is to explore, create, and coauthor the evolving story of his or her life at a deep sense of meaning. The role of the consultant is to establish and create a setting of mutual respect, of dialogue, of inquiry, of affirmation, and of goal seeking. The focus is about unfolding the preferred life the client would like to live, through asking different kinds of questions such as

- *Exception questions:* What's different when the problem is not occurring?
- *Coping questions:* With all you are going through, how do you keep going?
- *Scaling questions:* On a scale of one to ten, with one being the way you felt when you called me for an appointment, and ten feeling really great about yourself, how are you doing right now?
- *Miracle questions:* If during your sleep tonight your "problem" were miraculously lifted from you, how would you be different tomorrow?
- *Future-oriented questions:* What will you do with all the time you save when you no longer have this problem?
- *Competence and resource questions:* How did you do that? How did you figure that out?

Narrative Therapy

Narrative therapy, first introduced by Michael White and David Epston several years ago, is based on the notion that personal problems are generated by social, cultural, and political contexts. Each person comes to understand his or her own life from the stories that are available in these contexts. To treat these problems, therapists help clients "redescribe" themselves, through their own stories, to take responsibility for their own scripts. The therapy moves from given stories to alternative stories, using self-talk, listening, deconstruction, and repositioning. Unlike traditional psychologists, narrative therapists share their authority with their clients as they work together to "coauthor new narratives." This orientation uses group work to accelerate the therapy process into new, self-driven conversations.

Narrative therapists distinguish their work of "uncovering people's stories" from those therapists who concentrate on skill development or problem solving. The narrative questioning style is in the form of nonjudging queries like these: How might your daily work experience affect how you see this conflict? How would you describe the place of work and of leisure in your life?, What are your expectations of your leisure time?, and What's the relationship between the stress you feel as a result of work and the kind of music you play? Through inquiry like this, the dialogue works toward an externalized description of the conflict issue presented by the client. Then an alternative story is generated by the client, in ordinary language, with the therapist asking such questions as, What steps could you put in place to ensure that next week is more trouble-free for you?, What is it like for both of you here now to be talking about cooperation?, and Could this kind of discussion we are having now indicate anything about the kind of relationship you would prefer to have as neighbors? As the therapy relationship concludes, written agreements are constructed to sustain the new story. The basic credo of this orientation: everybody has tales to tell, and everybody has a legitimate claim to his place in the world.

The similarities with coaching include working within the expressed language of the client's story, fostering discovery through nonjudgmental questions, and resulting in a new course of action. (See Basic Library: Brief Therapies and Narrative Therapies for references.)

 BASIC LIBRARY FOR COACHES

Psychoanalytical Theories

*Albert, A. *Understanding Human Nature.* New York: Fawcett, 1998. Discussion of the function of teleology in human life, as each life moves toward purpose.

Brenner, C. *An Elementary Textbook of Psychoanalysis.* New York: Anchor, 1974.

*Erikson, E. H. (ed.) *Adulthood.* New York: Norton, 1978. A book of original readings on adulthood.

Erikson, E. H. *Childhood and Society.* (2nd ed.) New York: Norton, 1993. A key Erikson book; valuable for coaches,

Erikson, E. H. *Identity and the Life Cycle.* New York: Norton, 1994. On how ego identity gets shaped.

*Erikson, E. H. *Identity: Youth and Crisis.* New York: Norton, 1994. Covers identity development in youth, a theory section on the ego, a section on womanhood and inner space, and a section on race and a wider identity.

Erikson, E. H. *The Life Cycle Completed.* New York: Norton, 1997.

Erikson, E. H., Erikson, J. M., and Kivnick, H. Q. *Vital Involvement in Old Age.* New York: Norton, 1994.

Freud, S. *New Introductory Lectures on Psychoanalysis.* New York: Norton, 1965.

Gay, P. *Freud, A Life for Our Time.* New York: Norton, 1998.

Gould, R. "The Phases of Adult Life: A Study in Developmental Psychology." *American Journal of Psychiatry,* 1972, *129,* 521ff. A brief summary of his theory.

Gould, R. *Transformations.* New York: Simon and Schuster, 1978. A bold, psychoanalytical theory about the myth of absolute safety and how healthy adults demythologize it.

Guntrip, H. *Psychoanalytic Theory, Therapy and the Self.* New York: Basic Books, 1973. A solid introduction to Freud, Erikson, Klein, Sullivan, Fairbain, Winnicott, and others.

*Jung, C. G. *Modern Man in Search of a Soul.* New York: Harcourt, Brace and World, 1953. A good place to begin to read Jung.

Jung, C. G. "The Stages of Life." In *Modern Man in Search of a Soul.* New York: Harvest, 1955. Essay comparing the issues of the first half of life with the issues of the second half.

Jung, C. G. *Two Essays on Analytical Psychology.* (2nd ed.) Princeton, N.J.: Princeton University Press, 1966.

Jung, C. G. *The Portable Jung.* New York: Viking, 1976. Originally published 1930.

Jung, C. G. *The Archetypes and the Collective Unconscious.* (2nd ed.) Princeton, N.J.: Princeton University Press, 1981.

Jung, C. G. *The Structure and Dynamics of the Psyche.* (2nd ed.) Princeton, N.J.: Princeton University Press, 1981.

Jung, C. G. *Synchronicity.* Princeton, N.J.: Princeton University Press, 1988.

Masterson, J. F. *The Real Self: A Developmental, Self, and Object Relations Approach.* New York: Brunner/Mazel, 1985.

Sulloway, F. J. *Freud, Biologist of the Mind.* New York: Basic Books, 1992.

Psychosocial Theories of Adult Development

*Levinson, D. J. *The Seasons of a Man's Life.* New York: Knopf, 1986. The breakthrough book on life structures and transitions that formed the starting point for the Hudson cycle of change.

*Levinson, D. J. *The Seasons of a Woman's Life.* New York: Knopf, 1996.

Neugarten, B. L. "Adult Personality: Toward a Psychology of the Life Cycle." In W. C. Sze (ed.), *The Human Life Cycle.* New York: Jason Aronson, 1975. A compendium with remarkable breadth of coverage by some of the best scholars in the field.

Neugarten, B. L. "Time, Age, and the Life Cycle." In *American Journal of Psychiatry,* 1979, *136,* 887ff.

*Neugarten, D. A. (ed.). *The Meanings of Age: Selected Papers of Bernice L. Neugarten.* Chicago: University of Chicago Press, 1996. Leading articles by Bernice Neugarten, one of the founders of the field of adult development.

*Van Gennep, A. *The Rites of Passage.* Chicago: University of Chicago Press, 1961. First analysis in English of a major transition in primitive tribes—the transition from boyhood to manhood.

Moral Development Theories

*Garrod, A. (ed.). *Approaches to Moral Development: New Research and Emerging Themes.* New York: Teachers College Press, 1993.

Gilligan, C. *In a Different Voice: Psychological Theory and Women's Development.* Cambridge, Mass.: Harvard University Press, 1993. A groundbreaking event, establishing a basis for understanding women's development separately from male development.

*Gilligan, C., Murphy, J. M., and Tappan, M. B. "Moral Development Beyond Adolescence." In C. N. Alexander and E. J. Langer (eds.), *Higher Stages of Human Development.* New York: Oxford University Press, 1990.

Kegan, R. *The Evolving Self.* San Francisco: Jossey-Bass, 1983. An original theory in esoteric language portraying the flow of the adult years as being toward the self and then away from the self, throughout the years.

Kegan, R. *In Over Our Heads: The Mental Demands of Modern Life.* Cambridge, Mass: Harvard University Press, 1994. An attempt to interpret developmental theory—particularly moral developmental theory—as a basis for making sense of our lives in the nineties.

Adult Development Theories

*Bee, H. *Journey of Adulthood.* (3rd ed.) Englewood Cliffs, N.J.: Prentice Hall, 1995. A sound introduction to adult issues, literature, and the human prospect.

Bergler, E. *The Revolt of the Middle-Aged Man.* Madison, Conn.: International Universities Press, 1985. Analysis of middle-age rebellion and ways to work it through constructively.

Birren, J., and Schaie, K. W. (eds.). *Handbook of the Psychology of Aging.* (4th ed.) New York: Van Nostrand Reinhold, 1996. A highly technical and accurate information source for coaching with elders.

Bridges, W. *Transitions.* Reading, Mass.: Addison-Wesley, 1980. A classic reader with literary, not psychological, references, about the gaps we all have between the chapters of our lives.

Brim, O. G., Jr., and Kagan, J. (eds.). *Constancy and Change in Human Development.* Cambridge, Mass.: Harvard University Press, 1980. Discusses a problem coaches have to fathom: What is changing and what is staying constant as my client prepares for the future?

Campbell, J. *The Hero with a Thousand Faces.* Princeton, N.J.: Bollingen Series, 1990. A standard reference for understanding cultural symbolism, human choices, and the roles of heroes.

Campbell, J. *The Inner Reaches of Outer Space.* New York: Van Der Marck, 1995.

Chinen, A. *In the Ever After: Fairy Tales in the Second Half of Life.* Wilmette, Ill.: Chiron, 1989. In the Jungian and Campbell tradition, telling new tales about growing older.

*Colarusso, C. A., and Nemiroff, R. A. *Adult Development.* New York: Plenum, 1981. One of the most concise and informative introductory texts on adult life.

Edward, J., and Ruskin, T. *Separation-Individuation: Theory and Application.* New York: Gardner, 1992. An important book on the separation-individuation process in the life cycle.

Erikson, E. H. (ed.). *Adulthood.* New York: Norton, 1978.

Erikson, E. H. *Childhood and Society.* (2nd ed.) New York: Norton, 1993. A key Erikson book which should be read by coaches.

Erikson, E. H. *Identity and the Life Cycle.* New York: Norton, 1994. On how ego identity gets shaped.

*Erikson, E. H. *Identity: Youth and Crisis.* New York: Norton, 1994. Covers identity development in youth, a theory section on the ego, a section on womanhood and inner space, and a section on race and a wider identity.

Fiske, M. "Changing Hierarchies of Commitment." In N. J. Smelser and E. H. Erikson (eds.), *Themes of Work and Love in Adulthood.* Cambridge, Mass.: Harvard University Press, 1980. A developmentalist has original notions of adult life, based on social research and lifelong study.

Fiske, M. "Tasks and Crises of the Second Half of Life: The Interrelationship of Commitment, Coping, and Adaptation." In J. E. Birren and R. B. Sloane (eds.), *Handbook of Mental Health and Aging.* . Englewood Cliffs, N.J.:

Prentice Hall, 1992. A good summary of Fiske's ideas and a good reference book.

Fiske, M., and Chiriboga, D. A. *Change and Continuity in Adult Life.* San Francisco: Jossey-Bass, 1990. A scholarly book, reporting research; a solid book of information that will help the coach trace client thoughts and memories toward productive futures.

*Gilligan, C. *In a Different Voice: Psychological Theory and Women's Development.* Cambridge, Mass.: Harvard University Press, 1993.

Goffman, E. *The Presentation of Self in Everyday Life.* New York: Doubleday, 1959. An original, nonpsychological interpretation of how the self works in ordinary life.

Golan, N. *Passing Through Transitions.* New York: The Free Press, 1984. A social worker's interpretation.

Gould, R. "The Phases of Adult Life: A Study in Developmental Psychology," *American Journal of Psychiatry,* 1972, *129,* 521ff. A brief summary of his theory.

Goulding, M. M., and Goulding, R. L. *Changing Lives Through Redecision Therapy.* New York: Brunner/Mazel, 1997.

Guntrip, H. *Psychoanalytic Theory, Therapy and the Self.* New York: Basic Books, 1973.

Gutmann, D. C. "The Cross-Cultural Perspective: Notes Toward a Comparative Psychology of Aging." In J. E. Birren and K. W. Schaie (eds.), *Handbook of the Psychology of Aging.* New York: Van Nostrand Reinhold, 1996. Has special importance for interpreting adult development in the post-parental years.

Horner, A. *Being and Loving.* Northvale, N.J.: Jason Aronson, 1990. A psychoanalytic treatment of how these two human modalities complement one another.

*Hudson, F. M. *The Adult Years: Mastering the Art of Self-Renewal.* (rev. ed.) San Francisco: Jossey-Bass, 1999. A book on adult life that focuses on the application of knowledge to the construction and deconstruction of adult life across the life cycle.

Hudson, F. M., and McLean, P. *LifeLaunch: A Passionate Guide to the Rest of Your Life.* Santa Barbara, Calif.: Hudson Institute Press, 1996 (rev. ed). An application of adult development material to the lives of adults; a workbook applying the principles of *The Adult Years.*

Jung, C. G. "The Stages of Life." In *Modern Man in Search of a Soul.* New York: Harvest, 1933.

*Jung, C. G. *Modern Man in Search of a Soul.* New York: Harcourt, Brace and World, 1955.

Jung, C. G. *Two Essays on Analytical Psychology.* (2nd ed.) Princeton, N.J.: Princeton University Press, 1966.

Jung, C. G. *The Portable Jung.* New York: Viking, 1976. Originally published 1930.

Jung, C. G. *The Archetypes and the Collective Unconscious.* (2nd ed.) Princeton, N.J.: Princeton University Press, 1981.

Jung, C. G. *The Structure and Dynamics of the Psyche.* (2nd ed.) Princeton, N.J.: Princeton University Press, 1981.

Jung, C. G. *Synchronicity.* Princeton: Princeton University Press, 1988.

Kegan, R. *The Evolving Self.* San Francisco: Jossey-Bass, 1982.

Kegan, R. *In Over Our Heads: The Mental Demands of Modern Life.* Cambridge: Harvard, 1994.

Kernberg, O. *Object Relations Theory and Clinical Practice.* New York: Aronson, 1995.

*Levinson, D. J. *The Seasons of a Man's Life.* New York: Knopf, 1986.

Levinson, D. J. *The Seasons of a Woman's Life.* New York: Knopf, 1996.

Loevinger, J. *Ego Development.* San Francisco: Jossey-Bass, 1977.

Mahler, M. S. *On Human Symbiosis: The Vicissitudes of Individuation.* New York: International University Press, 1971.

Mahler, M. S., Pine, F., and Bergman, A. *The Psychological Birth of the Human Infant.* New York: Basic Books, 1989. An original theory on the formation of infant identity.

Masterson, J. F. *The Real Self: A Developmental, Self, and Object Relations Approach.* New York: Brunner/Mazel, 1985.

*Murphy, J. S., and Hudson, F. M. *The Joy of Old: A Guide to Successful Elderhood.* Altadena, Calif.: Geode Press, 1998.

Nemiroff, R., and Colarusso, C. *The Race Against Time.* New York: Plenum, 1985. An elegant study of midlife males and how they deal with their increasing sense of mortality.

Norton, D. L. *Personal Destinies.* Princeton, N.J.: Princeton University Press, 1976. A systematic treatise on the individual's place in nature and society.

Parke, R. D., Ornstein, P. A., Rieser, J. J., and Zahn-Waxler, C. (eds.). *A Century of Developmental Psychology.* Washington, D.C.: American Psychological Association, 1994.

Perry, W. G., Jr. *Forms of Intellectual and Ethical Development in the College Years.* New York: Holt, Rinehart and Winston, 1998. An application of moral development to the college years.

Pollock, G. H., and Greenspan, S. L. *The Course of Life, Vol. V: Early Adulthood.* Madison, Conn.: International Universities Press, 1993. A largely psychoanalytic interpretation of early adult development.

Pollock, G. H., and Greenspan, S. L. *The Course of Life, Vol. VI: Late Adulthood.* Madison, Conn.: International Universities Press, 1993. Discussions of losses, diseases, and disorders along with transformative tasks, deepening of trust, and the keeping of promises.

Riegle, K. "The Dialectics of Human Development," *American Psychologist,* Oct. 1976. One of the best non-stage theory interpretations of adult change and development.

Schlossberg, N., and Entine, A. (eds.). *Counseling Adults.* Monterey, Calif.: Brooks/Cole Publishing, 1995. A fine set of essays. One of the earliest applications of adult development theory to practice.

*Smelser, N. J., and Erikson, E. H. *Themes of Work and Love in Adulthood.* Cambridge, Mass.: Harvard, 1981. One of the best readers on the key theories of adult life.

Stage Theories of Cognitive and Moral Development: Criticisms and Applications. Harvard Educational Review: Reprint No. 13, 1978. A good primer on moral development theory and applications.

Storr, A. *C. G. Jung.* New York: Viking, 1991. A solid and fair biography.

*Sze, W. C. *Human Life Cycle.* New York: Jason Aronson, 1975. A superb collection of readings on many topics.

Van Gennep, A. *The Rites of Passage.* Chicago: University of Chicago Press, 1960.

*Winnicott, D. W. *The Maturational Processes and the Facilitating Environment.* London: Hogarth Press; Toronto: Clarke, Irwin and CO., Ltd., 1965. Provides many "root metaphors" for the coaching profession.

Winnicott, D. W. *Playing and Reality.* New York: Routledge, 1982. Contains essays on transitional objects, the theory of playing, the role of playing in the search for the self, and the good-enough mother.

Winnicott, D. W. *Home Is Where We Start From.* New York: Norton, 1990. Selected writings published as a book.

Winnicott, D. W. *The Family and Individual Development.* New York: Routledge, 1996. Essays on human development from infancy to early childhood to latency to adolescence to young adulthood—all in relation to healthy and disruptive factors in family life.

Psychotherapy

Brown, G. W., and Harris, T. *Social Origins of Depression: A Study of Psychiatric Disorder in Women.* New York: Free Press, 1978. A search for the roots of depression in life events, social class, personality disorders, and loss.

*Bugental, J.F.T. *Psychotherapy and Process: The Fundamentals of an Existential-Humanistic Approach.* New York: McGraw-Hill, 1978. A view of the psychotherapist's task as taking a journey to discover and extend how the client gives meaning to life and grows into deeper awareness of life itself.

Bugental, J.F.T. *Intimate Journeys: Stories from Life-Changing Therapy.* San Francisco: Jossey-Bass, 1990. A book of stories of people who developed lasting, intimate relationships.

Garfield, S., and Bergin, A. (eds.). *Handbook of Psychotherapy and Behavior Change.* (4th ed.) New York: Wiley, 1993.

Halleck, S. L. *The Treatment of Emotional Disorders.* New York: Jason Aronson, 1978. An outstanding book for understanding clinical psychology practices.

Ivey, A. E. *Developmental Therapy.* San Francisco: Jossey-Bass, 1986. Shows how to integrate the research and insights of developmental theorists into daily practice; can be applied in one-on-one coaching sessions.

Miller, P. H. *Theories of Developmental Psychology.* New York: Freeman, 1993.

Millman, H. L., and Associates. *Therapies for Adults.* San Francisco: Jossey-Bass, 1983. Presents multiple psychotherapeutic approaches to depression, anxiety disorders, obsessive-compulsive disorders, and personality disorders.

Patterson, C. H. *Theories of Counseling and Psychotherapy.* (2nd ed.) New York: Harper & Row, 1995. Has brief interpretations of Frankl's logotherapy and Kelly's theory of personal constructs.

Phillips, A. *Winnicott.* Cambridge, Mass.: Harvard University Press, 1989. A biography of D. W. Winnicott, including notes on the self and the interpretation of the lives of others.

Rawling, E. I., and Carter, D. K. *Psychotherapy for Women: Treatment Toward Equality.* Springfield, Ill.: Charles C. Thomas, 1977. Book of readings that seek to form a post-clinical paradigm that is future-oriented and learning-based.

Brief Therapies

Cade, B., and O'Hanlon, W. H. *A Brief Guide to Brief Therapy.* New York: Norton, 1993.

Ecker, B., and Hulley, L. *Depth-Oriented Brief Therapy.* San Francisco: Jossey-Bass, 1996.

Fisch, R. "Basic Elements in the Brief Therapies." In M. F. Hoyt (ed.), *The Handbook of Constructive Therapies.* New York: Guilford Press, 1998.

Fisch, R., and Schlanger, K. *Changing the Unchangeable.* San Francisco:

Jossey-Bass, 1999. Reports the effectiveness of brief therapy with excessive and intimidating cases.

Hoyt, M. F. *Brief Therapy and Managed Care.* San Francisco: Jossey-Bass, 1995.

*Miller, S. D., Hubble, M. A., and Duncan, B. L. (eds.). *Handbook of Solution-Focused Brief Therapy.* San Francisco: Jossey-Bass, 1996. Relevant for coaches, as people take responsibility for their own changes in meaning and hope.

Zeig, J. K., and Gilligan, S. G. (eds.). *Brief Therapy: Myths, Methods, and Metaphors.* New York: Brunner/Mazel, 1990.

Narrative Therapies

Friedman, S. (ed.). *The New Language of Change: Constructive Collaboration in Psychotherapy.* New York: Guilford Press, 1993.

Gilligan, S., and Price, R. *Therapeutic Conversations.* New York: Norton, 1993.

*Monk, G., Wislade, J., Crocket, K., and Epston, D. *Narrative Therapy in Practice: The Archaeology of Hope.* San Francisco: Jossey-Bass, 1997. Shows how clients' stories can reveal the contexts of problems, along with ways to rewrite better script.

 CHAPTER FIVE 

Social Theories of Adult Development

Coaches are often asked to facilitate group process, team development, organizational planning, and corporate training. Many coaches also function as consultants, enabling them to work with both persons and systems. For those reasons, coaches often look to the major social theories of adult development for insight into their coaching tasks.

Human systems theories relate to the contexts and environments of human beings—coupling, families, work organizations, leisure activities, governments, networks and social movements, and natural environments. These theories examine the roles that humans play within, between, and among these systems. This is a sociological field that, like developmental theory, has not developed an applied wing.

Human systems theory contends that adult development occurs when complex human systems experience system change. It is the system change that triggers personal change, forcing people to adapt to new conditions and meanings for their lives. Adult development occurs when two or more systems (biological, psychological, interpersonal, familial, groups, political entities, economic forces, natural forces, and so on) trigger disequalibrium in a person's life, who in turn evokes new personal and social strategies for managing and balancing life.

In human systems theory it is the "timing of events" that leads either to growth and development or to regression and dysfunction. It is often a matter of being in the right place at the right time or the wrong place at the wrong time. Although most of these shifts "happen to us" and are experienced as out of our control, they can also be provoked and proactively guided. Typical timing-of-events triggers are school attendance, marriage, parenthood, a disease, an accident, or a divorce. Other possible triggers are being hired or fired, winning the lottery, making a geographic move or a career change, retiring, or going to war.

SOCIAL CONTEXT THEORIES

Within this perspective, adults are examined in the context of families, careers, leisure environments, socioeconomic systems, political systems, ecological systems, and so forth. A developmental "crisis" is a disruption of the way a person is used to thinking and behaving in the social systems of his or her life. Urie Brofenbrenner (1979) states: "Human development is the process through which the growing person acquires a more extended differentiated, and valid conception of the ecological environment. . . ." (p. 27). Although much of the writing on human systems is abstract and theoretical, the concepts are essential for coaches to apply to their understanding of clients. In this section I will examine the theories of Kurt Lewin, Gerard Egan and Michael Cowan, and Marjorie Fiske.

Kurt Lewin

Kurt Lewin invented new ways to view the human situation. A rigorous scientist, he pulled sociology into the personal realm, and visa versa. He invented applied sociology. Most of all he wanted scholars who were practical theorists, devoted to action research. Although he did not generate a complete theory, he proposed the concept of *reeducation,* which he felt adults needed to engage in throughout their lives. He proposed that adults learn, and keep learning, new ways of thinking and being in three modalities: cognitive change (perception, information, expectation, and beliefs), value modification (beliefs, feelings, and sense of approval and disapproval), and motoric actions (behavioral skills, interpersonal skills).

Lewin proposed several principles to guide the process of reeducation throughout the adult years, the chief ones being these:

- Reeducation for normal and superlative adults requires the same kind of depth learning that our culture has reserved for "sick" people. The wall between "education" and "therapy" must be removed.
- Personal experience alone is not reeducation. It is the context of reeducation. Reeducation requires information, conceptual constructs, reflection, and social interaction as minimal prerequisites.

- The goal of reeducation is to bring about change in culture. It aims neither at adjustment to culture nor at mere personal fulfillment. Reeducation itself is fundamentally social, and the social systems themselves will change when new learning takes place.
- The world in which we act is the world as we perceive it. If people are to change, they must first change the way they perceive themselves and their situations.
- Classroom learning is of limited value because it relies too much on the possession of knowledge. The possession of knowledge does not, by itself, rectify false perceptions, bad feelings, or social decision.
- Individuals accept new values and beliefs by accepting belongingness in a group. Groups are the medium of effective reeducation.

If he were alive today, Lewin would probably applaud the coaching field for its application of many of his ideas. In turn, studying Lewin would help coaches learn to think like practical theorists, by knowing how to apply the knowledge of the coaching field.

Gerard Egan and Michael A. Cowan

In their book, *People in Systems: A Model for Development in the Human-Service Professions and Education* (1979), Egan and Cowan provide the most explicit systems perspective that is relevant to adult development. Their premise is that human development is the effective interaction between people and human systems.

Marjorie Fiske

Marjorie Fiske, a leading longitudinal scholar of adult life, observes that as our society becomes more complex and affected by change, there are fewer autonomous, self-generating people. She suggests that there is an increasing need to be told how to think, feel, and behave. With people living longer and social change rampant, the potential for individual growth may be stunted, she suggests. She proposes four commitments which, in varying proportions, guide adult development:

- Interpersonal commitment to esprit de corps at work, and in marriages, families, and communities.
- Altruistic commitment to integrated and generative activities, including ethical, philosophical, and religious allegiances.
- Mastery commitment to autonomy and continuous skill development in basic human skills. There should be an abundance of elders capable of teaching these mastery skills.

- Self-protective commitment to guard against being overwhelmed and dictated to by the world around us. Adults need to maintain self-preservation—to reduce their role commitments when they need to in order to care for themselves.

The coaches whom I know stress "mastery commitment" over the other three commitments. Is that wise or effective for the long run of person's lives or organizational systems? Are not "interpersonal commitments," "altruistic commitments," and "self-protective commitments" also important for effective coaching? (See Basic Library: Social Theories for references.)

MARRIAGE AND COUPLES DEVELOPMENT THEORIES

Although much has been written about the development of families, comparatively little theory is available about the development of couples. Because intimacy maintenance is a major issue in adult life, and because coupling is a basic form of intimacy, more attention needs to be devoted to how couples develop throughout the life cycle.

Dym and Glenn (1993) propose three stages of couples development, which, when completed, begin again and repeat:

1. *Expansion and promise*—high expectations, positive hopes, expansiveness
2. *Contraction and betrayal*—times of trouble, disappointment, withdrawal
3. *Resolution*—compromise, negotiation, accommodation, and integration

There is a general consensus among family therapy theorists that couples develop something like this:

1. *Dependent Phase*—romantic, symbiotic, idealistic, naive, unrealistic
2. *Counterdependent Phase*—rebellious, angry, pushing away, feeling disappointed
3. *Independent Phase*—accepting a truce in order to individuate, leading separate lives with separate friends and a minimal meaning to the relationship
4. *Interdependent Phase*—accepting separateness and togetherness, committing to support one another, growing friendships beyond the coupling, seeking quality time together, becoming spiritual partners growing old together

Although some therapists specialize in couple development, there are few other professionals that couples can turn to who can renew and revitalize their relationships. This could be an important coaching specialty for coaches with the proper training. (See Basic Library: Theories of Couples Development.)

FAMILY DEVELOPMENT THEORIES

Monica McGoldrick and Elizabeth A. Carter (1990, second edition) have outlined the family life cycle and ways professionals can facilitate it. Family coaching will probably evolve along the lines of Virginia Satir's *Peoplemaking*. It will concentrate on training parents and working with couples to understand to "develop" the family in sound and challenging ways. It will provide support to single parents and keep clients future-oriented. (See Basic Library: Theories of Family Development for references.)

CAREER DEVELOPMENT THEORIES

The theories of career development that relate to adult development and coaching include those of John Holland, Donald Super, Gene Dalton, Paul Thompson, Raymond Price, and Edgar Schein.

John Holland

Holland suggests that people project themselves into careers that are like themselves. He proposes six personality orientations, each of which corresponds with specific occupational preferences.

1. *Realistic persons* deal with the environment as an objective, concrete, and physically manipulative manner. They avoid psychologisms, intellectual or artistic expressions, group leadership roles, and social involvement. They like masculine roles and are often unsociable, emotionally stable, materialistic, and traditional. They prefer agricultural, technical, mechanical, and engineering careers. They like to use their motor skills to do projects or to solve problems. They like athletics, scouting, and crafts, and they dislike verbal interaction and being the center of attention. They have a low self-image.

2. *Investigative people* deal with the environment through their intelligence, words, and symbols. These are the intellectuals who prefer theory, scientific vocations, languages, art, music, and sculpture. They are unsociable, masculine, persistent, scholarly, and introverted. They do poorly as leaders but are original, independent, and self-confident. They are also less practical, emotionally stable, and conventional than the realistic person.

3. *Artistic individuals* deal with the environment by creating art forms and products. They thrive on subjective impressions and fantasies, particularly in

careers in music, art, literature, drama, and other creative fields. They are unsociable, feminine, submissive, introspective, sensitive, impulsive, and flexible.

4. *Social people* handle the environment through interpersonal skills. They need and want social interaction. They like educational, therapeutic, and religious vocations, and jobs in government, community services, and dramatics. They are sociable, nurturant, cheerful, conservative, responsible, achieving, and self-accepting. They have a positive self-image and like leadership, speaking, and popularity.

5. *Enterprising people* deal with the environment through dominance, adventure, and impulse. They are persuasive, verbal, extroverted, self-accepting, self-confident, aggressive, and exhibitionistic. They do well in sales, supervisory, and leadership vocations. They like athletics, dramatics, public speaking, and interviewing. They dislike loner, nonsocial activities.

6. *Conventional persons* deal with the environment by engaging in socially approved activities. They imitate others, like to be correct and neat, but are unoriginal. They are masculine, shrewd, dominant, controlled, rigid, and stable. They differ from social types by possessing greater self-control and by being more hard-headed and less dominant and nurturant.

Holland then provides a list of occupations that provide environments that fit each personality type, following a blend of the six types. His widely used Self-Directed Search provides a quick diagnosis of personality types and vocational options, normed primarily for young adults just entering work systems.

Donald Super

Donald Super has a career theory that is highly congruent with much of adult developmental theory. These are his central points:

- People have abilities and strengths for careers in a number of occupations. Adults follow a maxicycle from age fifteen to age seventy or later, in which they focus on some phase of career development: growth (fifteen to twenty), exploration (twenty to twenty-five), establishment (twenty-five to forty-five), maintenance (forty-five to sixty-five), and decline (over sixty-five). In other words, people's careers are shaped around the developmental forces of the adult life cycle.
- When each phase peaks and declines, people begin a minicycle process that will either renew and deepen commitments to the same occupational area or move to a different one.
- The career pattern is often determined by the person's parental socioeconomic level, mental ability, personality characteristics, and the opportunities to which he or she is exposed.
- Career development is essentially that of developing and implementing

self-concepts and synthesizing those with environmental opportunities and conditions.

- Work and career provide a focus for personality organization.

Gene Dalton, Paul Thompson, and Raymond Price

These authors have created a model of career development around four stages of development within an organization:

1. *Apprentice:* dependency work of a routine nature, aimed at developing expertise and recognition.
2. *Colleague:* assumption of leadership, team work, and some coaching.
3. *Mentor:* supervisor, involved in training and evaluation; interdependent in relationships and systems; perceived as an expert, a leader in the field.
4. *Sponsor:* policymaker, involved in shaping the direction of the organization. This person sponsors younger individuals for getting ahead in the organization. People at this level must be willing to give up daily control of the operation and feel comfortable with delegating and exercising power.

Edgar H. Schein

Schein has outlined stages and career tasks that adults in general follow within organizations. (See Basic Library for references to Schein's work.)

Richard Bolles, Charles Handy, and Tom Peters

Since about 1985, career theory has moved away from linear concepts and the presumption of work system stability to entrepreneurial notions and the presumption of continuous change. Bolles, Handy, and Peters are examples of persons articulating a new approach to career planning.

Bolles stresses the importance of the person who wants a job or career assuming responsibility for making it happen. A man, for example, should know his personal mission, identify his skill sets, construct a résumé, network, and market himself into the best job he can find that is congruent with his interests and abilities.

Handy suggests that careers are mostly discontinuous, and that instead of careers, people will be stringing together jobs using different "portfolios" of strengths, skills, and interests. A portfolio would include all the "work" a person wants to be doing, including remunerative jobs, avocations, hobbies, and family times. Relying on a portfolio means seeing yourself as self-employed and viewing every job as temporary. If a woman, for example were at the end of a job, she would envision the next chapter of her life, conduct a skills analysis of competence areas, identify job areas of intrigue and potential financial rewards, and entrepreneur the next job—knowing that it too will be a short-term engagement.

Tom Peters talks about serial contracting as empowerment. The contract that workplaces used to promise—lifetime security for financial rewards and career development in exchange for company loyalty and intensive working—has gone out of existence. Workers and employees have to work out *pro tem* contracts that are fair both ways, job by job. Workers must assume responsibility for work design, marketing, contracting, and redesign throughout their lives.

Sooner or later, almost all coaches are asked by their clients to do career coaching, and this knowledge needs to be included in coaching training. Coaches also need to know how to refer to established career professionals across the country. (See the Basic Library: Career Development Throughout Adulthood for references.)

ADULT DEVELOPMENT WITHIN LEISURE SYSTEMS

One approach to a lifespan approach to work and leisure is that of McDaniels.

Carl McDaniels

McDaniels has outlined a lifespan approach to work and leisure in his important book on life planning:

Adulthood, 24–40: The Implementation Stage. Quite often young adults combine work and leisure so the two activities feed each other. Others identify their leisure habits through their marriages and families. In today's world it is not unusual in this age group for leisure to replace work as a major source of life satisfaction and may be valued more highly than work. Many adults choose a lifetime sport at this point.

Midlife: 40–60: The Involvement and Reassessment Stage. In midlife, adults are likely to find life meaning from multiple sources, not just work and home. Often, leisure grows in importance, not as an escape from work but as a source of personal competence, friendship connections, and renewal. Leisure is a way to prepare for elderhood and to make readjustments to the work-play balance.

Retirement: 60+: The Reawareness and Reexploration Stage. With retirement, an adult can have total identification with and fulfillment through leisure. Although reduced income may change a person's leisure activities, there are more and more alternatives for retired people. (See Basic Library: Leisure in Adulthood for references.)

GROUP (TEAM) DEVELOPMENT THEORIES

Many coaches use coaching groups to facilitate deeper work and more rapid results. Peer interaction is invaluable for learning. Consider the possibility of using groups as a coaching venue in addition to one-on-one coaching. First get training in leading groups, if you don't already have it. (See Basic Library: Group Development Theories for references.)

ORGANIZATION DEVELOPMENT THEORIES

The field of human and organization development informs the coaching practice by providing insight into human systems and their functions. This includes couple and family systems, work systems, community systems, and larger systems. (See Basic Library: Organization Development Theories for references.)

 BASIC LIBRARY FOR COACHES

Social Theories

*Bennis, W. *Organizing Genius: The Secrets of Creative Collaboration.* Reading, Mass.: Addison-Wesley, 1998. Gives examples of how a great leader evokes the greatness of followers as colleagues.

Brofenbrenner, U. *The Ecology of Human Development: Experiments by Nature and Design.* Cambridge, Mass.: Harvard University Press, 1981.

Brofenbrenner, U., and Ceci, S. J. "Nature-Nurture Reconceptualized in Developmental Perspective: A Bioecological Model." *Psychological Review,* 1994, *10,* 568–586.

Fiske, M. "Changing Hierarchies of Commitment," In N. J. Smelser and E. H. Erikson (eds.), *Themes of Work and Love in Adulthood.* Cambridge, Mass.: Harvard University Press, 1984.

Fiske, M. "Tasks and Crises of the Second Half of Life: The Interrelationship of Commitment, Coping, and Adaptation." In J. E. Birren and R. B. Sloane (eds.), *Handbook of Mental Health and Aging.* Englewood Cliffs, N.J.: Prentice Hall, 1992.

Fiske, M., and Chiriboga, D. A. *Change and Continuity in Adult Life.* San Francisco: Jossey-Bass, 1990.

French, W. L., and Bell, C. H., Jr. *Organization Development: Behavioral Science Interventions for Organization Improvement.* (3rd ed.) Englewood

Cliffs, N.J.: Prentice Hall, 1994. A good manual for developing strategies within organizations.

*Fritts, P. *The New Managerial Mentor.* Palo Alto, Calif.: Davies-Black, 1998. Views mentoring as a force for collaborative decision making.

Lewin, K., and Grabbe, P. "Conduct, Knowledge, and Acceptance of New Values." *The Journal of Social Issues,* Aug. 1945, *1*(3).

*Simonsen, P. *Promoting a Development Culture in Your Organization.* Palo Alto, Calif.: Davies-Black, 1997. Describes ways to develop people and organizational systems simultaneously.

Weisbord, M. R. *Productive Workplaces: Organizing and Managing for Dignity, Meaning, and Community.* San Francisco: Jossey-Bass, 1981.

Theories of Couples Development

Bader, E., and Pearson, P. T. *In Quest of the Mythical Mate: A Developmental Approach to Diagnosis and Treatment in Couples Therapy.* New York: Brunner/Mazel, 1988. An original and useful theory.

Brody, S., and Brody, C. *Renew Your Marriage at Midlife.* New York: Putnam, 1999.

*Bugental, J. F. *Intimate Journeys: Stories from Life-Changing Therapy.* San Francisco: Jossey-Bass, 1990. A book of stories of people who developed lasting, intimate relationships.

*Cherlin, A. J. *Marriage, Divorce, Remarriage.* Cambridge, Mass.: Harvard University Press. 1992. A lucid and useful book on these topics.

Cosby, F. J. (ed.). *Spouse, Parent, Worker: On Gender and Multiple Roles.* New Haven, Conn.: Yale University Press, 1987. Cutting-edge reading on multiple role issues by the leading scholars.

*Davidson, C. *Staying Home Instead: Alternatives to the Two-Paycheck Family.* San Francisco: Jossey-Bass, 1998. Maps out ways that mothers can stay at home and manage to keep their sanity, self-esteem, and checking account balance.

Dym, B., and Glenn, M. L. *Couples: Exploring and Understanding the Cycles of Intimate Relationships.* New York: HarperCollins, 1993.

*Everett, C., and Everett, S. *Healthy Divorce.* San Francisco: Jossey-Bass, 1998. Suggests ways a couple and their children can successfully process the phases of the divorce process.

Fisher, R., and Brown, S. *Getting Together: Building Relationships as We Negotiate.* New York: Penguin, 1989. Discusses negotiation skills within relationships.

*Gottman, J. M. *Why Marriages Succeed or Fail.* New York: Simon and Schuster, 1994. Simply written and full of examples.

*Hendrix, H. *Getting the Love You Want: A Guide for Couples.* New York: Holt, 1992. Clear descriptions of what makes coupling succeed.

Hendrix, H. *Keeping the Love You Find: A Guide for Singles.* New York: Pocket, 1993. Well written and applicable to married couples as well as singles.

James, P. *The Divorce Mediation Handbook: Everything You Need to Know.* San Francisco: Jossey-Bass, 1998. Takes readers step by step through the supportive process of divorce mediation.

*Kaslow, F. W., and Schwartz, L. L. *The Dynamics of Divorce: A Life Cycle Perspective.* New York: Brunner/Mazel, 1987. Combines a life cycle approach with family systems, and looks at the impact divorce has on the husband and wife, the children, and extended family for many years.

McGoldrick, M., and Associates. *Ethnicity and Family Therapy.* New York: Guilford Press, 1996. A collection of writing representing family structures in many nations, cultures, and ethnic groups.

Moore, T. *Soul Makes: Honoring the Mysteries of Love and Relationship.* New York: HarperCollins, 1994.

*Schnarch, D. *Passionate Marriage: Keeping Love & Intimacy Alive in Committed Relationships.* New York: Holt, 1997. A unique approach to individuation and coupling.

*Sekaran, U. *Dual-Career Families.* San Francisco, Jossey-Bass, 1986. A problem-solving book aimed at helping minimize the negative issues in dual-career couples.

*Stahmann, R. F., and Hiebert, W. J. *Pre-Marital and Remarital Counseling: The Professional's Handbook.* San Francisco: Jossey-Bass, 1998. A fine resource for couple coaches, particularly with premarital coaching.

*Wallerstein, J. S., and Blakeslee, S. *The Good Marriage: How and Why Love Lasts.* New York: Warner, 1995. Shows how to work backward from the qualities of a good marriage to constructing those qualities.

Welwood, J. *Journey of the Heart: The Path of Conscious Love.* New York: HarperPerennial, 1996. Beautifully written, with clarity and passion.

Theories of Family Development

*Blakely, M. K. *American Mom.* Chapel Hill, N.C.: Algonquin, 1994. Describes motherhood with insight, humor, and power.

Carter, E. A., and McGoldrick, M. (eds.). *The Changing Family Life Cycle: A Framework for Family Therapy.* (2nd ed.) Boston: Allyn & Bacon, 1990. A gold mine of information on all kinds of family systems, economic groupings, and situations.

Einstein, E. *The Stepfamily: Living, Loving, Learning.* New York: Macmillan, 1994.

*Elium, D., and Elium, J. *Raising a Son: Parents and the Making of a Healthy Man.* Berkeley, Calif.: Celestial Arts, 1996. A book for staying in the trenches through thick and thin.

*Galinsky, E. *The Six Stages of Parenthood.* Reading, Mass.: Addison-Wesley, 1990. An outstanding overview of the parenting years.

Glick, P. C. "The Family Life Cycle and Social Change." *Family Relations,* 1992, *38,* 123–129.

Heitler, S. M. *From Conflict to Resolution: Skills and Strategies for Individual, Couple, and Family Therapy.* New York: Norton, 1990.

Hibbs, E. (ed.). *Adoption: International Perspectives.* Madison, Conn.: International Universities Press, 1991. Provides a broad overview of adoption issues in several countries.

*Lerner, H. *The Mother Dance: How Children Change Your Life.* New York: HarperCollins, 1998.

Miller, A. *For Your Own Good: Hidden Cruelty in Child-rearing and the Roots of Violence.* New York: Farrar, Straus, and Giroux, 1990.

Silverstein, O. *The Courage to Raise Good Men.* New York: Viking, 1995.

Visher, E. B., and Visher, J. S. *Step-Families: A Guide to Working with Step-parents and Step Children.* New York: Brunner/Mazel, 1979. A good reference book for understanding the step-family.

*Winnicott, D. W. *The Family and Individual Development.* New York: Routledge, 1996. Essays on human development from infancy to early childhood to latency to adolescence to young adulthood—all in relation to healthy and disruptive factors in family life.

Wolf, A. E. *Get Out of My Life: But First Could You Drive Me and Cheryl to the Mall? A Parent's Guide to the New Teenager.* New York: Noonday Press, 1992. A rude awakening to successful parenting during the teenage years.

Career Development Throughout Adulthood

*Bolles, R. *The 1999 What Color Is Your Parachute?* Berkeley, Calif.: Ten Speed Press, 1999. The most complete book on how to conduct a successful job hunt.

*Borchard, D., Kelly, J. J., and Weaver, N.-P. *Your Career: Choices and Changes.* (7th ed.) Dubuque, Iowa: Kendall/Hunt, 1998. An outstanding book for choosing or redesigning a career.

Bridges, W. *Jobshift: How to Prosper in a Workplace Without Jobs.* Reading, Mass.: Addison-Wesley, 1995.

Career Planning and Adult Development Journal, 4965 Sierra Road, San Jose, CA 95132. A journal covering a wide range of career development issues, aimed at human resources professionals and career counselors.

Dalton, G., Thompson, P., and Price, R. "Career Stages: A Model of Professional Careers in Organizations." *Organizational Dynamics*: *6,* 19–42.

Dent, H. S., Jr. *Job Shock: Four New Principles Transforming Our Work and Business.* New York: St. Martin's Press, 1995. Theorizes that the real meaning of "downsizing" in corporate America is to prepare for global entrepreneurism.

*Feller, R., and Walz, G. (eds.). *Career Transitions in Turbulent Times: Exploring Work, Learning and Careers.* Brief chapters by the giants of the field: Krumboltz, Gyspers, Osipow, Tiedeman, Schlossberg, Gelatt, Campbell, and Hudson. 1996. An ERIC book; order at 800-414-9769.

Fox, M. *The Reinvention of Work: A New Vision of Livelihood for Our Time.* New York: HarperCollins, 1995. A spiritual, value-based interpretation of getting your "work" in balance with the rest of your life.

*Gysbers, N. C., and Associates. *Designing Careers.* San Francisco: Jossey-Bass, 1984. Probably the best single book on how to design a career for yourself or for others.

Hall, D. T., and Associates. *Career Development in Organizations.* San Francisco: Jossey-Bass, 1986. A scholarly book on promoting career development within organizations.

*Hansen, L. S., and Rapoza, R. S. *Career Development and Counseling of Women.* New York: Charles C. Thomas, 1978. Probably the most complete book ever done on women's career issues.

Herr, E. L., and Cramer, S. H. *Career Guidance and Counseling Through the Lifespan: Systematic Approaches.* New York: HarperCollins, 1995.

Holland, J. "A Theory of Vocational Choice." *Journal of Counseling Psychology,* 1959, *6,* 35–45.

Holland, J. "A Theory-Ridden, Computerless, Impersonal, Vocational Guidance System." *Journal of Vocational Behavior,* 1971, *1,* 167–176.

Leong, F.T.L. *Career Development and Vocational Behavior of Racial and Ethnic Minorities.* Hillsdale, N.J.: Erlbaum, 1995.

*McKenna, E. P. *When Work Doesn't Work Anymore: Women, Work, and Identity.* New York: Delacorte, 1997.

*Newman, B. K. *Now That You're All Grown Up, What Do You Want to Be?: A Career Transition Guide.* Dubuque, Iowa: Kendall/Hunt, 1996. Useful exercises for career coaching.

*Osipow, S. H. *Theories of Career Development.* (3rd ed.) Englewood Cliffs, N.J.: Prentice Hall, 1995. The bible on theories of career development.

Savickas, M. L., and Lent, R. W. *Convergence in Career Development Theories.* Palo Alto, Calif.: Consulting Psychologists Press, 1994.

*Schein, E. H. *Career Dynamics: Matching Individual and Organizational Needs.* New York: Addison-Wesley, 1978.

Super, D. "A Theory of Vocational Development." *American Psychologist,* 1953, *8,* 185–190. Super's basic career theory at the beginning of his career.

*Super, D. "Career and Life Development." In D. Brown and L. Brooks (eds.) *Career Choice and Development,* 192–234. San Francisco: Jossey-Bass, 1996. Super's career theory today; uses life cycle information in his model.

Super, D. E. "A Life-span, Life-space Approach to Career Development." *Journal of Vocational Behavior,* 1980, *16,* 282–298.

*Super, D. E., and Sverko, B. (eds.). *Life Roles, Values, and Careers.* San Francisco: Jossey-Bass, 1995. Based on an innovative, cross-national project; reports how values, roles, and careers combine to forge the process of human development across the lifespan; includes valuable instruments that coaches can use.

*Waterman, R., Jr., Waterman, J. A., and Collard, B. A. "Toward a Career-Resilient Workforce." *Harvard Business Review,* Jul./Aug. 1994, 87–95.

Leisure in Adulthood

Anderson, N. *Man's Work and Leisure.* Leiden, Netherlands: E. J. Brill, 1997.

Csikszentmihalyi, M. *Beyond Boredom and Anxiety: The Experience of Play in Work and Games.* San Francisco: Jossey-Bass, 1975.

*Kelly, J. R. *Leisure.* Englewood Cliffs, N.J.: Prentice Hall, 1995. The most comprehensive book in the area of leisure and easy to read.

*Lederman, E. *Vacations That Can Change Your Life: Adventures, Retreats and Workshops for the Mind, Body and Spirit.* Naperville, Ill.: Sourcebooks, 1998. An outstanding collection of resources for renewal and learning.

Group Development Theories

Corey, G. *Theory and Practice of Group Counseling.* Pacific Grove, Calif.: Brooks/Cole, 1990. Combined with previous two books, provides a comprehensive grounding in theory and practice of group work.

*Corey, G. *Group Techniques.* (2nd ed.) Pacific Grove, Calif.: Brooks/Cole, 1992. Written for practitioners; promotes training models for obtaining necessary techniques throughout the group process; includes ethical considerations, termination guidelines, and a good reading list.

*Corey, M. S., and Corey, G. *Groups: Process and Practice.* (5th ed.) Pacific Grove, Calif.: Brooks/Cole, 1997. Written to guide coaches or counselors into and through the group process, step by step.

*Dyer, W. G. *Team Building: Issues and Alternatives.* (2nd ed.) Reading, Mass.: Addison-Wesley, 1995. A simple and straightforward book on small groups, teams, and corporate applications.

Journal for Specialists in Group Work. American Counseling Association, 5999 Stevenson Avenue, Alexandria, VA 22304. Good journal for coaches.

*Lacoursiere, R. *The Life Cycle of Groups: Group Developmental Stage Theory.* New York: Human Sciences Press, 1980. An excellent book on the ongoing process of group work, from orientation to dissatisfaction to resolution to production to termination.

Munroe, R. L., and Munroe, R. H. *Cross-Cultural Human Development.* Monterey, Calif.: Brooks/Cole, 1994. A critical examination of cultural, ethnic, and national identifications and how they influence adult development.

*Schwarz, R. M. *The Skilled Facilitator: Practical Wisdom for Developing Effective Groups.* San Francisco: Jossey-Bass, 1994. An excellent introduction to group leadership, stressing process and facilitation.

Yalom, I. D. *Encounter Groups: First Facts.* New York: Basic, 1973. A good source for understanding the different kinds of groups, their goals, and their effectiveness.

Organization Development Theories

*Argyris, C. *Knowledge for Action.* San Francisco: Jossey-Bass, 1993.

Argyris, C., Putnam, R., and Smith, D. M. *Action Science.* San Francisco: Jossey-Bass, 1985. Promotes learning for action and change within the organizations of the society.

Boulding, K. E. *The World as a Total System.* Newbury Park, Calif.: Sage, 1985. Provides the basic concepts of how individuals interface with everything else as a total system.

Bronfenbrenner, U. *The Ecology of Human Development.* Cambridge, Mass.: Harvard University Press, 1981. Proposes a unique theory for understanding human development. (Creative Education Foundation, 1050 Union Road, Buffalo, NY 14224, 800-447-2774)

*French, W. L., and Bell, C. H., Jr. *Organization Development: Behavioral Science Interventions for Organization Improvement.* (3rd ed.) Englewood Cliffs, N.J.: Prentice Hall, 1994. A good manual for developing strategies within organizations.

Goffman, E. *The Presentation of Self in Everyday Life.* New York: Doubleday, 1959. Treats the social self as a person with many masks that shift from activity to activity.

Human Resource Development Quarterly, sponsored by the American Society for Training and Development and The American Academy of Human Resource Development. San Francisco: Jossey-Bass. Brief reports of new research in how human development issues intersect with corporate performance.

Jackson, C. N. (ed.). *Targeting Change: Organizational Development.* Alexandria, Va.: ASTD, 1989. Brief chapters by many authors on organizational themes.

Jacobs, R. L. (ed.). *Human Resource Development Quarterly.* San Francisco: Jossey-Bass.

Kauffman, D., Jr. *Systems 1: An Introduction to Systems Thinking.* Minneapolis, Minn.: Future Systems Inc., 1980.

Magnusson, D. (ed.). *Toward a Psychology of Situations: An Interactional Perspective.* Hillsdale, N.J.: Erlbaum, 1981. Collected essays on how environments and situations affect human behavior, and visa versa.

Sarason, S. B. *The Psychological Sense of Community: Prospects for a Community Psychology.* San Francisco: Jossey-Bass, 1988.

Sarason, S. B. *The Creation of Settings and the Future Societies.* San Francisco: Jossey-Bass, 1989. Describes ways adults interface around the creation of events and places.

*Straus, R. A. *Using Sociology.* Bayside, N.Y.: General Hall, Inc., 1994. Solid information for coaches as social engineers.

Strauss, W., and Howe, N. *The History of America's Future Generations.* New York: Morrow, 1991. Proposes a generational sequencing that keeps repeating itself, from the founding of America until now which can be used to plot the future.

Toulmin, S. *Cosmopolis: The Hidden Agenda of Modernity.* New York: Free Press, 1992. Reviews how previous societies have sustained a vision of their future and proposes that we do the same within a global and cosmopolitan context.

*Van Eynde, D. F., Hoy, J. C., and Van Eynde, D. (eds.). *Organization Development Classics: The Practice and Theory of Change.* San Francisco: Jossey-Bass, 1997. Essays spanning the second half of the twentieth century by major leaders in the OD field.

VonBertalanffy, L. "General Systems Theory and Psychiatry." In Silvano Arieti (ed.), *American Handbook of Psychiatry* (Vol. 1, pp. 1095–1117). New York: Basic Books, 1974.

White, R. K. (ed.). *Psychology and the Prevention of Nuclear War.* New York: New York University, 1986. A remarkable book on strategies that people in the helping professions can take to prevent nuclear war.

Whittaker, J. K. *Social Treatment: An Approach to Interpersonal Helping.* Chicago: Aldine, 1989. A family systems pioneer who taught others how to intervene in systems as well as with individuals.

 PART THREE 

A CONCEPTUAL MODEL FOR COACHING

 CHAPTER SIX 

Coaching Through Life Transitions

In the post-modern world, continuous change flows directly from its sources into our minds and lives. Huge supermarkets and megamarkets present us with an enormous range of choices; television, movies, and the Internet expand the number of choices infinitely. The intensity and dimensions of change will increase throughout the twenty-first century, and the ability of our human systems (marriages, families, occupations, communities, nations) to protect us or to guide us will continue to decrease.

Each person must learn to be responsible for making the best choices in whatever social context presents itself. Coaches can help clients do that. In this section I discuss my own model for change—how adult lives follow change cycles—and suggest specific ways to coach people who are in different phases of a change cycle. First I introduce my conception of how adults experience change (see Figure 2) for reference. Then I discuss the phases of the change cycle and show how knowing about them can facilitate the coaching task.

HOW CHANGE IS EXPERIENCED

Good coaches should take into account that adults experience their lives in two basic patterns: either they are in a *life chapter* or they are in a *life transition*. Life chapters and life transitions are experienced as cycles of

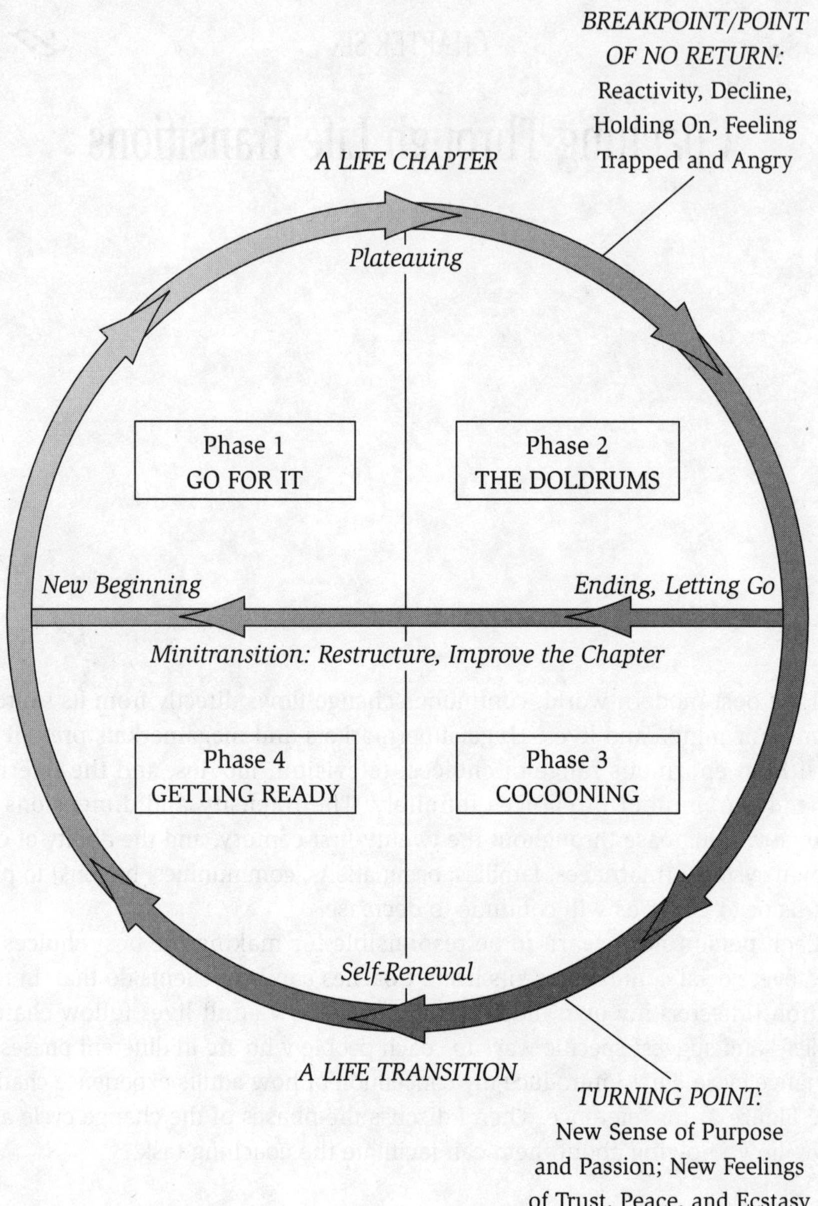

Figure 2. Phases of an Adult's Experience of Change.

change that are repeated over and over. The old way of expecting a linear progression of predictable life events to unfold no longer serves as a model for adult life.

Life Chapters

In a life chapter, the world seems basically stable, with opportunities to grow and live well. A person's dominant behavior pattern is most likely to be upbeat, high-energy, and optimistic. Change seems like a reliable flow of resources and opportunities for fulfilling life's purpose. Performing certain action steps seems to be a way to serve those purposes and reach those goals.

For a person in a life chapter, the flow of change provides opportunities to soar. A woman, for example, may be eager to advance at work, to begin a family, to get recognized and rewarded. Her life seems full of outer challenges. The focus of coaching people who are in a life chapter, both for men and women, is mostly about performing, doing, achieving.

Life Transitions

In a life transition, people experience the world as basically unreliable, chaotic, and punishing. They are likely to feel discouraged, have low energy, and be pessimistic. For example, if a man experiences abrupt change—loses his job, mate, or health—he could also lose his moorings and find himself withdrawing from his usual coping mechanisms; he may envelop himself in a full-time life review. His effort then goes to finding new resources and tools for managing his life.

A person in a life transition turns inward and disengages from as much "busyness" as possible; inner voices begin to seem more reliable than outer signals. The inner journey of a life transition deconstructs the former chapter; a person then matures and eventually grows into a new chapter, much as a butterfly does when it cocoons. I call this *cocooning* because it is a time filled with opportunities for transformation, amazing growth, and renewal.

The model I'm proposing views change and continuity as continuous, positive forces in adult and social life. According to the model, adults can and should be trained to manage both life chapters and life transitions. We learn from all places in the change cycle, and the most important lesson of this model is that there are no permanent arrival points, only a continuous journey as we navigate continuous change. Coaches help clients understand how to manage change, wherever they are in the cycle.

The human systems to which we belong (families, work organizations, communities, and so forth) also move through chapters and transitions. This kind of systems change is what organizational coaches most often work with.

PHASES WITHIN LIFE CHAPTERS AND TRANSITIONS

In my model, each life chapter has two phases: Go for It (working for goals and experiencing success) and The Doldrums (managing disenchantment and restlessness). Each life transition also has two phases: Cocooning (reconstructing the self) and Getting Ready for the Next Chapter (training, experimenting, and networking). These are four phases of adult life that coaches should understand if they are to coach their adult clients effectively.

Life Chapter: Phases One and Two

Phase One is a period of success and stability. The elements and forces of change cohere in what *seems* to be a linear and permanent life chapter. Coaches need to know how to motivate and guide clients who are in Phase One toward legitimate goals (see Figure 3).

Phase Two is marked by a period of boredom and restlessness. Phase Two ends with either a minitransition that serves to improve life in Phase One or with a longer life transition that leads a person to seek new directions.

In Phase Two, the elements and forces that seemed so promising at the beginning of Phase One now seem heavy, less promising, and a burden. A person has a been-there-done-that feeling and may ask, "Is this all there is?" In fact, the career the person is in may have become obsolete, and there may be no option other than to get new training and direction. Whatever the specific circumstance, coaches need to know how to challenge people who are stuck in Phase Two to seek out new options.

Coaching strategies for people in Phase Two are very different from the ones that work with clients in Phase One (see Figure 4).

The best choice for Phase Two clients is for the coach to facilitate designing an exit plan and departing from Phase Two to either a minitransition or to a life transition in Phase Three. For references see (1) Basic Library: Coaching Clients in Phase One and (2) Basic Library: Coaching Clients in Phase Two.

A Minitransition

When people in Phase Two choose to leave, they almost always choose to make a minitransition, which is some minor revision in the chapter they are already in: change of geographic location, change of job, change of spouse, or return to school. A minitransition is a time of strategic planning, renewing the chapter of life with new strategies to improve what's working and change what's not, introducing new options, and getting launched again. Minitransitions are a restructuring of what already exists in the service of improving it. Minitransitions are not of less value than life transitions. They are simply different and serve to renew the chapter a person is in, whereas a life transition renews and transforms the person.

If this is the phase your client is in, indicate here the planning steps you might take:

1. ________________
2. ________________
3. ________________
4. ________________
5. ________________
6. ________________
7. ________________
8. ________________
9. ________________
10. ________________

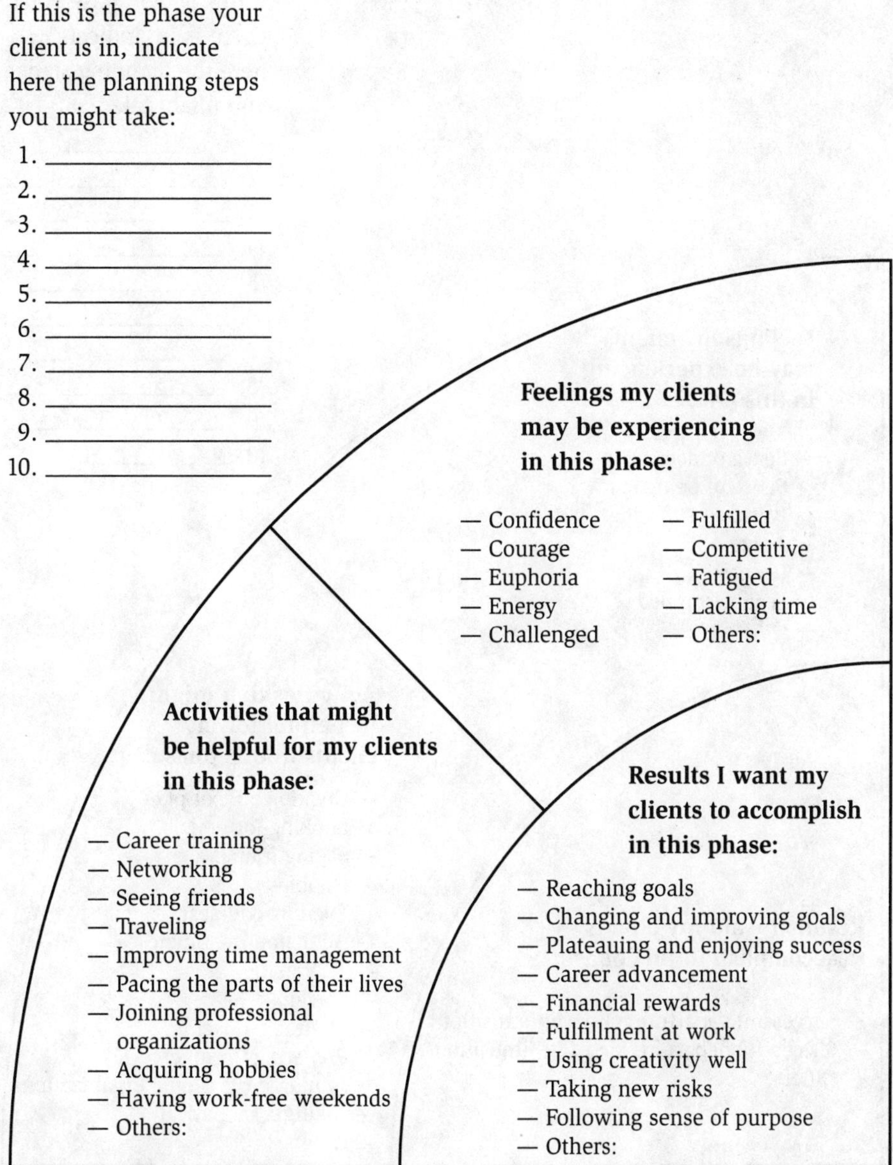

Figure 3. Coaching Clients in Phase One.

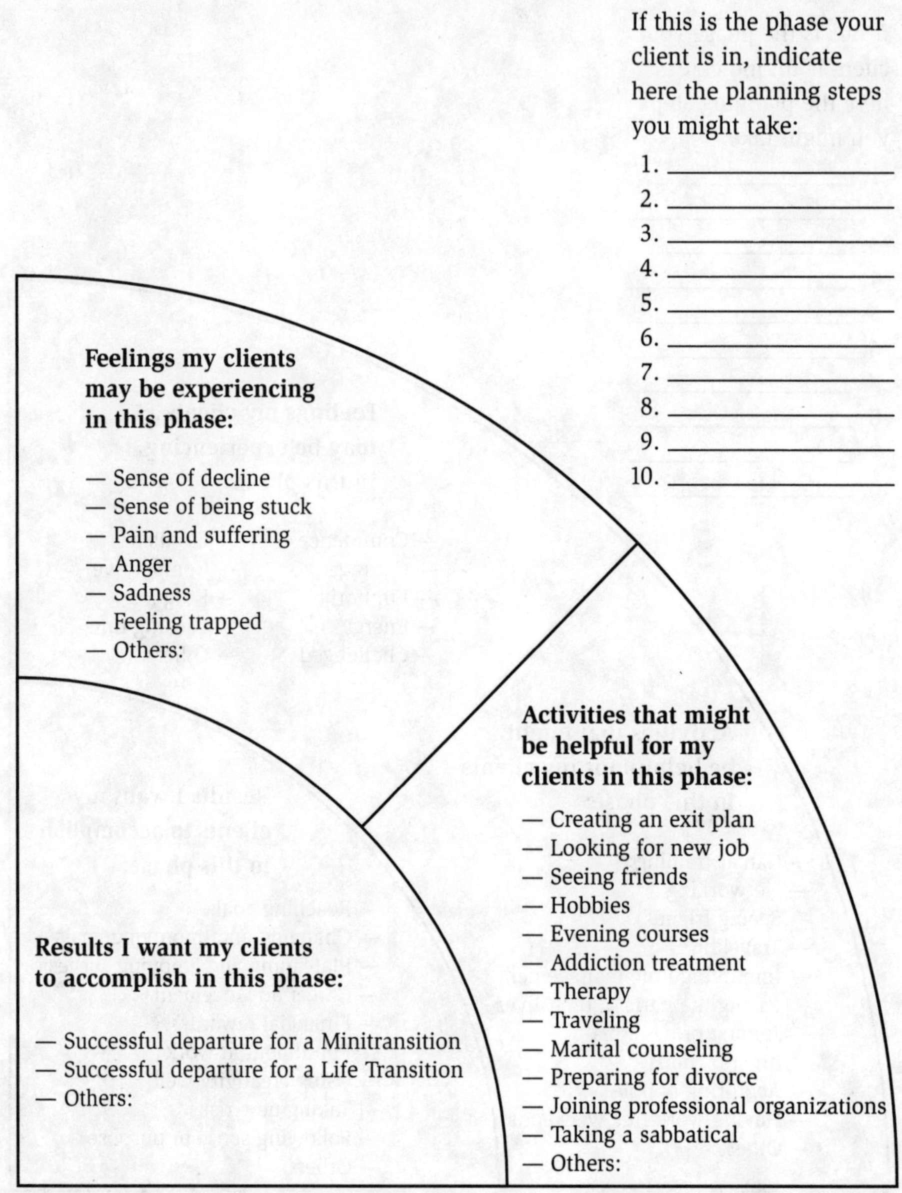

Figure 4. Coaching Clients in Phase Two.

Life Transition: Phases Three and Four

In Phase Three the self is explored at a deeper level through introspection; a person searches for deep meaning as well as for new resources for the future. This is a transition space and time for starting over, while deepening the maturity of the self and its dreams. Coaches need to be able to work with people and organizations in transition and to foster transformation and viable directions for where they are with their lives. This is a time for spiritual coaching and for getting to core values and beliefs (see Figure 5).

Some people arrive at Phase Three not by choice but by emotional default. Sometimes an ending triggers an emotional response that, in turn, triggers a cocooning process, observable as turning inward and being emotionally labile. It feels like an uninvited ending has happened—a little death. People who cocoon come to terms with who they are without their previous roles dominating them. They work through an identity crisis and take time out, psychologically speaking, for soul searching. Little by little, out of solitude grows a resilient self, anchored in core values and inner peace, and challenged by new purpose and passion. Life is transformed. Coaching Phase Three people is ontological, spiritual, and transformative. People leave this phase when they are anchored to deep meaning within themselves.

The major products of Phase Three are self-esteem, self-renewing resilience, the courage to be, and a trust in a force beyond one's ego. In fact, just as the person in Phase One turns to "doing" as the primary vehicle for fulfillment, the person in Phase Three turns to "being." Being seeks doing for its own fulfillment, and doing seeks being for its own sustenance; this is the forceful dynamic of the continuous cycle.

In Phase Four—Getting Ready—people are slowly moving out of the transition space and devoting their time to getting ready for new challenges. Phase Four people usually have amazing energy and thirst for creative activities, networking, and learning. Even though people who have cocooned for some time feel ready to move on, they don't want to be exactly who they were, doing what they did. They want new directions, with significant changes from past ways of living and being. So they set about investigating options, investing in learning, experimenting with ideas, networking, and getting trained. It's a fun, busy, optimistic time but it is lacking in clear goals. A life transition takes time, and coaches who facilitate transitions trust the process and do not rush (see Figure 6).

The cycle of change is a never-ending process throughout the adult years. This cycle is explained in detail in two books by Frederic M. Hudson: *The Adult Years* (1999) and *LifeLaunch* (1996).

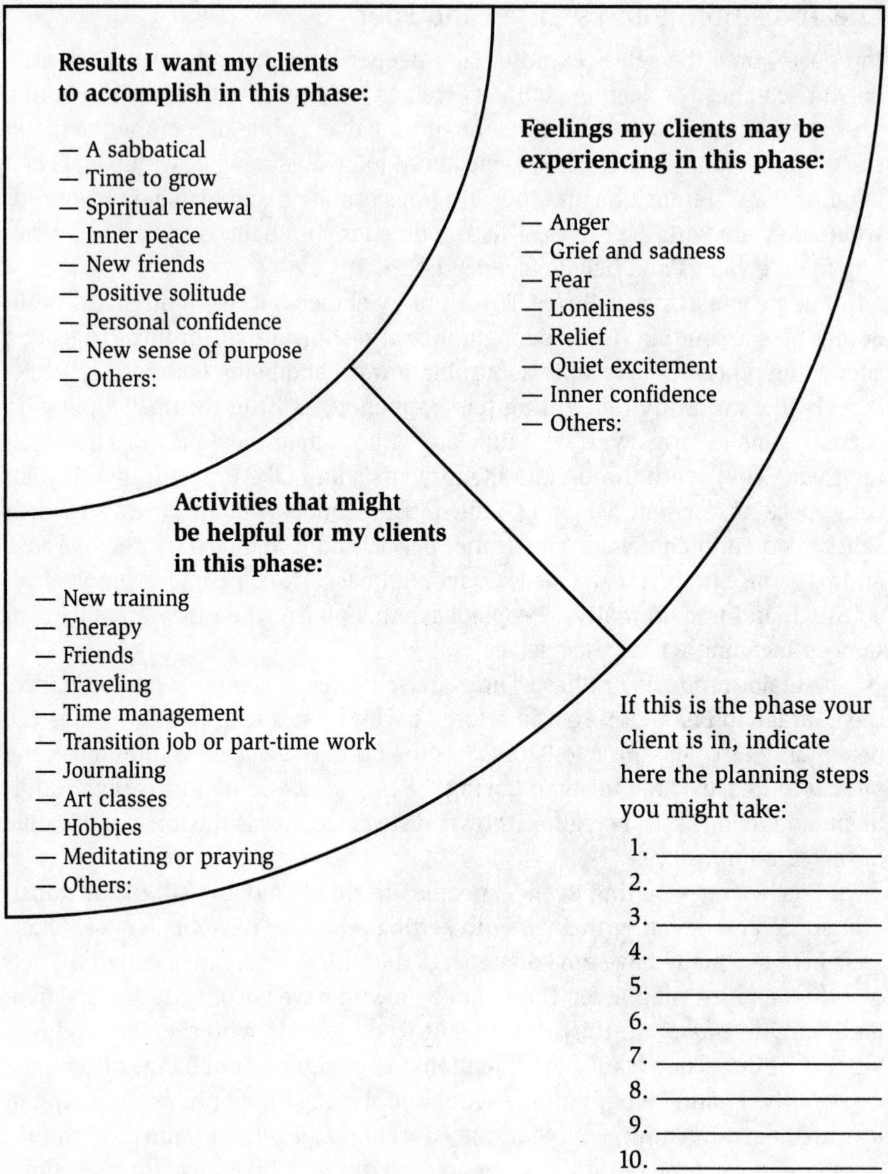

Results I want my clients to accomplish in this phase:

— A sabbatical
— Time to grow
— Spiritual renewal
— Inner peace
— New friends
— Positive solitude
— Personal confidence
— New sense of purpose
— Others:

Feelings my clients may be experiencing in this phase:

— Anger
— Grief and sadness
— Fear
— Loneliness
— Relief
— Quiet excitement
— Inner confidence
— Others:

Activities that might be helpful for my clients in this phase:

— New training
— Therapy
— Friends
— Traveling
— Time management
— Transition job or part-time work
— Journaling
— Art classes
— Hobbies
— Meditating or praying
— Others:

If this is the phase your client is in, indicate here the planning steps you might take:

1. ____________
2. ____________
3. ____________
4. ____________
5. ____________
6. ____________
7. ____________
8. ____________
9. ____________
10. ____________

Figure 5. Coaching Clients in Phase Three.

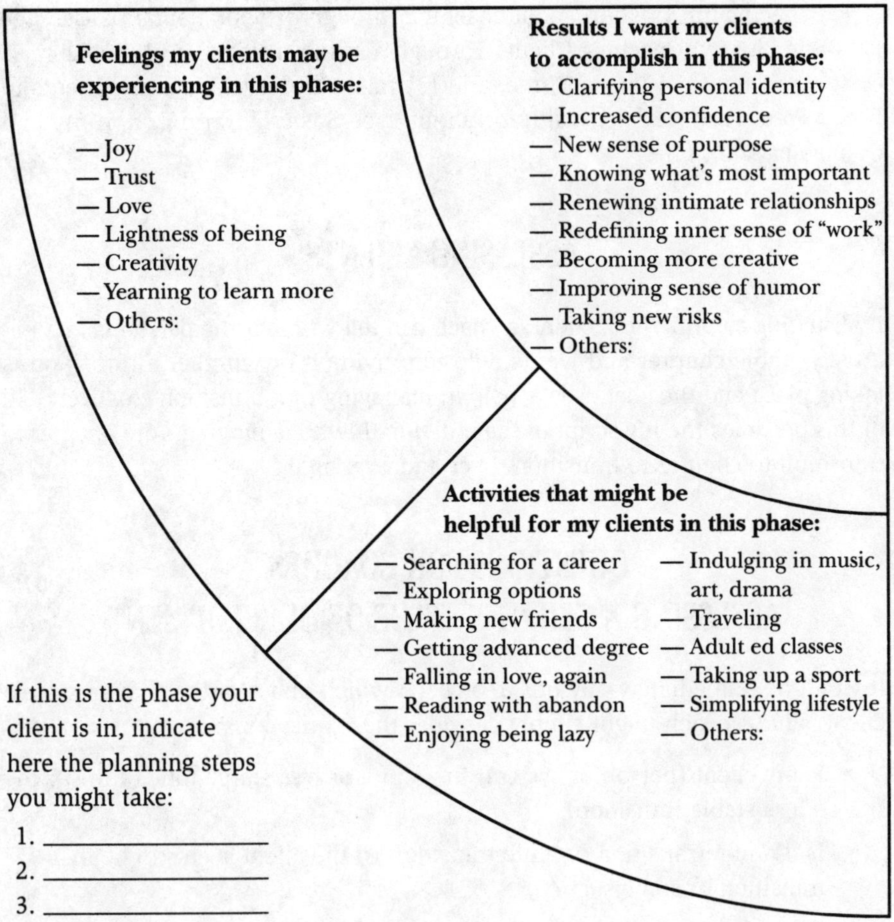

Feelings my clients may be experiencing in this phase:

— Joy
— Trust
— Love
— Lightness of being
— Creativity
— Yearning to learn more
— Others:

Results I want my clients to accomplish in this phase:

— Clarifying personal identity
— Increased confidence
— New sense of purpose
— Knowing what's most important
— Renewing intimate relationships
— Redefining inner sense of "work"
— Becoming more creative
— Improving sense of humor
— Taking new risks
— Others:

Activities that might be helpful for my clients in this phase:

— Searching for a career
— Exploring options
— Making new friends
— Getting advanced degree
— Falling in love, again
— Reading with abandon
— Enjoying being lazy
— Indulging in music, art, drama
— Traveling
— Adult ed classes
— Taking up a sport
— Simplifying lifestyle
— Others:

If this is the phase your client is in, indicate here the planning steps you might take:

1. ____________________
2. ____________________
3. ____________________
4. ____________________
5. ____________________
6. ____________________
7. ____________________
8. ____________________
9. ____________________
10. ____________________

Figure 6. Coaching Clients in Phase Four.

For specific information about coaching through developmental phases, see (1) Basic Library: Coaching Clients Through a Minitransition; (2) Basic Library: Coaching Clients in Phase Three, and (3) Basic Library: Coaching Clients in Phase Four. For more general information, see Basic Library: Continuity and Change in Adult Life.

ASSESSING CLIENTS

By listening carefully to a client, a coach can tell whether the person is in a relatively stable chapter and wants help improving it or whether a transition is taking place and the client seeks help in managing that transition creatively. All of this becomes the life script of the individual, who is moving from chapter to transition to chapter to transition, over and over again.

QUESTIONS FOR COACHES: ASSESSING A CLIENT'S STAGE OF DEVELOPMENT

It won't be immediately obvious to a coach which phase of the change cycle a client is in. A coach might simply consider these questions:

- Is my client (person or system) in a more or less stable time of life or in a less-stable transition?
- Is it a minitransition or a life transition (if the client seems to be in a transition of some sort)?
- Which of the four phases illustrated in the model is my client in? What specific life skills can I encourage my client to consider at this time?
- What critical developmental activities would promote growth and discovery for my client?
- What is my client's resistance to moving ahead in the renewal cycle, and how can I make future-oriented rewards more compelling?
- What strengths does my client have that might be vehicles for growth and development at this time?
- What is my client's vision of the future—dreams, expectations, hopes, yearnings? Has my client a sense of purpose or mission? Where does the client want to be five years from now?
- How can I use the group process most strategically with my client?
- If my client is committed to a minitransition or restructuring, how can I assist in promoting an accurate evaluation of what to hold on to, let go of, or take on?

- Are there external sources of change triggering a transition in my client? If so, how do I encourage self-management at this time?
- What does my client want from me? Am I willing and able to fulfill that contract?
- What planning items are being identified by my client for his or her next chapter of life?
- What follow-up coaching or referral items are being identified by my client for his or her next chapter of life?

COACHING AND BIOGRAPHY, RITUALS, RITES OF PASSAGE

In addition to their understanding of change cycles, coaches are grounded in an intimate understanding of biography, rituals, and rites of passage—all of which are manifestations of change.

Biography

Coaching could be seen as the art of facilitating life scripts. A coach gets inside a client's "story" and "plots" in order to question and explore how the story can best evolve and develop. Effective coaching connects the past, present, and future aspects of a client's story, whether the client is a person or an organization. Sometimes coaching has to do with only one "scene" in a client's life, such as performance at work, but more often it involves relating that scene to the whole of the person's or organization's story. (See Basic Library: Biography.)

Rituals

Rituals help socialize and validate biographical changes. Rituals are a way to keep people who are in radical change connected to the communities of their lives. (See Basic Library: Rituals.)

Rites of Passage

Some rituals facilitate the rites of passage from one stage of life to another within the life cycle. Transitions often function as a rite of passage, from some earlier point of development to a more mature point of development. These rites provide personal and social validation for life's turning points.

See the following references as guides to more in-depth information: (1) Basic Library: Mythic Origins of Personal Stories; (2) Basic Library: Construction and Deconstruction of Stable Chapters; (3) Basic Library: Sample Biographies and Autobiographies; (4) Basic Library: Understanding Biographical Transitions.

BASIC LIBRARY FOR COACHES

Coaching Clients in Phase One

*Block, P. *The Empowered Manager.* San Francisco: Jossey-Bass, 1991. A clear and brief treatise on how healthy, awake people lead and create a future.

Campbell, D. *If You Don't Know Where You're Going, You'll Probably End Up Somewhere Else.* Allen, Tex.: Tabor, 1990. A fun book on planning your life.

Douglass, M. E., and Douglass, D. N. *Manage Your Time, Manage Your Work, Manage Yourself.* New York: AMACOM, 1993.

Garfield, C. *Peak Performers: The New Heroes of American Business.* New York: Avon, 1991. Shows how to use visioning, planning, and training to keep performance on a winning track.

Morrisey, G. L. *Creating Your Future: Personal Strategic Planning for Professionals.* San Francisco: Berrett-Koehler, 1992. A clear and thorough guide to planning.

*Morrisey, G. L. *Morrisey on Planning: A Guide to Strategic Thinking, Building Your Planning Foundation.* San Francisco: Jossey-Bass, 1996. A sound planning guide that teaches "strategic thinking" as a skill set.

Waitley, D. *The New Dynamics of Winning: Gain the Mind-set of a Champion for Unlimited Success in Business and Life.* New York: Morrow, 1995. Presents a formula for success when the world is ready and waiting for you.

Coaching Clients in Phase Two

*Barwick, J. M. *The Plateauing Trap.* New York: AMACOM, 1986. A wise and timely book for plateaued people.

Bradshaw, J. *Healing the Shame That Binds You.* Deerfield Beach, Fla.: Health Communications, 1988. Description of toxic shame and how to liberate your healthy inner child for a new spiritual awakening.

Bradshaw, J. *Homecoming: Reclaiming and Championing Your Inner Child.* New York: Bantam, 1990. More ways to move out of dysfunctional behaviors into renewal and healing.

Carter-Scott, C. *Negaholics: How to Recover from Your Addiction to Negativity and Turn Your Life Around.* New York: Villard, 1996. An easy read about a difficult subject—dealing with people with sustained negative communication patterns.

Evans, P. *The Verbally Abusive Relationship: How to Recognize It and How to Respond.* (2nd ed.) Holbrook, Mass.: Adams Media, 1996.

*Geber, S. Z. *How to Manage Stress for Success.* New York: AMACOM, 1996. A highly applicable how-to book.

Hughes, R. *Culture of Complaint: The Fraying of America.* New York: Oxford, 1993.

*Hyatt, C., and Gottlieb, L. *When Smart People Fail: Rebuilding Yourself for Success.* (rev. ed.) New York: Penguin, 1993. A book on how to cope with life when you don't get the life you think you deserve.

Juster, N. *The Phantom Tollbooth.* New York: Knopf, 1988. A children's book that describes the doldrums briefly.

*Kanter, D. L., and Mirvis, P. H. *The Cynical Americans: Living and Working in an Age of Discontent and Disillusion.* San Francisco: Jossey-Bass, 1989.

Katz, S. J., and Liu, A. E. *Success Trap: Rethink Your Ambitions to Achieve Greater Personal and Professional Fulfillment.* New York: Ticknor and Fields, 1990. Success viewed as an addictive habit that traps us in yesterday's dreams.

Kets de Vries, M.F.R., and Miller, D. *The Neurotic Organization.* San Francisco: Jossey-Bass, 1984. Discusses how organizations, like people, develop irrational forces that sustain dysfunctional behaviors.

Killinger, B. *Workaholics: The Respectable Addicts: A Family Survival Guide.* New York: Fireside, 1992. Argument made that workaholics—to make themselves feel powerful and useful—reduce their focus of energy to their "work"; a recovery program is outlined.

Lasch, C. *The Culture of Narcissism: American Life in an Age of Diminishing Expectations.* New York: Norton, 1991.

*O'Neil, J. R. *The Paradox of Success: When Winning at Work Means Losing at Life.* Los Angeles: Tarcher, 1993. A book for leaders who need renewal.

Peck, M. S. *The People of the Lie: The Hope for Healing Human Evil.* New York: Touchstone Books, 1997.

Robinson, B. E. *Chained to the Desk: A Guidebook for Workaholics.* New York: New York University Press, 1998. A thorough description of work addiction and how it affects marriages, families, and friendships.

Schumacher, E. F. *A Guide for the Perplexed.* New York: Harper & Row, 1977.

Seligman, M. *Helplessness.* San Francisco: W. H. Freeman, 1992. A pioneering effort, establishing that some forms of depression are little more than learned behavior.

Tjosvold, D. *Learning to Manage Conflict: Getting People to Work Together.* New York: Lexington, 1993.

Coaching Clients Through a Minitransition

Covey, S. R. *The Seven Habits of Highly Effective People: Restoring the Character Ethic.* New York: Simon and Schuster, 1989. Basic reading for sustaining personal effectiveness.

Gumpert D. E. *How to Create a Successful Business Plan.* Boston: *Inc.* (magazine), 1996. How to write one followed by stories of some successful business plans.

*Morrisey, G. L. *Morrisey on Planning: A Guide to Strategic Thinking: Building Your Planning Foundation.* San Francisco: Jossey-Bass, 1996. A solid book for understanding the role of planning and discipline for achieving.

*Rusk, T. *Instead of Therapy: Help Yourself Change and Change the Help You're Getting.* Carson, Calif.: Hay House, 1991.

Coaching Clients in Phase Three

Ashe, A. *Days of Grace.* New York: Knopf, 1993. A biography revealing chapters and transitions, the final one being most difficult.

Belf, T.-E., and Ward, C. *Simply Live It UP: Brief Solutions.* Bethesda, Md.: Purposeful Press, 1997. A fun book of exercises for growth and renewal.

*Carter, J., and Carter, R. *Everything to Gain: Making the Most of the Rest of Your Life.* New York: Random House, 1995. The story of how the Carters worked through their defeat as they left the White House.

*Culp, S. *Streamlining Your Life: A Plan for Uncomplicated Living.* Cincinnati: *Writers Digest,* 1991. A neat set of suggestions for getting organized and staying that way.

Dowrick, S. *Intimacy and Solitude.* New York: Norton, 1996. Presents the language of inner space—knowing yourself, knowing the other.

Grof, S. *The Adventure of Self-Discovery.* Albany: State University of New York, 1988. A transpersonal interpretation of the far reaches of the self.

Johnson, R. A. *Inner Work.* New York: Harper & Row, 1989. A well-known Jungian writing on the use of dreams and active imagination for personal growth.

Keleman, S. *Living Your Dying.* New York: Random House, 1985. A description of the healthy process of dying—little by little—from the day we are born.

*Leider, R. J., and Shapiro, D. A. *Repacking Your Bags: Lighten Your Load for the Rest of Your Life.* San Francisco: Berrett-Koehler, 1994. How to reevaluate your life and begin again.

Masten, A. S., Best, K. M., and Garmezy, Norman. "Resilience and Development: Contributions from Children who Overcome Adversity." *Development and Psychopathology,* 1990, *2,* 425–444.

May, R. *The Discovery of Being.* New York: Norton, 1994. A classic essay in existential thinking.

Mecca, A. M., Smelser, N. J., and Vasconcellos, J. *The Social Importance of Self-Esteem.* Berkeley: University of California Press, 1989.

Mindell, A. *Working on Yourself Alone.* New York: Viking, 1989. An invitation to introspect and clarify your agenda.

Parkes, C. M. *Bereavement: Studies of Grief in Adult Life.* New York: International Universities Press, 1998. A discussion about the normal grieving that follows a lost commitment, a broken heart, sudden alarm, anger and guilt, gaining a new identity, types of grief, and other types of loss.

*Prather, H. *Notes to Myself.* Moab, Utah: Real People Press, 1983. About the struggle to be yourself.

Richards, M. C. *Centering: in Pottery, Poetry, and the Person.* Middletown, Conn.: Wesleyan Press, 1989.

Shuchter, S. R. *Dimensions of Grief: Adjusting to the Death of a Spouse.* San Francisco: Jossey-Bass, 1986. A scholarly analysis.

Sonnenfeld, J. *The Hero's Farewell: What Happens When CEOs Retire.* New York: Oxford, 1988. A brilliant book on four ways CEOs leave: the monarch, the general, the ambassador, and the governor.

Spencer, S. A., and Adams, J. D. *Life Changes: Growing Through Personal Transitions.* San Luis Obispo, Calif.: Impact, 1990.

*Tatelbaum, J. *The Courage to Grieve: Creative Living, Recovery, and Growth Through Grief.* New York: Harper & Row, 1980. A masterpiece.

*Viorst, J. *Necessary Losses.* New York: Simon and Schuster, 1998. Tough talk by a caring writer about a difficult subject.

Wallace, M. *Retreat: The Dynamic New Answer for Your Firm's Successful Future in These Uncertain Times.* Pacific Palisades, Calif.: Wintergreen and Advance, 1979. A good book on how to use a retreat to renew a company.

Wanderer, Z., and Cabot, T. *Letting Go: How to Overcome a Broken Heart.* New York: Putnam, 1987.

Watts, A. *The Book: On the Taboo Against Knowing Who You Are.* New York: Vintage, 1989.

Coaching Clients in Phase Four

Gottlieb, B. H. (ed.). *Social Networks and Social Support.* Newbury Park, Calif.: Sage, 1981. Description of a form of social support for facilitating future life styles, careers, communities, and health.

*Hagberg, J., and Leider, R. *The Inventurers: Excursions in Life and Career Renewal.* (3rd ed.) Reading, Mass.: Addison-Wesley, 1988. A profound manual that works.

McCay, J. T. *The Management of Time.* Englewood Cliffs, N.J.: Prentice Hall, 1995. An old book with very up-to-date advice.

Newman, B. K. *Now That You're All Grown Up, What Do You Want to Be?* Dubuque, Iowa: Kendall/Hunt, 1996. A solid book on how to knit your life back together after it has unraveled.

Senge, P. *The Fifth Discipline.* New York: Doubleday, 1994. A convincing argument on the importance of learning in the process of remaking ourselves and the future.

Tregoe, B. B., and Associates. *Vision in Action: Putting a Winning Strategy to Work.* New York: Simon and Schuster, 1999. A corporate book on how to link vision to action.

*Whyte, D. *The Heart Aroused.* New York: Doubleday, 1994. An inspiring book by a poet about the meaning of work.

Continuity and Change in Adult Life

Bandura, A. *Self-Efficacy in Changing Societies.* New York: Cambridge University Press, 1995.

*Beck, D. E., and Cowan, C. C. *Spiral Dynamics: Mastering Values, Leadership, and Change.* Cambridge, Mass.: Blackwell, 1996. A creative theory to understanding change as a flow of ever-deepening values and possibilities for the human adventure.

Bergquist, W. *The Postmodern Organization: Mastering the Art of Irreversible Change.* San Francisco: Jossey-Bass, 1993. A book written with the assumption that change is here to stay; suggests organizational models for the future.

Briggs, J., and Peat, F. D. *Turbulent Mirror: An Illustrated Guide to Chaos Theory and the Science of Wholeness.* New York: Harper & Row, 1989. An original description of the tension we all live with, between chaos and order.

Colin, V. L. *Human Attachment.* Philadelphia: Temple University Press, 1996.

*Csikszentmihalyi, M. *Flow: The Psychology of Optimal Experience: Steps Toward Enhancing the Quality of Life.* New York: Harper & Row, 1990. The result of a long study on "optimal experience," during which people report feelings of concentration and deep enjoyment, no matter what is going on around them.

Galpin, T. J. *The Human Side of Change: A Practical Guide to Organization Redesign.* San Francisco: Jossey-Bass, 1996. Good book for corporate coaches.

Gleick, J. *Chaos: Making a New Science.* New York: Penguin, 1988. A scientific book on the meaning of "chaos."

*Handy, C. *The Age of Unreason.* Boston: Harvard Business School, 1991. A prophetic book about our cultural shift from managing continuities to managing discontinuities.

Handy, C. *The Age of Paradox.* Boston: Harvard Business School, 1994. The work of a prophet for our times.

*Hudson, F. M. *The Adult Years: Mastering the Art of Self-Renewal.* (rev. ed.) San Francisco: Jossey-Bass, 1999. This book provides the basic conceptual tools for understanding successful living at every age throughout the adult life cycle.

*Hudson, F. M., and McLean, P. *LifeLaunch: A Passionate Guide to the Rest of Your Life.* (rev. ed.) Santa Barbara, Calif.: Hudson Institute Press, 1996. An application of adult development material to the lives of adults.

*Johnson, B. *Polarity Management: Identifying and Managing Unsolvable Problems.* Amherst, Mass.: HRD Press, 1997. An important book for recognizing the difference between problems to be solved and polarities to be managed.

*Land, G., and Jarman, B. *Breakpoint and Beyond: Mastering the Future, Today.* New York: HarperBusiness, 1992. Puts the present in perspective with the future.

Peters, T. *Thriving on Chaos.* New York: Knopf, 1987. One of the first popular books on chaos as our normal social environment.

Peters, T. *The Tom Peters Seminar: Crazy Times Call for Crazy Organizations.* New York: Vintage, 1994. Describes a management system for a change-dominated world.

Riegel, K. F., and Meacham, J. A. (eds.). *The Developing Individual in a Changing World, Vol. 2: Social and Environmental Issues.* Chicago: Aldine, 1976. A study of social, environmental, educational, and other issues that affect the developing individual throughout the world.

Strebel, P. *Breakpoints: How Managers Exploit Radical Business Change.* Cambridge, Mass.: Harvard Business School Press, 1992. A model of change that takes advantage of discontinuities.

*Vaill, P. B. *Learning as a Way of Being: Strategies for Survival in a World of Permanent White Water.* San Francisco: Jossey-Bass, 1996. A unique book on learning, in that it stresses the integration of learning into the being of the learner.

Biography

*Aftel, M. *The Story of Your Life: Becoming the Author of Your Experience.* New York: Simon and Schuster, 1996. A popular and effective statement of how to take conscious responsibility for your own life story.

Brown, L. M., and Gilligan, C. *Meeting at the Crossroads: The Landmark Book About the Turning Points in Girls' and Women's Lives.* New York: Ballantine, 1992. A beautifully written book on female development, using many case studies and excellent research.

*Heilbrun, C. G. *Writing a Woman's Life.* New York: Ballantine, 1988. A provocative book suggesting that women learn to write their own scripts.

Monk, G., Wislade, J., Crocket, K., and Epston, D. *Narrative Therapy in Practice: The Archaeology of Hope.* San Francisco: Jossey-Bass, 1997.

Norton, D. L. *Personal Destinies: A Philosophy of Ethical Individualism.* Princeton, N.J.: Princeton University Press, 1976. A philosophical treatise on the evolution of the person.

*Steiner, C. *Scripts People Live: Transactional Analysis of Life Scripts.* New York: Grove Press, 1990. An excellent summary of script analysis from a TA perspective.

Wimberly, E. P. *Recalling Our Own Stories: Spiritual Renewal for Religious Caregivers.* San Francisco: Jossey-Bass, 1998. Aimed at renewing the mission of religious leaders; method produces renewal for anyone willing to piece together their life stories.

Rituals

Brown, J. E. *The Sacred Pipe: Black Elk's Account of the Seven Rites of the Ogala Sioux.* New York: Penguin, 1989.

Foster, S. *The Book of the Vision Quest: Personal Transformation in the Wilderness.* Englewood Cliffs, N.J.: Prentice Hall, 1992. An old Indian custom as a rite into adulthood.

*Hammerschlag, C. A., and Silverman, H. D. *Healing Ceremonies: Creating Personal Rituals for Spiritual, Emotional, Physical, and Mental Health.* New York: Perigree, 1997. A practical book written by two physicians who are passionately concerned about the social power of life's turning points throughout the life cycle.

*Imber-Black, E., and Roberts, R. F. *Rituals for Our Times: Celebrating, Healing, and Changing Our Lives and Our Relationships.* New York: HarperCollins, 1998. Suggests a wide variety of ways that people can devise to symbolize their rites of passage and profound events throughout their lives.

Schwartz, P. *The Art of the Long View: Planning for the Future in an Uncertain World.* New York: Currency, 1996. Teaches the reader how to build future scenarios with individuals and organizations.

Turner, V. *The Ritual Process.* Chicago: Aldine, 1995.

Walker, B. G. *Women's Rituals: A Sourcebook.* New York: Harper & Row, 1990. Provides information on how and when to conduct rituals, make mandalas, and link rituals to rites of passage.

Rites of Passage

Christopher, N. G. *Right of Passage: The Heroic Journey to Adulthood.* Washington, D.C.: Cornell University Press, 1996.

*Mahdi, L. C., Christopher, N. G., and Meade, M. *Crossroads: The Quest for Contemporary Rites of Passage.* Chicago: Open Court, 1996. A large tome on ancient practices, youth-related contemporary rituals, women's rituals, group rituals, individual rites of passage for various points in the life cycle, and how to create rituals.

*Van Gennep, A. *The Rites of Passage.* Chicago: University of Chicago Press, 1960. Analyzes a major transition in primitive tribes, the transition from boyhood to manhood.

Mythic Origins of Personal Stories

*Campbell, J. *The Power of Myth.* New York: Doubleday, 1991.

Campbell, J. *Myths to Live By.* New York: Viking, 1993.

May, R. *The Cry for Myth.* New York: Norton, 1991. An excellent introduction to the positive role myths play in our lives.

Stevens, A. *Private Myths: Dreams and Dreaming.* London: Penguin, 1995.

Construction and Deconstruction of Stable Chapters

*Bateson, M. C. *Composing a Life.* New York: Plume, 1990. A useful book about how several well-known women composed their lives.

Cars, J. P. *Finite and Infinite Games: A Vision of Life as Play and Possibility.* New York: Ballantine Books, 1994. A brief but potent metaphysical book on how human beings frame their experience.

Ellis, D. B. *Creating Your Future: A Guide to Long-Range Visioning.* Rapid City, S.D.: Breakthrough Enterprises, 1997. A down-to-earth, practical guide to generating a future scenario.

Funder, D. C., Parke, R. D., Tomlinson-Keasy, C., and Widaman, K. (eds.). *Studying Lives Through Time.* Washington, D.C.: American Psychological Association, 1997.

Grundin, R. *Time and the Art of Living.* New York: Houghton Mifflin, 1982. Musings about how time influences who we are and how we live.

Hall, E. T. *The Dance of Life: The Other Dimension of Time.* New York: Anchor, 1984. A look by an anthropologist at the many cultural meanings of "time" as a basis for understanding why people are the way they are.

*Josselson, R., and Lieblich, A. *The Narrative Study of Lives.* Newbury Park, Calif.: Sage, 1993.

Miller, S. D, Hubble, M. A., and Duncan, B. L. (eds.). *Handbook of Solution-Focused Brief Therapy.* San Francisco: Jossey-Bass, 1996. Relevant for coaches, as people take responsibility for their own changes in meaning and hope.

Monk, G., Wislade, J., Crocket, K., and Epston, D. *Narrative Therapy in Practice: The Archaeology of Hope.* San Francisco: Jossey-Bass, 1997. By examining the stories of clients, the contexts of problems can be identified, along with ways to rewrite better scripts.

Sample Biographies and Autobiographies

Ashe, A. *Days of Grace.* New York: Knopf, 1993. A bold autobiography about a famous man who has a young family and AIDS.

*Baker, R. *Growing Up.* New York: Plume, 1991. A moving autobiography by a gifted writer and thinker.

Benson, J. J. *Wallace Stegner: His Life and Work.* New York: Viking, 1997. A creatively crafted biography of a great writer.

Berry, W. *The Memory of Old Jack.* New York: Harcourt Brace, 1985.

Buhler, C. "The Curve of Life as Studied in Biographies." *Journal of Applied Psychology,* 1935, *19,* 405–409.

Field, J. *A Life of One's Own.* Los Angeles: Tarcher, 1981. An autobiography begun in 1926, published in this form in 1951.

Leeming, D. *James Baldwin: A Biography.* New York: Knopf, 1994.

*L'Engle, M. *A Circle of Quiet.* New York: Seabury, 1986. A story about one person's experience of the life cycle.

*Mandela, N. *Long Walk to Freedom.* Boston: Little, Brown, 1995. The most important autobiography of the twentieth century.

Newton, J. *Uncommon Friends: Life with Thomas Edison, Henry Ford, Harvey Firestone, Alexis Carrel and Charles Lindbergh.* New York: Harcourt Brace, 1989. Stories of what these people meant to the author.

Phillips, A. *Winnicott.* Cambridge, Mass.: Harvard University Press, 1988. A biography of D. W. Winnicott, including notes on the "self" and the interpretation of the lives of others.

Understanding Biographical Transitions

*Beckhard, R., and Harris, R. T. *Organizational Transitions: Managing Complex Change.* (2nd ed.) Reading, Mass.: Addison-Wesley, 1987. A clear structural model for managing organizational change.

Bridges, W. *Managing Transitions: Making the Most of Change.* Reading, Mass.: Addison-Wesley, 1991. How to get inside the change process within the people already experiencing it.

*Carter, J., and Carter, R. *Everything to Gain: Making the Most of the Rest of Your Life.* New York: Random House, 1995. A beautiful description of a major transition by a couple who have walked their talk after leaving the White House.

Ehrlich, G. *A Match to the Heart.* New York: Pantheon, 1994. An outstanding description of a profound personal transition, written by a professional writer, not a psychologist.

George, L. K. "Sociological Perspectives on Life Transition." *Annual Review of Sociology,* 1993, *19,* 353–373.

Helson, R."Women's Difficult Times and the Rewriting of the Life Story." *Psychology of Women Quarterly,* 1995, *16,* 331–347.

*Hudson, F. M. *The Adult Years: Mastering the Art of Self-Renewal.* (rev. ed.) San Francisco: Jossey-Bass, 1999. "The most compelling book ever written on personal transition and transformation," wrote reviewer James M. Kouzes.

L'Engle, M. *A Circle of Quiet*. New York: Seabury, 1986. A story of the author's last summer with her dying mother, and what they learned.

St. James, E. *Simplify Your Life: 100 Ways to Slow Down and Enjoy the Things that Really Matter.* New York: Hyperion, 1994. A practical book on ways to downsize your life and enjoy it more.

CHAPTER SEVEN 

Coaching for Basic Values

The previous chapter was about understanding how coaches can help clients manage their experience of change. Now I want to discuss coaching for human core values. My colleagues and I have examined 250 biographies of successful adults over the past twenty years, searching for the dominant inner anchors that guided people toward realizing their own greatness. We found the successful persons to be those who measured their lives with one or more of six basic core values, often in combination.

The six core values compete for our loyalty and passionate commitment throughout the life course, and we often shift gears throughout the adult years from familiar, accomplished value areas to new, challenging ones. (See Basic Library: General References to Human Values.)

The six core values are

1. *Personal power: claiming yourself.* Self-esteem, confidence, identity, inner motivation, a positive sense of self, clear ego boundaries, self-love, courage
2. *Achievement: proving yourself.* Reaching goals, conducting projects, working, winning, playing in organized sports, having ambition, getting results and recognition, being purposive, doing
3. *Intimacy: sharing yourself.* Loving, bonding, caring, being intimate, making relationships work, touching, feeling close, nesting, coupling, parenting, being a friend

4. *Play and creativity: expressing yourself.* Being imaginative, intuitive, playful, spontaneous, original, expressive, humorous, artistic, celebrative, re-creative, funny, curious, childlike, and nonpurposive
5. *Search for meaning: integrating yourself.* Finding wholeness, unity, integrity, peace, an inner connection to all things, spirituality, trust in the flow of life, inner wisdom, a sense of transcendence, bliss
6. *Compassion and contribution: giving yourself.* Improving, helping, feeding, reforming, leaving the world a better place, bequeathing, being generative, serving, feeding, social and environmental caring, institution building, volunteering

Most of the persons we studied combined two or three of these values (never more than three) to form an alliance that produced energy and direction for living and sustaining their sense of purpose, chapter by chapter. In a life transition, persons (or organizations) go through a reevaluation of core values, making a conscious selection based on the reconstructed self at the end of the cocooning process. This choice of values in the middle of a transition generates immense energy and sense of purpose, which join together to prepare persons to evolve as they move on successfully into the creation of new visions and plans. Coaches facilitate this process of values clarification, commitment, and action around their clients' emerging core values.

Each core value or passion draws on a different aspect of our human abilities, but every adult has the capacity to tap all six passions at various times in the life cycle by way of sustaining vitality and purpose. Too often we lock ourselves into the passions and values of our young adult years and "burn out" on them during midlife. A better approach is to keep evaluating our priorities and preferences to be sure that at any time in our lives we are marching to our own drumbeats, empowered by the values we honor in our hearts at any given time.

QUESTIONS FOR COACHES: HELPING A CLIENT ASSESS VALUES

A coach won't necessarily know from casual conversation what values a client holds dear. The following questions for a coach to consider will help focus his or her approach to dealing with values.

- Which of the six passions does my client feel drawn toward?
- Which of the passions seem to produce energy for life in my client?
- Which of the six passions are negative or neutral for my client at this time?

- What are the core values and beliefs that my client is struggling with?
- What are some passionate destinations (goals or results) that my client would like to reach with his or her top three passions?
- How can I enable my client to move from an articulation of values to a statement of purpose for the next chapter of life?

QUESTIONS FOR CLIENTS: COACHING THE SIX CORE VALUES

Often clients are not sure how they feel about values. A coach often must ask probing questions. Following are questions pertaining to each of the six values that a coach could ask a client to consider. With each set of questions, I've suggested some goals a coach might reach for in the questioning process.

Core Value One: Personal Identity

Basic questions: Who am I? What do I like most about being me? What are my boundaries? What is my sense of purpose? Where am I going? Who is going with me? How will I get there? Will I have a place in it? What do I need to learn? What is my "work"? How shall I measure my success? How am I evolving as a person?

Possible coaching goals: Increasing self-confidence or self-esteem, improving personal performance, developing better relationships, managing conflict, increasing trust in the future, embracing the maturation process, developing leadership and spiritual awareness, wellness planning, financial planning, developing a career, becoming more introspective, deepening a sense of self, increasing self-esteem and confidence, maintaining clear boundaries, becoming more assertive, using solitude time creatively, spending time alone in nature, joining a vision quest

Core Value Two: Achievement

Basic questions: What are my gifts? What is my compelling sense of purpose? If I could leave a "mark," what would it look like? If I should reach my goals, what would I do next? What rewards am I really seeking? What training do I need to be at my best? How much is enough? How do I count what counts? What is my legacy?

Possible coaching goals: Promoting personal vision, reaching goals, getting results, being dependable, collaborating, gaining leadership skills, pursuing continuous training, motivating others, collaborating, obtaining business skills, knowing how to make and conduct strategic plans, learning time management skills

Core Value Three: Intimacy

Basic questions: What matters most to me? How do I love myself and remain my own best friend? What are the bonds I honor most in my life? How am I investing in those bonds this year? How do I attach to others? How do I want others to attach to me? Am I a good friend to others? Are my friends available to me in ways I want them to be? How is my love evolving and growing? What would add value to my expressions of intimacy?

Possible coaching goals: Maintaining healthy self-love, sustaining affective bonds, knowing how to attach to love objects, investing in friendships, renewing long-term love or sex, succeeding in father-mother-helper roles, sustaining a high level of empathy for others

Core Value Four: Play and Creativity

Basic questions: How often does my mind wander outside of the box? How do I have fun being me? What are my favorite forms of spontaneous expression? How am I creative? How am I playful? What learning would deepen my creativity? With which friends am I most naturally playful and creative?

Possible coaching goals: Eliciting intuition, processing client dreams, future visioning with clients, indulging in nonsense, laughing, risk taking, being playful, allowing spontaneous laughing, being inventive, creating new forms of things or ideas, being spontaneous, having fun, finding flow in everyday life

Core Value Five: Search for Meaning

Basic questions: What am I doing here? What is my ultimate concern? What can I rely on? How do I arrive at inner peace? What are my basic beliefs and how do I express them? What are the settings that help me experience the unity of all things? What forms of caring are part of my spiritual beliefs? What do I feel called to do with my life? How do I express reverence for life?

Possible coaching goals: Looking for connections and unities, purpose, inner peace, profound spirituality; tapping the soulful part of a client (not the ego)

Core Value Six: Compassion and Contribution

Basic questions: What is my legacy? What will live on long after I am gone? How can I support the needs of others, not merely my own needs? What are the important contributions I want to make? How can I express the compassion I feel? What causes am I willing to support? How can I volunteer my time to make a difference.

Possible coaching goals: Finding meaningful ways to express social caring, becoming compassionate, becoming concerned beyond oneself, wanting to leave a legacy, seeking fairness in treatment of all people, becoming socially active or politically connected

BASIC LIBRARY FOR COACHES

General References to Human Values

Adler, A. *Understanding Human Nature.* New York: Hazelden, 1998. About the function of "teleology" in human life, as each life moves toward purpose.

Ashby, W. *A Comprehensive History of Western Ethics: What Do We Believe?* New York: Prometheus, 1997.

Bloom, A. *The Closing of the American Mind.* New York: Touchstone, 1987. Makes a strong argument for conserving America's values.

Boorstin, D. J. *The Americans: The National Experience.* New York: Random House, 1988. Looks for core values in the experience of Americans from our founding days to the present.

Bronowski, J. *Science and Human Values.* New York: Harper, 1990.

Burke, K. *Permanence and Change: An Anatomy of Purpose.* Indianapolis: Bobbs-Merrill, 1984.

Cochran, T. C. *Challenges to American Values: Society, Business and Religion.* New York: Oxford University Press, 1985. A historical review of American values.

*Goldthwait, J. T. *Value, Language, and Life.* New York: Prometheus, 1992.

Goldthwait, J. T. *Values: What They Are and How We Know Them.* New York: Prometheus, 1994.

*Hudson, F. M. *The Adult Years: Mastering the Art of Self-Renewal.* (rev. ed.) San Francisco: Jossey-Bass, 1999. A basic resource for understanding the dynamics of adult development.

*Keeney, R. L. *Value-Focused Thinking: A Path to Creative Decisionmaking.* Cambridge, Mass.: Harvard University Press, 1996. A brilliant writing on how individuals can apply value-based thinking to all of their decisions.

*Kidder, R. M. *Shared Values for a Troubled World: Conversations with Men and Women of Conscience.* San Francisco: Jossey-Bass, 1994.

*Killen, M., and Hart, D. (eds.). *Morality in Everyday Life: Developmental Perspectives.* Cambridge, England: Cambridge University Press, 1995.

*Leider, R. J. *The Power of Purpose.* (rev. ed.). San Francisco: Berrett-Koehler, 1997. A simple but powerful book by a visionary on the meaning of purpose.

Maslow, A. *Religions, Values, and Peak-Experiences.* New York: Penguin, 1976.

McCarthy, K. W. *The On-Purpose Person: Making Your Life Make Sense.* Colorado Springs, Colo.: Pinon, 1992.

O'Toole, J. *Leading Change: Overcoming the Ideology of Comfort and the Tyranny of Custom.* San Francisco: Jossey-Bass, 1995. A philosophical triumph for the concept of value-based leadership.

Rokeach, M. *Understanding Human Values: Individual and Societal.* New York: Free Press, 1979.

Rokeach, M. "Inducing Change and Stability in Belief Systems and Personality Structures." *Journal of Social Issues,* 1985, *41*(1), 153–171.

*Simon, S. B., Howe, L. W., and Kirschenbaum, H. *Values Clarification: A Handbook of Practical Strategies for Teachers and Students.* New York: Warner Books, 1995. The groundbreaking book of applying values to America's school systems.

Value One: Personal Identity

Adams, K. *Journal to the Self. How to Keep a Journal That Will Grow Your Undiscovered Self.* New York: Warner, 1990.

Cross, W. W., Jr. *Shades of Black: Diversity in African-American Identity.* Philadelphia: Temple University Press, 1991.

*Csikszentmihalyi, M. *Finding Flow: The Psychology of Engagement with Everyday Life.* New York.: Basic Books, 1997.

Erikson, E. H. *Identity and the Life Cycle.* New York: Norton, 1994. His best book on identity and the life cycle.

Field, J. *A Life of One's Own.* New York: St. Martins Press, 1981. An autobiography originally written in 1936.

Gallwey, W. T. *Inner Tennis: Playing the Game.* New York: Random House, 1997. All about being centered, having self-esteem, having the ability to be in the moment.

Gardner, J. W. *Self-Renewal: The Individual and the Innovative Society.* (rev. ed.) New York: Norton, 1995. A treatise, written by one of the first people to use the term *self-renewal,* which became a buzz word.

Grof, S. *The Adventure of Self-Discovery: Dimensions of Consciousness.* New York: SUNY, 1988.

Hammarskjold, D. *Markings.* New York: Knopf, 1966. The collected inner thoughts of the man who served as the first general secretary of the United Nations.

Herman, S. M. *A Force of Ones: Reclaiming Individual Power in a Time of Teams, Work Groups, and Other Crowds.* San Francisco: Jossey-Bass, 1994.

*Johnson, R. A. *Inner Work.* New York: Harper & Row, 1986. A well-known Jungian writing on the use of dreams and active imagination for personal growth.

Kohut, H. *The Restoration of the Self.* New York: International Universities Press, 1977. A major contribution to neoanalytic theory.

Krusell, J., and Associates. *Personal and Interpersonal Development: A Self-Administered Workbook.* San Diego, Calif.: University Associates, 1981. Simple exercises for learning basic personal skills.

Levine, S. *A Gradual Awakening.* New York: Anchor, 1989. A book on being conscious, in the here and now, with an introduction by Ram Dass.

Maslow, A. *The Farther Reaches of Human Nature.* New York: Peter Smith, 1983. A posthumous publication of an unfinished text on the extraordinary capabilities of human beings.

*Maslow, A. *Toward a Psychology of Being.* New York: Wiley, 1998.

Masterson, J. F. *The Real Self: A Developmental, Self, and Object Relations Approach.* New York: Brunner/Mazel, 1985. Working out of object relations' theory, Masterson constructs the positive attributes of the real self.

May, R. *Man's Search for Himself.* New York: Delacorte, 1992. One of May's best books, all about the courage to be yourself.

Perlmutter, M., and Hall, E. *Adult Development and Aging.* New York: Wiley, 1994. An undergraduate overview.

Prather, H. *Notes to Myself.* New York: Bantam Books, 1983.

Robbins, H. A. *How to Speak and Listen Effectively.* New York: AMACOM, 1992. Exercises on speaking and listening.

*Rogers, C. *On Becoming a Person.* Boston: Houghton Mifflin, 1995. A basic book for understanding persons.

*Scott, C. D., and Jaffee, D. T. *Managing Personal Change.* Menlo Park, Calif.: Crisp, 1989. An elementary primer for moving through transitions.

Steinem, G. *Revolution from Within: A Book of Self-Esteem.* Boston: Little, Brown, 1993. A generous sharing of her journey into the resilience of self-esteem.

*Storr, A. *Solitude: A Return to the Self.* New York: Free Press, 1988. A superbly written book about the value of being alone.

The Stress Management Handbook. Shawnee Mission, Kans.: National Press Publications, 1991. How to recognize stress and reduce it.

Having a Private Life

Blumenfeld, W. J., and Raymond, D. *Looking at Gay and Lesbian Life.* (rev. ed.) Boston: Beacon, 1993.

*Booher, D. *Get a Life Without Sacrificing Your Career: How to Make More Time for What's Really Important.* New York: McGraw-Hill, 1996. A practical book for simplifying your life.

*Csikszentmihalyi, M. *Finding Flow: The Psychology of Engagement with Everyday Life.* New York: Basic Books, 1997.

Falbo, T., and Polit, D. F. "Quantitative Review of the Only-Child Literature: Research Evidence and Theory Development." *Psychology Bulletin,* 1986, *100,* 176–189.

Galvin, R. M. "The Nature of Shyness." *Harvard Magazine,* 1992, *94*(4), 40–45.

Grof, S. *The Adventure of Self-Discovery.* Albany, N.Y.: SUNY, 1988. A mystical approach to understanding the core of one's consciousness.

Horn, F. *I Want One Thing.* Marina del Rey, Calif.: DeVorss, 1981. A beautiful story of one woman's wake-up call and personal transformation.

Leider, R. J. *Life Skills: Taking Charge of Your Personal and Professional Growth.* Englewood Cliffs, N.J.: Prentice Hall, 1994. A practical guide to coaching yourself.

*Leider, R. J. *The Power of Purpose.* (rev. ed.) San Francisco: Berrett-Koehler, 1997. A simple but powerful book by a visionary on the meaning of purpose.

*Lifton, R. J. *The Life of the Self.* New York: Touchstone, 1976. A concept of self is proposed that is self-renewing and developmental.

Newman, M., and Berkowitz, B. *How to Be Your Own Best Friend.* New York: Ballantine, 1990. A simple, straightforward, amazingly popular book on self-empowerment.

Perkins-Reed, M. A. *Discovering Your Life's Purpose.* Audiotape. Hay House, 1991.

*Quinn, R. E. *Deep Change: Discovering the Leader Within.* San Francisco: Jossey-Bass, 1996. How to use the depths of your personal reality in the outer work of your life.

*Rogers, C. *On Becoming a Person.* Boston: Houghton Mifflin, 1995. A classic in the field.

Sustaining Personal Resilience

*Hudson, F. M. *The Adult Years: Mastering the Art of Self-Renewal.* (rev. ed.) San Francisco: Jossey-Bass, 1999. A basic resource for understanding coaching and adult development.

*Lederman, E. *Vacations That Can Change Your Life: Adventures, Retreats, and Workshops for the Mind, Body, and Spirit.* Naperville, Ill.: Sourcebooks, 1998. A unique book listing hundreds of ways to invest in your own growth and development.

Developing People Skills

Alberti, R. E. (ed.). *Assertiveness.* San Louis Obispo, Calif.: Impact Publishers, 1990.

Belf, T-E, and Ward, C. *Simply Live It UP: Brief Solutions.* Bethesda, Md.: Purposeful Press, 1997. A fun book of exercises for growth and renewal.

*Bolton, R. *People Skills: How to Assert Yourself, Listen to Others, and Resolve Conflicts.* New York: Simon and Schuster, 1980. Excellent guide for learning coaching skills.

Goleman, D. *Emotional Intelligence: Why It Can Matter More than IQ.* New York: Bantam, 1995. One of the most important books for coaches in training to read.

*Goleman, D. *Working with Emotional Intelligence.* New York: Bantam, 1998. Identifies the skills of top performers: self-awareness, self-confidence, self-control, commitment and integrity, the ability to communicate and influence, the ability to initiate and accept change.

Hutchins, D. E., and Cole, C. G. *Helping Relationships and Strategies.* Monterey, Calif.: Brooks/Cole, 1996. A very good book for understanding and acquiring the basic skills of listening, asking questions, clarification, reflection, using silence, and confrontation.

Johnson, D. W. *Reaching Out: Interpersonal Effectiveness and Self-Actualization.* Boston: Allyn & Bacon, 1996. Basic skills needed by effective coaches.

Krusell, J., and Associates. *Personal and Interpersonal Development.* San Diego, Calif.: University Associates, 1982.

Robbins, H. A. *How to Speak and Listen Effectively.* New York: AMACOM, 1992. A good place to begin learning these skills.

*Steinem, G. *Revolution from Within: A Book of Self-Esteem.* Boston: Little, Brown, 1993. A fine book on self-esteem.

*Tannen, D. *You Just Don't Understand: Women and Men in Conversation.* New York: Ballantine, 1990. Excellent for skill development in understanding the similarities and difference in communication styles of men and women.

Tannen, D. *Talking from Nine to Five.* New York: Morrow, 1994. Corporate applications of male-female communication and miscommunication.

Simplifying Your Life

Berner, J. *The Joy of Working from Home: Making a Life While Making a Living.* San Francisco: Berrett-Koehler, 1994. A simple, direct book full of helpful advice and inspiration.

Steenhouse, A. V. *A Woman's Guide to a Simpler Life.* New York: Harmony, 1996.

St. James, E. *Simplify Your Life: 100 Ways to Slow Down and Enjoy the Things that Really Matter.* New York: Hyperion, 1994.

Value Two: Achievement

Business Ethics. Bi-monthly magazine on business and values. Minneapolis.

Davis, S., and Meyer, C. *BLUR: The Speed of Change in the Connected Economy.* Reading, Mass.: Perseus, 1998. Insights given into the radical implications for the way we make decisions—about strategy, investments, products, and people.

Davis, S. M. *Future Perfect.* Reading, Mass.: Addison-Wesley, 1987. A comprehensive approach to sustained achievement.

*Ellis, D. B. *Creating Your Future: A Guide to Long-Range Visioning.* Rapid City, S.D.: Breakthrough Enterprises, 1997. A step-by-step manual for becoming a high achiever.

Garfield, C. A. *Peak Performers: The New Heroes of American Business.* New York: Avon, 1991. Living examples of peak performers.

Gates, W. (Bill). *The Road Ahead.* New York: Viking, 1995. Weaves together achievement and technology.

*Hesselbein, F., Goldsmith, M., and Beckhard, R. *The Leader of the Future: New Visions, Strategies, and Practices for the Next Era.* San Francisco: Jossey-Bass, 1996. A book of readings by top scholars in the field.

*Jaffe, D. T., Scott, C. D., and Tobe, G. R. *Rekindling Commitment: How to Revitalize Yourself, Your Work, and Your Organization.* San Francisco: Jossey-Bass, 1994. How to sustain high performance and to stay renewed.

*Knoke, W. *Bold New World: The Essential Road Map to the Twenty-First Century.* New York: Kodansha, 1996. An achieving triumph.

Kotter, J. P. *Leading Change.* Boston, Mass.: Harvard Business School Press, 1996. A strategic plan for leading change.

Maxwell, J. C. *Developing the Leader Within You.* New York: Nelson, 1993.

Morrisey, G. L. *Morrisey on Planning: A Guide to Strategic Thinking: Building Your Planning Foundation.* San Francisco: Jossey-Bass, 1996. A solid book for understanding the role of planning and discipline for achieving.

Waitley, D. *The New Dynamics of Winning.* New York: Quill, 1995. A motivational guide to inner leadership.

*White, R. P., Hodgson, P., and Crainer, S. *The Future of Leadership: Riding* *the Corporate Rapids into the 21st Century.* London: Pitman, 1996. Discusses five critical skills of the new achiever: seeking difficult learning, maximizing energy, resonant simplicity, multiple focus, and mastering inner sense.

Value Three: Intimacy

Beck, U., and Beck-Gernsheim, E. *The Normal Chaos of Love.* Cambridge, England: Polity Press, 1995. A realistic portrayal of the wonders of love.

*Blieszner, R., and Adams, R. G. *Adult Friendships.* Newbury Park, Calif.: Sage, 1992. A concise summary of the current studies of adult friendships.

Bowlby, J. *The Making and Breaking of Affectional Bonds.* Bungay, Suffolk, England: Chaucer Press, 1979. A technical book on the formation of and separation from affectional bonds.

Fisher, M., and Stricker, G. *Intimacy.* New York: Plenum Press, 1982. Perhaps the most ambitious book on intimacy ever issued.

Fromm, E. *The Art of Loving.* New York: HarperCollins, 1989. A theory of love and its disintegration.

Fromme, A. *The Ability to Love.* New York: Wilshire Books, 1992. A layman's bible on love.

Keen, S. *The Passionate Life: Stages of Loving.* San Francisco: HarperCollins, 1992. A veritable outline of erotic development, by a man self-appointed as a philosopher to our culture.

*Lerner, H. *The Dance of Intimacy: A Woman's Guide to Courageous Acts of Change in Key Relationships.* New York: HarperPerennial, 1990. Focuses on the importance of "self-focus" in the development of intimate bonds in adult women.

Luthman, S. G. *Intimacy: The Essence of Male and Female.* San Rafael, Calif.: Mehetabel and Co., 1977. A practical book on how maleness and femaleness intertwine in the real lives of couples.

*Osherson, S. *Wrestling with Love: How Men Struggle with Intimacy.* New York: Ballantine, 1992.

Rubin, L. B. *Just Friends: The Role of Friendship in Our Lives.* New York: HarperCollins: 1993. A study of the meaning of friendships.

Sternberg, R. J., and Barnes, M. L. (eds.). *The Psychology of Love.* New Haven, Conn.: Yale University Press, 1988.

*Welwood, J. *Journey of the Heart: The Path of Conscious Love.* New York: HarperPerennial, 1996. A fresh and beautiful statement of what intimacy is all about.

Value Four: Play and Creativity

*Adams, J. L. *The Care and Feeding of Ideas: A Guide to Encouraging Creativity.* Reading, Mass.: Addison-Wesley, 1986. A training book for finding and sustaining creativity.

Adams-Price, C. (ed.). *Creativity and Aging.* New York: Springer, 1998.

*Ayan, J. *Aha! Ten Ways to Free Your Creative Spirit and Find Your Great Ideas.* New York: Three Rivers, 1997. Creativity described as the most powerful resource we have for inventing the future.

Cameron, J. *The Artist's Way: A Spiritual Path to Higher Creativity.* Los Angeles: Tarcher, 1992. A course in discovering and recovering your creative self.

Creative Education Foundation, 1050 Union Road, Buffalo, NY 14224, 800-447-2774. Excellent resource for materials on and training opportunities in creative problem solving, using group techniques.

Creativity Coaching: Creative Education Foundation, 1050 Union Road, Buffalo, NY 14224, 800-447-2774. An excellent resource for materials on and training opportunities in applying creativity to many social settings.

*Csikszentmihalyi, M. *Finding Flow: The Psychology of Engagement with Everyday Life* . New York: Basic Books, 1997. A powerful argument that human life is an evolving process and that choosing optimal experiences for our growth is always available in the flow of our daily lives.

Dilts, R. B. *Skills for the Future: Managing Creativity and Innovation.* Capitola, Calif.: Meta, 1993. Applying creativity to problem solving of all types.

*Fritz, R. *The Path of Least Resistance: Learning to Become the Creative Force in Your Own Life.* (rev. ed.) New York: Fawcett, 1989. A compelling book that will benefit coaches.

*Fritz, R. *Creating: A Guide to the Creative Process.* New York: Fawcett Columbine, 1991. An embellishment on his former book.

Ghiselin, B. *The Creative Process.* Berkeley: University of California Press, 1996. Thirty-eight creative people express their own views on creativity.

Grundin, R. *The Grace of Great Things: Creativity and Innovation.* New York: Ticknor and Fields, 1997. Philosophical, original, and useful.

Harman, W., and Rheingold, H. *Higher Creativity: Liberating the Unconscious for Breakthrough Insights.* Los Angeles: Jeremy Tarcher, 1984.

May, R. *The Courage to Create.* New York: Norton, 1994. A creative existentialist's treatise on creativity.

Merritt, S. *Mind, Music, and Imagery.* New York: Aslan, 1996. Forty exercises using music to stimulate creativity.

Oech, R. von. *A Whack on the Side of the Head: How to Unlock Your Mind for Innovation.* New York: Warner, 1998. All about creative discovery in corporate environments.

Ray, M., and Myers, R. *Creativity in Business.* New York: Doubleday, 1989. Shows how creativity can be a major source for success in business ventures.

Watkins, M. *Invisible Guests: The Development of Imaginal Dialogues.* Hillsdale, N.J.: Continuum Press, 1999.

Value Five: Search for Meaning

*Baumeister, R. F. *Meanings of Life.* New York: Guilford Press, 1991. An extraordinary book on life's meaning; interdisciplinary, with studies of four themes: purpose, value, efficacy, and self-worth.

Bohm, D. *Unfolding Meaning.* New York: Routledge, 1996. An original theory of how we find meaning.

*Bolman, L. G., and Deal, T. E. *Leading with Soul: An Uncommon Journey of Spirit.* San Francisco: Jossey-Bass, 1995.

Bonhoeffer, D. *The Cost of Discipleship.* New York: Simon and Schuster, 1995. A profound theological and ethical point of view.

*Brussat, F., and Brussat, M. A. *Spiritual Literacy: Reading the Sacred in Everyday Life.* New York: Touchstone, 1998. Readings for finding sacredness in the ordinary experiences of our lives.

Frankl, V. E. *The Doctor and the Soul.* New York: Random House, 1986.

*Frankl, V. E. *Man's Search for Meaning: An Introduction to Logotherapy.* New York: Washington Square Press, 1998. Sets forth the principles of logotherapy, an approach to finding meaning in life.

Hillman, J. *Insearch: Psychology and Religion.* New York: Springer Publications, 1994.

Hillman, J. *The Soul's Code: In Search of Character and Calling.* New York: Random House, 1996.

Hope, J. *The Secret Language of the Soul: A Visual Guide to the Spiritual World.* San Francisco: Chronicle, 1997. Narrative and illustrations of how various cultures portray the soul.

Hunsberger, B. "Religion, Age, Life Satisfaction, and Perceived Sources of Religiousness: A Study of Older Persons." *Journal of Gerontology,* 1985, *40,* 615–620.

Hyde, K. E. *Religion in Childhood and Adolescence: A Comprehensive Review of the Research.* Birmingham, Ala.: Religious Education Press, 1990.

James, W. *The Varieties of Religious Experience.* New York: Macmillan, 1997. (Originally published 1902). A good overview of humanity's quest for higher meaning.

Maslow, A. H. *Religions, Values, and Peak-Experiences.* New York: Viking, 1994. A humanistic perspective.

Maslow, A. H. *Toward a Psychology of Being.* New York: Wiley, 1998. Classic book on peak experiences and the hierarchy of values.

Needleman, J. *Time and the Soul: Where Has All the Meaningful Time Gone . . . and How to Get It Back.* New York: Doubleday, 1998. Short, well written, profound.

Otto, R. *The Idea of the Holy.* New York: Oxford, 1967. A perennial essay on the natural human attraction to the numinous, mysterious, rapturous forces in nature, history, and in our own imagination.

*Pauchant, T. C., and Associates. *In Search of Meaning: Managing for the Health of Our Organizations, Our Communities, and the Natural World.* San Francisco: Jossey-Bass, 1995. An existential perspective on the daily practice of management aimed at reuniting the self, the organization, and the natural environment.

Progoff, I. "Translation and Introductory Commentary." *The Cloud of Unknowing: A 14th Century Spiritual Experience.* New York: Delta, 1957. A mystical guide.

Smith, H. *Forgotten Truth: The Common Vision of the World's Religions.* New York: HarperCollins, 1992.

Thompson, F. *The Hound of Heaven.* Mount Vernon, NY: Vital Issues Press, 1997. A poem about a person besieged by meaning.

*Thompson, P. *Finding Your Own Spiritual Path.* San Francisco: Harper, 1994. A how-to book for connecting with the sacred and learning how to stay related through prayer, community, rituals and service.

Tillich, P. *The Courage to Be.* New Haven, Conn.: Yale University Press, 1952. Suggests that the courage to be is the only way to survive the strong pull of nonbeing.

Vaughan, F. *The Inward Arc: Healing and Wholeness in Psychotherapy and Spirituality.* New York: Blue Dolphin Press, 1994. A transpersonal perspective.

Value Six: Compassion and Contribution

*Bellah, R. N., and Associates. *Habits of the Heart: Individualism and Commitment in American Life.* Berkeley: University of California Press, 1996. An important position paper on the American bifurcation between individualism and social caring.

*Block, P. *Stewardship: Choosing Service Over Self-Interest.* San Francisco: Berrett-Koehler, 1993. A passionate plea for corporate caring.

Greenleaf, R. K. *Servant Leadership.* Mahwah, N.J.: Paulist, 1983. An important book for its original thoughts on what constitutes legitimate power and greatness.

*Hesselbein, F., Goldsmith, M., Beckhard, R., and Schubert, R. F. *The Community of the Future.* San Francisco: Jossey-Bass, 1998. A major book of readings on community building, including Peter Drucker, Margaret Wheatley, Lester Thurow, Stephen Covey, Gifford Pinchot, Noel Tichy, and Elie Wiesel.

Hwang, P. O. *Other-Esteem: A Creative Response to a Society Obsessed with Promoting the Self.* La Jolla, Calif.: Black Forest Press, 1995. Argues that self-esteem requires valuing and promoting others, just as other-esteem requires valuing the self.

*Kidder, R. M. *Shared Values for a Troubled World: Conversations with Men and Women of Conscience.* San Francisco: Jossey-Bass, 1994. Descriptions of ways to find common ground in religion, education, business, journalism, government, and humanity.

*Mecca, A. M., Smelser, N. J., and Vasconcellos, J. *The Social Importance of Self-Esteem.* Berkeley: University of California Press, 1989. A landmark book connecting the personal self-esteem knowledge to the social consequences.

*Mindell, A. *The Leader as Martial Artist: Techniques and Strategies for Resolving Conflict and Creating Community.* San Francisco: Harper San Francisco, 1993. A guide for empowering and preserving the ecological well-being of human beings.

Sarason, S. B. *Caring and Compassion in Clinical Practice: Issues in the Selection, Training, and Behavior of Helping Professionals.* Northvale, N.J.: Jason Aronson, 1995. Expresses a variety of ways that "social caring" can be built into the preparation of the training of lawyers, teachers, psychiatrists.

General References: Coaching Individuals

Gerzon, M. *Listening to Midlife: Turning Your Crisis into a Quest.* Boston: Shambhala, 1996. A warm, forthright conversation on midlife issues and how to deal with them.

Gould, R. "Transformational Tasks in Adulthood." In S. Greenspan and G. Pollock (eds.), *The Course of Life: Psychoanalytic Contributions Toward an*

Understanding of Personality Development; Volume 3, Adulthood and Aging. Md.: U.S. Department of Health and Human Services, 1981.

*Spencer, S. A., and Adams, J. D. *Life Changes: Growing Through Personal Transitions.* San Luis Obispo, Calif.: Impact, 1990. A concise outline of personal transitions.

 CHAPTER EIGHT 

Coaching for High Performance in Human Systems

A coach can help clients perform as well as possible within a *system,* by which I mean a family, work or volunteer organization, profession, community. All are groups that give context to life. Adults need to be, and to feel, effective within the systems that surround and support life. Just as fish cannot live without water to swim in, we cannot live without the systems we're in and the environments they provide. In fact, our lives are *embedded* in systems, through the roles we have in them. Systems shape the way we think and feel, provide us with arenas for our own fulfillment, and program us with roles and expectations.

During our adult years we can define the roles we prefer and choose how to leave or diminish the roles that become burdensome. Coaches can facilitate that process. Sometimes coaches can help clients transcend system roles temporarily by reflecting on the roles the clients prefer in the years ahead. Specifically, coaches can help clients see what their own roles are within a system, gain perspective on their involvement, and see ways to change roles if they are no longer satisfactory. Or clients might want to improve an unhappy situation by rearranging priorities and achieving balance. Another possibility is to de-role entirely and move on, either inside or outside the system, when roles no longer satisfy or remain available. Coaches can help clients understand their options and feel empowered to pursue new-found goals.

ORGANIZATION OF THE CHAPTER

I've organized the discussion of, and the references for, the area of coaching for high performance in systems into five sections—five major areas of coaching within systems: *personal, couples, family and friends, work,* and *community.*

GETTING STARTED WITH SYSTEMS COACHING

Coaches must first determine their clients' status in and feelings about the system or systems they're in that are of concern. Considering these questions can be useful:

- Which of the five systems (personal, coupling, family, work, and social connections) concern my client the most?
- To what extent is my client helped and supported by this system, and to what extent is the system dominating my client's life?
- To what extent is my client contained by, defined by, and driven by the rules and values of one or more of the human systems in which he or she is embedded?
- If my client is role-bound, how can I provoke a dialogue with the real self without being perceived as being against the role?
- How do the system concerns of my client correlate with the information I have about his or her place in the cycle of change?
- How do my client's system concerns correlate with the information I have about his or her commitments to core values? Are the major positive system concerns related to the top three or four core values?
- Is my client experiencing role overload? If so, what steps might I imagine to reduce investment in this role and get control of it?
- Is my client experiencing a hunger to explore a different system or role?
- Is my client experiencing a conflict between or among the roles and systems of life?
- What is the balance my client would like with roles and systems in the next chapter of life?

FIRST COACHING AREA: PERSONAL CARE

Coaches can help clients learn to care for themselves—along with their belongings, health, personal space, friends, time alone, spirituality, nutrition, finances, and physical exercise. Included in this area is training for personal growth, self-nurturing, and development.

Personal coaching is directed to fostering holistic, self-responsible, personal care. The better clients do with this system, the more likely they are to do well with the other four. Managing personal roles effectively prepares them for managing larger roles. (See Basic Library: Personal Care.)

SECOND COACHING AREA: COUPLES

The couple is probably the most neglected human system in adult life. Typically, we give more attention and have more professional assistance for work roles and family roles than we do for couple roles. Coaches should look for what is working in a client's life as part of a couple and promote that. A coach should look for the ties that bind currently. Be ready to refer a couple to a trained therapist if that seems appropriate.

Possible coaching goals in this area include redefining what it means to be a couple and discovering how to sustain individuation within the couple. Other goals include redefining parenting, understanding the cycle of couple renewal, exploring post-parental social roles, caring for clients' own parents, designing a leisure life, working through health issues, financial planning, pursuing new learning, and growing older together.

Coaches should encourage nurturing, fun, and intimate contact with a client's significant other. This includes

- Having regular times for talking and touching
- Sharing roles, tasks, and fun at home
- Respecting and honoring each other's work
- Enjoying couple friendships and commitments
- Sharing projects and activities outside the home
- Managing shared health needs
- Finding time for intimacy and sex
- Enjoying recreation and leisure activities such as adventuring, learning, traveling, and watching TV and movies

The possibility of being single often arises for clients who are being coached as part of a couple. Possible coaching goals in this area include looking for ways to promote a visionary future by building on what is already working in a client's life. Another option is to explore the advantages of having freedom, along with ways to have abiding friendships and temporary attachments. (See

Basic Library: Being Single; Dual-Career Couples; Sex and Sexuality; Separation, Divorce, and Remarriage.)

THIRD COACHING AREA: FAMILY AND FRIENDS

Coaching a family system requires training in the field, and coaches who aren't trained sufficiently shouldn't try it. For those who have the skills, however, this can be a rewarding field. A coach should help clients form visions and plans for the future, coaching individual members separately and then the family as a whole. (See Basic Library: Families.)

Parenting

Most people who become parents have little training in that role, so they parent along the lines that their own parents did—or they do the very opposite. Women tend to learn mothering skills faster than men learn fathering skills, probably because they often have the primary bond to the children, and they seek out other mothers to learn from.

Some possible coaching goals include training couples to be effective parents, teaching the life cycle of parenting, leading family reunions, developing family rituals, conducting vision quests or other rites of passage experiences, helping parents receive validation and appreciation, and coaching participants in family-owned businesses. Coaches who really enjoy parenting may also enjoy coaching other parents. (See Basic Library: Parenting; Mothering; Fathering.)

Grandparenting

Grandparenting gets redefined by every generation, and the current version is to be active, independent, vital, and connected to the grandchildren episodically. That said, many grandparents volunteer to raise their children's children because of all kinds of complications. Grandmothers and grandfathers are a wonderful target audience for coaches, although the financial rewards are slim. Because the nuclear family ties are weakening, grandparents have to renew their commitment to perform essential functions with their kin while maintaining independent lives. Grandparent coaching groups can be exciting. Groups can be about rituals, mentoring, trips, reunions, hobbies, sports. Possibilities abound. (See Basic Library: Grandparenting.)

Extended Families

Topics generated by the extended intimate relationships and responsibilities that come with caring for children, parents, and others include parenting, managing money, cooking and eating, taking vacations and holidays, watching TV and going to movies, participating in sports activities and hobbies, maintaining a home, developing spiritually and religiously, educating children, maintaining family friendships, managing family health needs, and caring for parents and parents-in-law. (See Basic Library: Coaching Parents and Families.)

Adult Friendships

There is considerable interest in adult friendships at this time, when so many of us are in midlife or beyond. Typically, women have more friends in general and more "life" friends in particular, that is, the friendships aren't based on work or career. Men tend to develop friendships around work- or career-related contacts and around sports interests. But as men and women move into their fifties and sixties, friends play more important roles in their lives. Clients can be coached to find ways to enlist, maintain, and terminate friendships. The most difficult friendships, to the surprise of few, are cross-gender friendships. (See Basic Library: Adult Friendships.)

FOURTH COACHING AREA: WORK

Coaching in work systems—jobs, careers, or volunteer efforts—can relate to making a living or to finding meaning through work roles. Some possible topics in this coaching area are commuting, making volunteer commitments, completing work assignments effectively, finding work friends, training in a career, doing work chores, performing week-end work and special assignments, negotiating for a salary. The reading list (see Basic Library) describes conditions in the workplace that inform coaches how to provide services. Collaboration is an essential concept. Working at home is a popular trend. Creating a "development culture" in the workplace is a win-win idea.

Organizational Culture

If the culture is vital and supportive of the company's goals, a coach should find ways to sustain and renew it; he or she should inspire, promote, and expand what is already working well as a climate and value base for the workforce. However, if there are legitimate changes to be made in the culture, and members of the workforce are resisting change, a coach can lead the way with transition coaching and help the company come up with a revised version of their culture. (See Basic Library: Organizational Culture.)

Leadership Coaching

Possible coaching goals in this area include performance coaching to meet specific corporate results, personal coaching to help achieve balance and perspective, skill training in specific areas (conflict management, technical skills, people skills), exit planning or succession planning; helping with managing a downturn; finding new vision. (See Basic Library: Leadership Coaching.)

High Performance of Individuals and Teams

When the idea of *quality circles* led to work teams during the 1980s, the need for team coaching began. Work teams were an organizational innovation experimenting with motivational processes that could outproduce top-down, control-management structures. Work teams are semi-autonomous units with assignments to produce high-quality results in a timely fashion. The team decides how to tackle the assignment, seek imaginative solutions, assign work, implement decisions, and manage disagreements and group relationships. A team coach facilitates this process, working with individuals as well as groups; learning systems lead toward excellence within the framework of the group assignment. When one team completes its work, an evaluation is made—usually focusing on the group as a whole rather than individual performances. After that, members choose or are assigned to new teams. The best single resource for understanding team coaching is Donna Deeprose's *The Team Coach* (1995).

Possible coaching goals include challenging individuals and teams to take more ownership of what is possible within their organizations, training individuals and teams with high-performance skills, and training others to be self-motivated with their own visions and sense of purpose. (See Basic Library: Coaching for High Performance of Individuals and Teams.)

Organizational Learning

To develop, with clients, a learning program that facilitates their future personal or professional plans is a coaching task. Such a plan would include specific learning designs to deepen self-directed learning, learning within intimate relationships, learning within work organizations and career areas, learning within community contexts, technical learning, and learning about future possibilities. All coaches are engaged in a learning process with their clients, and the more they can understand the learning agenda of their clients, along with the social sources of learning, the more effective they will be as coaches. These social sources include formal instructional and degree programs, on-line learning sources, tutoring or mentoring roles, and discovery that comes from informal learning groups, adventure travel, and creativity training. (See Basic Library: Organizational Learning.)

Career Coaching

Career coaches sometimes work directly with individual clients and sometimes work within organizations. Tom Peters (*A Passion for Excellence,* 1986) identifies five coaching roles for career coaches working within organizations: educating, sponsoring, coaching, counseling, and confronting. All five of these work toward the same goal, says Peters, "to facilitate learning and elicit creative contributions from all hands to the organization's overarching purpose" (p. 398).

The five coaching roles are

- *Educate*: Emphasize learning and applying specific new knowledge, acquiring new skills, articulating performance expectations, finding "learning laboratories" wherever they may be.
- *Sponsor*: Focus on the future by fine-tuning, emphasizing long-term development and contribution, advocating for clients, and dismantling barriers to performance.
- *Coach*: Mentor, encourage, motivate, listen, instill confidence, improve performance.
- *Counsel*: Problem solve, support, dialogue, enhance ownership and accountability, renew commitment.
- *Confront*: Give direct, useful feedback; discuss sensitive issues; challenge, reassign, or dismiss clients.

Donna Deeprose (*The Team Coach,* 1995) adds "team coaching" to this list. A team coach

- Facilitates communication among teams
- Conducts long-term planning
- Supports the career development of team members
- Coaches for conflict resolution
- Measures performance

Peggy Simonsen makes a compelling case that career development can be used as a change agent with organizations (*Promoting a Development Culture in Your Organization,* 1997). She proposes a three-step career development process within organizations:

Step 1: Looking Inward (self-insight)—self-assessment and feedback (p. 204)

Step 2: Looking Outward (career focus)—department, company, and industry information and realities (p. 213)

Step 3: Looking Forward (action plan)—goals and implementation (p. 218)

She puts forth excellent coaching questions for implementing this type of career development:

- What career development philosophy and approach will you communicate?
- How will you inform and educate employees and managers so they understand the purpose and scope of the program?

- How do you get attention without leaving the impression that career development is an "event"?
- How will you communicate the effect the process is having on achieving business results? On contributing to a development culture?
- How can you use outcomes from the career development program to contribute to an overall culture change?

Because few linear careers are left, adults will have to learn, throughout the life cycle, how to reevaluate their work roles and preferred rewards for work in order to formulate a personal business plan that extends themselves and their overall responsibilities into a challenging future. This is what career coaches do. They help clients formulate self-directed plans for successfully integrating the work dimensions of their lives into their total life designs. (See Basic Library: Career Coaching.)

Coaching Corporate Managers

Possible coaching goals include training high-performance teams, career coaching, facilitating a strategic plan, working with morale issues, resilience coaching, dealing with resistance, forging collaborative decisions, personal coaching. (See Basic Library: Coaching Corporate Managers.)

Entrepreneurism

Becoming an entrepreneur is a popular way to create the career a person wants, but not everyone has the skills and inner tolerance for running a business. Coaches in this area may want to know how to evaluate prerequisite skills and abilities, how to train clients with entrepreneurial skills, and how to be a business coach to clients' companies. (See Basic Library: Entrepreneurism.)

Organizational Development

Possible coaching goals: coach the strategic leaders of an organization to deepen the human and business dimensions as gateways to the future; train others to understand system coaching, role analysis, and retooling; and emphasize the centrality of personal leadership for the future of an organization. (See Basic Library: Organizational Development; Coaching for Corporate Change; Coaching Organizational Transitions; Restructuring, Downsizing, and Outplacement; Coaching Organizational Transformation.)

FIFTH COACHING AREA: COMMUNITY

A coach might help a client evaluate his or her social system connections, including involvement in community organizations and activities.

Coaching for Community Building

The following topics might be generated in the coach-client relationship surrounding this topic:

- Participation in community organizations
- Volunteer activities in the community
- Membership in professional groups
- Commitments to neighborhood
- Participation in religious institutions
- Participation in network groups, including electronic networks
- Participation in social causes
- Leisure activities and roles, political groups, and environmental concerns

Possible coaching goals: developing community leadership, facilitating community forums, conducting future search workshops, promoting clarification of political issues, leading debates on environmental issues, seeking new solutions for homeless people, talk radio discussions on domestic violence, and other topics. (See Basic Library: Coaching for Community Building; Leisure Coaching; Coaching for Society-at-Large Roles.)

 BASIC LIBRARY FOR COACHES

Personal Care

Fiske, M., and Chiriboga, D. A. *Change and Continuity in Adult Life.* San Francisco: Jossey-Bass, 1990.

Gilmour, R., and Duck, S. (eds.). *The Emerging Field of Personal Relationships.* Hillsdale, N.J.: Erlbaum, 1986.

*Herman, S. M. *A Force of Ones: Reclaiming Individual Power in a Time of Teams, Work Groups, and Other Crowds.* San Francisco: Jossey-Bass, 1994. A practical book on how to tap into your singular vision, stay centered in work relationships, deal with conflict, and thrive on the spirit of individualism.

Johnson, R. A. *Inner Work: Using Dreams and Active Imagination for Personal Growth.* New York: Harper & Row, 1986. A Jungian approach to inner development.

*Kalbfleisch, P. J. (ed.). *Interpersonal Communication: Evolving Interpersonal Relationships.* Hillsdale, N.J.: Erlbaum, 1993.

Lidz, T. *The Person: His Development Throughout the Life Cycle.* New York: Basic Books, 1968. A standard reference.

Orsborn, C. *Inner Excellence.* San Rafael, Calif.: New World Library, 1992. Relates spirituality to corporate excellence.

Rosenberg, M., and Kaplan, H. B. (eds.). *Social Psychology of the Self-Concept.* Arlington Heights, Ill.: Harlan Davidson, 1982. A large book with many readings on how the self-concept gets formed, how it links to a social context and institutions.

Couples

Bader, E., and Pearson, P. T. *In Quest of the Mythical Mate: A Developmental Approach to Diagnosis and Treatment in Couples Therapy.* New York: Brunner/Mazel, 1988. An original and useful theory, written by the directors of The Couples' Institute of Menlo Park, California.

Booth, A., and Edwards, J. N. "Starting Over: Why Remarriages are More Unstable." *Journal of Family Issues,* 1992, *13,* 179–194.

Booth, A., and Johnson, E. "Premarital Cohabitation and Marital Success." *Journal of Family Issues,* 1988, *9,* 387–394.

*Brody, W., and Brody, C. *Renew Your Marriage at Midlife.* New York: Putnam, 1999.

*Bugental, J. F. *Intimate Journeys: Stories from Life-Changing Therapy.* San Francisco: Jossey-Bass, 1990. A book of stories of people who developed lasting, intimate relationships.

Cabaj, R. P., and Purcell, D. W. (eds.). *On the Road to Same-Sex Marriage.* San Francisco: Jossey-Bass, 1998. An excellent and comprehensive resource for lesbians and gays who look forward to legalized same-sex marriage and for coaches who work with them.

DeMaris, A., and Rao, A. "Premarital Cohabitation and Subsequent Marital Stability in the United States: A Reassessment." *Journal of Marriage and the Family,* 1992, *54,* 178–190.

*Dym, B., and Glenn, M. L. *Couples: Exploring and Understanding the Cycles of Intimate Relationships.* San Francisco: Harper/Collins, 1993. The best new book on understanding coupling, its phases of development, and how to grow within a couple's system.

Everett, C., and Everett, S. *Healthy Divorce.* San Francisco: Jossey-Bass, 1998. Suggests ways a couple and their children can successfully process the phases of the divorce process.

Fisher, R., and Brown, S. *Getting Together: Building Relationships as We Negotiate.* (2nd ed.) New York: Penguin, 1991. Discusses negotiation skills within relationships.

Freeman, S. *The Complete Guide to Fertility and Family Planning.* New York: Prometheus, 1992.

*Hendrix, H. *Getting the Love You Want: A Guide for Couples.* New York: Holt, 1988. A self-help book for couples.

*Hendrix, H. *Keeping the Love You Find.* New York: Pocket Books, 1992. A book for singles and for committed couples.

James, P. *The Divorce Mediation Handbook: Everything You Need to Know.* San Francisco: Jossey-Bass, 1998. Takes readers step-by-step through the supportive process of divorce mediation.

Kaslow, F. W., and Schwartz, L. L. *The Dynamics of Divorce: A Life Cycle Perspective.* New York: Brunner/Mazel, 1987. Combines a life cycle approach with family systems and looks at the impact divorce has on the husband-wife, the children, and extended family for many years.

*Kottler, J. *Beyond Blame: A New Way of Resolving Conflicts in Relationships.* San Francisco: Jossey-Bass, 1997. Written by an eminent psychologist for resolving problems between friends, fellow workers, lovers, bosses, husbands and wives, and parents and children.

Laird, J., and Green, R.-J. (eds.). *Lesbians and Gays in Couples and Families.* San Francisco: Jossey-Bass, 1996. Provides sound recommendations and suggestions for coaching gay couples and families.

Louden, J. *The Couple's Comfort Book: A Creative Guide for Renewing Passion, Pleasure and Commitment.* San Francisco: HarperCollins, 1994. Excellent exercises for couples' renewal.

Markman, H., Stanley, S., and Blumberg, S. L. *Fighting for Your Marriage: Positive Steps for Preempting Divorce and Preserving a Lasting Love.* San Francisco: Jossey-Bass, 1997. Teaches positive ways to manage conflict in marriages.

*McKay, M., Fanning, P., and Paleg, K. *Couple Skills: Making Your Relationship Work.* Oakland, Calif.: New Harbinger, 1994. Begins with listening and expressing feelings, moves to communication and negotiation skills, then goes to managing anger and conflict, and concludes with changing the patterns in our heads that keep the old tapes alive.

Miller, S., and Associates. *Couple Workbook: Increasing Awareness and Communication Skills.* Minneapolis, Minn.: Interpersonal Communication Programs, Inc., 1978.

*Napier, A. Y. *The Fragile Bond: In Search of an Equal, Intimate, and Enduring Marriage.* New York: HarperPerennial, 1988. Especially useful for understanding the healthy developmental process of male and female roles in a linear marriage.

Rogers, C. *Becoming Partners: Marriage and Its Alternatives.* New York:

Delacorte, 1972. Written during the explosive sixties and offers candid advice to all kinds of couples.

Sanford, J. A. *The Invisible Partners: How the Male and Female in Each of Us Affects Our Relationships.* New York: Paulist Press, 1980.

*Schnarch, D. *Passionate Marriage: Keeping Love and Intimacy Alive in Committed Relationships.* New York: Holt, 1998.

*Stahmann, R. F., and Hiebert, W. J. *Marital and Remarital Counseling: The Professional's Handbook.* San Francisco: Jossey-Bass, 1998. A fine resource for couple coaches, particularly with premarital coaching.

Stuart, R. B. *Helping Couples Change: A Social Learning Approach to Marital Therapy.* New York: Guilford Press, 1980.

*Taylor, R. *Love Affairs: Marriage and Infidelity.* New York: Prometheus, 1996. Explores in depth the affair and its often painful consequences; stresses the importance of marriage, fidelity and lasting love as the basis for true happiness.

Weiss, R. L. Two cassette tapes: *Coupling Skills,* T–387, BMA Audio Cassette Programs, 1980.

Weiss, R. S. *Marital Separation.* New York: Harper Colophon, 1975. A first-rate presentation by a marital expert.

*Wheeler, G., and Backman, S. (eds.). *On Intimate Ground: A Gestalt Approach to Working with Couples.* San Francisco: Jossey-Bass, 1994. An outstanding application of gestalt theory and practice to all kinds of couples.

Zoldbrod, A. P. *Men, Women, and Infertility: Intervention and Treatment Strategies.* San Francisco: Jossey-Bass, 1990. Written for the helping professional.

Being Single

*Amador, X., and Kiersky, J. *Being Single in a Couple's World.* New York: Free Press, 1998.

*Broder, M. *The Art of Living Single.* New York: Avon, 1988.

Brody, S., and Brody, C. *Renew Your Marriage at Midlife.* New York: Putnam, 1998. Very useful.

Clements, M. *Improvised Woman: Living Single in an Age of Uncertainty.* New York: Norton, 1998.

Davis, L. *Black & Single.* New York: Ballantine, 1998.

Hudson, P. *You Can Get Over Divorce.* Rocklin, Calif.: Prima, 1998.

Campbell, S. M. *The Couple's Journey: Intimacy as a Path to Wholeness.* San

Luis Obispo, Calif.: Impact, 1987. Especially useful for defining the meaning of coupling in the second half of life.

Carlson, R., and Bailey, J. *Slowing Down to the Speed of Life.* San Francisco: Harper San Francisco, 1998. Shows how to get more satisfaction in life from less rushing around.

Cosby, F. J. (ed.). *Spouse, Parent, Worker: On Gender and Multiple Roles.* New Haven, Conn.: Yale University Press, 1987. Cutting-edge writing on multiple role issues by leading scholars.

*Covey, S. *The Seven Habits of Highly Effective Families.* New York: Golden Books, 1997. Practical steps for making families successful.

*Dym, B., and Glenn, M. L. *Couples: Exploring and Understanding the Cycles of Intimate Relationships.* New York: HarperCollins, 1993.

Fisher, R., and Brown, S. *Getting Together: Building Relationships as We Negotiate.* New York: Penguin, 1988. About negotiation skills within relationships.

Gottman, J. M. *Why Marriages Succeed or Fail.* New York: Simon and Schuster, 1994. How to recognize attitudes that build or doom a marriage.

Gurman, A. S. (ed.). *Casebook of Marital Therapy.* New York: Guilford Press, 1985. A large collection of writings.

*Hendrix, H. *Getting the Love You Want: A Guide for Couples.* New York: Holt, 1988. Clear descriptions of what makes coupling succeed.

Hendrix, H. *Keeping the Love You Find: A Guide for Singles.* New York: Pocket, 1992. Applicable to married couples as well as singles.

Hope, M. *The Psychology of Ritual.* Longmead, Shaftesbury, Dorset, England: Element Books, 1988. A classic review of the importance of ritual to the human family throughout history.

Houts, R. M., Robins, E., and Huston, T. L. "Compatibility and the Development of Premarital Relationships." *Journal of Marriage and the Family,* 1996, *58,* 7–20.

*Imber-Black, E., and Roberts, J. *Rituals for Our Times: Celebrating, Healing, and Changing Our Lives and Our Relationships.* New York: HarperCollins, 1992. Conveys the importance of rituals and how to invent them.

McKay, M., Fanning, P., and Paleg, K. *Couple Skills.* Oakland, Calif.: New Harbinger Publications, 1994.

Moore, T. *Soul Makes: Honoring the Mysteries of Love and Relationship.* New York: HarperCollins, 1994. A gentle book on coupling.

Mornell, P. *Passive Men, Wild Women.* New York: Ballantine, 1973. About midlife changes in men and women, as many men become active at work but passive at home, while their mates are becoming active in the world outside the home.

*Murstein, B. I. (ed.). *Exploring Intimate Life Styles.* New York: Springer, 1978. Covers contracts, open marriage, communes, comarital sex, group marriage, singlehood, cohabitation, homosexuality, and life styles of the future.

*Ornish, D. *Love & Survival: The Scientific Basis for the Healing Power of Intimacy.* New York: HarperCollins, 1997. A sound guide to how healthy relationships contribute to health and well-being.

Popenoe, D., Elshtain, J. B., and Blankenhorn, D. (eds.). *Promises to Keep: Decline and Renewal of Marriage in America.* Lanham, Md.: Rowman & Littlefield, 1996.

Porcino, J. *Growing Older, Getting Better: A Handbook for Women in the Second Half of Life.* Reading, Mass.: Addison-Wesley, 1988.

Rice, D. G. *Dual-Career Marriage: Conflict and Treatment.* New York: Free Press, 1979. Focuses on the impact of dual careers on the marital bond itself, for better and for worse.

Rogers, C. R. *Becoming Partners: Marriage and Its Alternatives.* New York: Delacorte, 1972.

Rosenman, M. F. *Loving Styles: A Guide for Increasing Intimacy.* Englewood Cliffs, N.J.: Prentice Hall, 1979. Conveys the styles of loving, how to become intimate with yourself, and how to risk-trust-share.

Sager, C. J. *Marriage Contracts and Couple Therapy: Hidden Forces in Intimate Relationships.* New York: Brunner/Mazel, 1976.

*Schnarch, D. *Passionate Marriage: Keeping Love & Intimacy Alive in Committed Relationships.* New York: Holt, 1997. A unique approach to individuation and coupling.

Schneider, E. L., and Rowe, J. W. (eds.). *Handbook of the Biology of Aging.* (3rd ed.) San Diego: Academic Press, 1990.

Sholevar, G. P. (ed.). *The Handbook of Marriage and Marital Therapy.* New York: Spectrum, 1981. A compendium of all the basic approaches to marital improvement.

Stahmann, R. F., and Hiebert, W. J. *Marital and Remarital Counseling: The Professional's Handbook.* San Francisco: Jossey-Bass, 1998. A fine resource for couple coaches, particularly with premarital coaching.

Stuart, R. B. *Helping Couples Change: A Social Learning Approach to Marital Therapy.* New York: Guilford Press, 1980.

*Wallerstein, J. S., and Blakeslee, S. *The Good Marriage: How and Why Love Lasts.* New York: Warner, 1995. Shows how the qualities that make a good marriage can be constructed.

Welwood, J. *Journey of the Heart: The Path of Conscious Love.* New York: HarperPerennial, 1990. Beautifully written, with clarity and passion.

Wheeler, G., and Backman, S. (eds.). *On Intimate Ground: A Gestalt Approach to Working with Couples.* San Francisco: Jossey-Bass, 1994. An outstanding application of gestalt theory and practice to all kinds of couples.

Dual-Career Couples

Culp, S. *Streamlining Your Life: A Plan for Uncomplicated Living.* Cincinnati: *Writers Digest,* 1991. A neat set of suggestions for simplifying your life, getting organized, and staying that way.

*Davidson, C. *Staying Home Instead: Alternatives to the Two-Paycheck Family.* San Francisco: Jossey-Bass, 1995. Maps out ways that mothers can stay at home and also manage to keep their sanity, self-esteem, and checking account balance.

Hoffman, L. W. "Effects of Maternal Employment in the Two-parent Family: Accounting for Sibling Differences." *Psychological Bulletin,* 1991, *110,* 187–203.

McGoldrick, M., and Associates. *Ethnicity and Family Therapy.* New York: Guilford Press, 1982. A large collection of writing representing family structures in many nations, cultures, and ethnic groups.

Moore, T. *Soul Mates: Honoring the Mysteries of Love and Relationship.* New York: HarperCollins, 1994.

*Napier, A. Y. *The Fragile Bond: In Search of an Equal, Intimate, and Enduring Marriage.* New York: HarperPerennial, 1988. Especially useful for understanding the healthy developmental process of male and female roles in a linear marriage.

Rice, D. G. *Dual-Career Marriage: Conflict and Treatment.* New York: Free Press, 1979.

Rogers, C. R. *Becoming Partners: Marriage and Its Alternatives.* New York: Delacorte, 1972.

Rosenman, M. F. *Loving Styles: A Guide for Increasing Intimacy.* Englewood Cliffs, N.J.: Prentice Hall, 1979.

Sager, C. J. *Marriage Contracts and Couple Therapy: Hidden Forces in Intimate Relationships.* New York: Brunner/Mazel, 1976.

*Sekaran, U. *Dual-Career Families.* San Francisco, Jossey-Bass, 1986. A problem-solving book aimed at helping minimize the negative issues in dual-career couples.

Sholevar, G. P. (ed.). *The Handbook of Marriage and Marital Therapy.* New York: Spectrum, 1981. A compendium of all the basic approaches to marital improvement.

Stuart, R. B. *Helping Couples Change: A Social Learning Approach to Marital Therapy.* New York: Guilford Press, 1980.

Wallerstein, J. S., and Blakeslee, S. *The Good Marriage: How and Why Love Lasts.* New York: Warner, 1995.

Welwood, J. *Journey of the Heart: The Path of Conscious Love.* New York: HarperPerennial, 1990.

*Wheeler, G., and Backman, S. (eds.). *On Intimate Ground: A Gestalt Approach to Working with Couples.* San Francisco: Jossey-Bass, 1994.

Sex and Sexuality

Baker, R. B., and Associates. *Philosophy and Sex.* (3rd. ed.) New York: Prometheus, 1996.

Comfort, A. *The Joy of Sex: A Gourmet Guide to Love Making.* New York: Fireside, 1972.

Eisenberg, A., Murkoff, H. E., and Hathaway, S. E. *What to Expect When You're Expecting.* Hathaway, N.Y.: Workman, 1996. Updated, practical, and helpful to understand and manage pregnancy creatively.

Fisher, P. (ed.). *Age Erasers for Women: Actions You Can Take Right Now to Look Younger and Feel Great.* Emmaus, Penn.: Rodale, 1994.

Freeman, E. W., and Rickels, K. *Early Childbearing: Perspectives on Black Adolescents and Pregnancy.* Newbury Park, Calif.: Sage, 1993.

Hoffman, S. D., Foster, E. M., and Furstenberg, F. F. "Reevaluating the Costs of Teenage Childbearing." *Demography,* 1993, *30,* 1–13.

Hooper, A. *Sexual Intimacy: How to Build a Lasting and Loving Relationship.* New York: D.K. Publishing, 1996.

Jacobowitz, R. S. *150 Most-Asked Questions About Sex, Love and Intimacy.* New York: Hearst, 1995.

Kaplan, H. S. *The New Sex Therapy: Active Treatment of Sexual Dysfunctions.* New York: Brunner/Mazel, 1974. The standard reference.

*Katchadourian, H. A., and Lunde, D. T. *Fundamentals of Human Sexuality.* New York: Holt, Rinehart and Winston, 1990. Standard reference book for professionals.

Masters, W. H., and Johnson, V. E. "Sex and the Aging Process." *Journal of the American Geriatrics Society,* 1981, *29,* 385–390.

*Masters, W. H., Johnson, V. E., and Kolodny, R. C. *Heterosexuality.* New York: HarperCollins, 1994.

May, R. *Sex and Fantasy: Patterns of Male and Female Development.* New York: Norton, 1980.

Montagu, A. *Touching: The Human Significance of the Skin.* New York: Perennial Library, 1986. A classic by an acclaimed anthropologist.

*Rossi, A. S. (ed.). *Sexuality Across the Life Course.* Chicago: University of Chicago Press, 1994.

*Sadock, B., Kaplan, J., Harold I., and Freedman, A. M. *The Sexual Experience.* Baltimore, Md.: Williams and Wilkins, 1976. An encyclopedia of sexual functions, practices, and therapies.

Silverstein, J. L. *Sexual Enhancement for Men.* New York: Vantage Press, 1986.

Slupik, R. I. (ed.). *Complete Guide to Women's Health.* New York: Random House, 1996. A most complete single volume on this topic.

Stanton, A. L., and Dunkel-Schetter, C. (eds.). *Infertility.* New York: Plenum, 1991.

Separation, Divorce, and Remarriage

Allison, P. D., and Furstenberg, F. F., Jr. "How Marital Dissolution Affects Children." *Developmental Psychology,* 1989, *25,* 540–549.

*Amato, P. R. "A Prospective Study of Divorce and Parent-child Relationships." *Journal of Marriage and the Family,* 1996, *58,* 356–365.

Arendell, T. *Fathers and Divorce.* Newbury Park, Calif.: Sage, 1995.

*Cherlin, A. J. *Marriage, Divorce, Remarriage.* Cambridge, Mass.: Harvard University Press. 1992. A lucid and useful book on these topics.

Chiriboga, D. A., and Catron, L. A. *Divorce: Crisis, Challenge or Relief?* New York: New York University Press, 1992.

*Everett, C., and Everett, S. *Healthy Divorce.* San Francisco: Jossey-Bass, 1998. Suggests ways a couple and their children can successfully process the phases of the divorce process.

Furstenberg, F. F., Jr., Brooks-Gunn, J., and Morgan, P. A. *Adolescent Mothers in Later Life.* New York: Cambridge University Press, 1987.

Furstenberg, F. F., Jr., and Cherlin, A. J. *Divided Families: What Happens to Children When Parents Part.* Cambridge, Mass.: Harvard University Press, 1991.

Furstenberg, F. F., Jr., and Nord, C. W. "Parenting Apart: Patterns of Childbearing after Marital Disruption." *Journal of Marriage and the Family,* 1985, *47,* 893–912.

*Ganong, L. H., and Coleman, M. *Remarried Family Relationships.* Newbury Park, Calif.: Sage, 1994.

Heaton, T., and Albrecht, S. L. "Unhappy Marriages." *Journal of Marriage and the Family,* 1991, *53,* 747–758.

Hetherington, E. M., and Aresteh, J. D. (eds.). *Impact of Divorce, Single Parenting, and Step-Parenting on Children.* Hillsdale, N.J.: Erlbaum, 1988.

Hetherington, E. M., and Clingempeel, W. G. "Coping with Marital Transitions." *Monographs of the Society for Research in Child Development,* 1992, *57*(2–3, Serial No. 227).

*James, P. *The Divorce Mediation Handbook: Everything You Need to Know.* San Francisco: Jossey-Bass, 1998. Takes the reader step by step through the supportive process of divorce mediation.

*Kaslow, F. W., and Schwartz, L. L. *The Dynamics of Divorce: A Life Cycle Perspective.* New York: Brunner/Mazel, 1987. Combines a life cycle approach with family systems; looks at the impact divorce has on the husband and wife, the children, and extended family.

Montague, L. *A New Life Plan: A Guide for the Divorced Woman.* New York: Doubleday, 1978. A sound planning guide.

Spanier, G., and Thompson, L. *Parting: The Aftermath of Separation and Divorce.* Newbury Park, Calif.: Sage, 1984.

*Weiss, R. S. *Marital Separation: Coping with the End of a Marriage and the Transition to Being Single Again.* New York: Basic Books, 1975. Written by a leading expert on the social-psychological aspects of adult issues.

Families

*Blieszner, R., and Bedford, V. H. (eds.). *Handbook of Aging and the Family.* Westport, Conn.: Greenwood Press, 1995.

*Carter, E. A., and McGoldrick, M. (eds.). *The Changing Family Life Cycle: A Framework for Family Therapy.* (2nd ed.) Boston: Allyn & Bacon, 1990. A gold mine of information on all kinds of family systems, economic groupings, and situations.

Cicirelli, V. G. *Sibling Relationships Across the Life Span.* New York: Plenum Press, 1995.

Clausen, J. A. *American Lives: Looking Back at the Children of the Great Depression.* Berkeley: University of California Press, 1995. A retrospective study of how the great depression affected the lives of children across the nation.

Coulson, R. *Family Mediation: Managing Conflict, Resolving Disputes.* San Francisco: Jossey-Bass, 1996. Written by an expert in arbitration and mediation.

*Einstein, E. *The Stepfamily: Living, Loving, Learning.* New York: Macmillan, 1994. The book most used to understand this new reality.

Elium, D., and Elium, J. *Raising a Son: Parents and the Making of a Healthy Man.* Berkeley: Celestial Arts, 1996. A book for staying in the trenches through thick and thin.

Fein, E. "Issues in Foster Family Care: Where Do We Stand?" *American Journal of Orthopsychiatry,* 1991, *61,* 578–583.

Gottfried, A. E., and Gottfried, A. W. (eds.). *Redefining Families: Implications for Children's Development.* New York: Plenum, 1994.

Grossman, F. K., Pollack, W. S., and Golding, E. "Fathers and Children: Predicting the Quality and Quantity of Fathering." *Developmental Psychology,* 1988, *24,* 82–91.

Haley, J. *Problem-Solving Therapy.* San Francisco: Jossey-Bass, 1991.

Haley, J. *Leaving Home: The Therapy of Disturbed Young People.* New York: Brunner/Mazel, 1997. A classic book that underscores the importance of parenting throughout the leaving-home period of about ten years.

Hetherington, E. M., Reiss, D., and Plomin, R. (eds.). *Separate Social Worlds of Siblings: The Impact of Nonshared Environments on Development.* Hillsdale, N.J.: Erlbaum, 1994.

Hibbs, E. (ed.). *Adoption: International Perspectives.* Madison, Conn.: International Universities Press, 1991.

Higgins, C., Duxbury, L., and Lee, C. "Impact of Life-Cycle Stage and Gender on the Ability to Balance Work and Family Responsibilities." *Family Relations,* 1994, *43,* 144–150.

Hochschild, A. R. *The Second Shift: Working Parents and the Revolution at Home.* New York: Avon, 1997.

Hochschild, A. R. *The Time Bind: When Work Becomes Home and Home Becomes Work.* New York: Holt, 1997.

Hoffman, L. *Foundations of Family Therapy.* (2nd ed.) New York: Basic Books, 1981.

Jacobs, J. E., Bennett, M. A., and Flanagan, C. "Decision-making in One-parent and Two-parent Families: Influence and Information Selection." *Journal of Early Adolescence, 13,* 245–266.

Kantor, D., and Lehr, W. *Inside the Family: Toward a Theory of Family Process.* San Francisco: Jossey-Bass, 1975. A system approach to understanding how families function.

Madanes, C. *Strategic Family Therapy.* San Francisco: Jossey-Bass, 1991.

McLanahan, S. S., and Sandefur, G. *Growing Up with a Single Parent: What Hurts, What Helps.* Cambridge, Mass.: Harvard University Press, 1994.

Miller, A. *For Your Own Good: Hidden Cruelty in Child-Rearing and the Roots of Violence.* New York: Noonday Press, 1990.

Milne, A. M., Myers, D. E., Rosenthal, A. S., and Ginsburg, A. "Single Parents, Working Mothers, and the Educational Achievement of School Children." *Sociology of Education,* 1986, *59,* 125–139.

Mindel, C. J., Haberstein, R. W., and Roosevelt, W., Jr. *Ethnic Families in America.* (3rd ed.) Englewood Cliffs, N.J.: Prentice Hall, 1997.

Minuchin, S., and Nichols, M. P. *Family Healing: Tales of Hope and Renewal from Family Therapy.* New York: Free Press, 1993.

Parcel, T. L., and Menaghan, E. G. *Parents' Jobs and Children's Lives.* New York: Aldine de Gruyter, 1995.

Peters, D. L., and Pence, A. R. *Family Day Care: Current Research for Informed Public Policy.* New York: Teachers College Press, 1992.

Satir, V. *Conjoint Family Therapy.* Palo Alto, Calif.: Science and Behavior Books, 1983.

Silverstein, O. *The Courage to Raise Good Men.* New York: Viking, 1994.

*Skolnick, A. *Embattled Paradise: The American Family in an Age of Uncertainty.* New York: Basic Books, 1993.

Staples, R., and Johnson, L. B. *Black Families at the Crossroads.* San Francisco: Jossey-Bass, 1993.

Steinmetz, S. K. (ed.). *Family and Support Systems across the Life Span.* New York: Plenum, 1988.

Stewart, R. B. *The Second Child: Family Transitions and Adjustment.* Newbury Park, Calif.: Sage, 1990.

Visher, E. B., and Visher, J. S. *Step-Families: A Guide to Working with Stepparents and Step Children.* New York: Brunner/Mazel, 1979. Considered by many the best reference book for understanding the step-family.

*Winnicott, D. W. *The Family and Individual Development.* New York: Routledge, 1996. Essays on human development from infancy to early childhood to latency to adolescence to young adulthood: all in relation to healthy and disruptive factors in family life.

Zedeck, S. (ed.). *Work, Families, and Organizations.* San Francisco: Jossey-Bass, 1992.

Coaching Parents and Families

Abidin, R. R. *Parenting Skills.* New York: Human Sciences Press, 1982. An excellent workbook on developing parent skills in oneself and in others.

Aigaki, D. M. *Trouble in Paradise: A Survival Manual for Couples Who Are Parents.* Napa, Calif.: Dry Creek, 1988.

Anderson, B. "Effects of Public Day Care: A Longitudinal Study." *Child Development,* 1989, *273,* 124–128.

Angel, R. J., and Angel, J. L. *Painful Inheritance: Health and the New Generation of Fatherless Families.* Madison: University of Wisconsin Press, 1994.

Barret, R. L., and Robinson, B. E. *Gay Fathers.* San Francisco: Jossey-Bass, 1996. Provides valuable insights into the full range of life experiences that such families encounter along with an accurate picture of the personal, societal, and legal issues accompanying gay fatherhood.

Belsky, J., and Kelley, J. *The Transition to Parenthood.* New York: Delacorte, 1994.

Belsky, J., and Vondra, J. "Lessons from Child Abuse: The Determinants of Parenting." In D. Cicchetti and V. Carlson (eds.), *Child Maltreatment: Theory and Research on the Causes and Consequences of Child Abuse and Neglect.* Cambridge, England: Cambridge University Press, 1989.

Caron, A. F. *Don't Stop Loving Me: A Reassuring Guide for Mothers of Adolescent Daughters.* New York: HarperPerennial, 1992.

Caron, A. F. *Strong Mothers, Strong Sons: Raising the Next Generation of Men.* New York: HarperPerennial, 1994. Excellent, clearheaded advice for raising healthy, loving sons.

*Carter, E. A., and McGoldrick, M. (eds.). *The Changing Family Life Cycle: A Framework for Family Therapy.* (2nd ed.) Boston: Allyn & Bacon, 1990. Outlines the changes in all kinds of family systems, through the life cycles of families, emphasizing social as well as interpersonal issues.

Cummings, E. M., and Davies, P. *Children and Marital Conflict: The Impact of Family Dispute and Resolution.* New York: Guilford Press, 1994.

Daro, D. *Confronting Child Abuse.* New York: Free Press, 1998.

Davis, J. M., and Sandoval, J. *Suicidal Youth: School-Based Intervention and Prevention.* San Francisco: Jossey-Bass, 1991.

Davis-Floyd, R. E. *Birth as an American Rite of Passage.* Berkeley: University of California Press, 1992.

*Elium, D., and Elium, J. *Raising a Son: Parents and the Making of a Healthy Man.* Berkeley, Calif.: Celestial Arts, 1996.

Gordon, T. *Parent Effectiveness Training.* New York: New American Library, 1990. The founder of Parent Effectiveness Training presents his model of self-focused communication.

*Imber-Black, E., and Roberts, J. *Rituals for Our Times: Celebrating, Healing, and Changing Our Lives and Our Relationships.* New York: Jason Aronson, 1998. An original invitation to create rituals that tap the meaning of changing life and relationships.

Laird, J., and Green, R.-J. (eds.). *Lesbians and Gays in Couples and Families.*

San Francisco: Jossey-Bass, 1996. Provides sound recommendations and suggestions for coaching gay couples and families.

Levine, J. A. *Working Fathers: New Strategies for Balancing Work and Family.* Reading, Mass.: Addison-Wesley, 1997. A practical book for working out parenting arrangements to achieve a balance in life.

Monahon, C. *Children and Trauma: A Guide to Parents and Professionals.* San Francisco: Jossey-Bass, 1994. Describes how coaches can offer hope and reassurance and restore a child's sense of safety and balance.

*Prather, H., and Prather, G. *Spiritual Parenting: A Guide to Understanding and Nurturing the Heart of Your Child.* New York: Harmony Books, 1997.

Shamoo, T. K., and Patros, P. G. *Helping Your Child Cope with Depression and Suicidal Thoughts.* San Francisco: Jossey-Bass, 1997. Shows caregivers how to talk, listen, communicate, intervene, and refer to an expert.

Staples, R., and Johnson, L. *Black Families at the Crossroads: Challenges and Prospects.* San Francisco: Jossey-Bass, 1993. Provides an overview for understanding black families in the context of economics, racism, culture, and politics.

Teber, E. *Helping Children Cope with Divorce.* San Francisco: Jossey-Bass, 1996. Helps parents handle children's problems at each stage of the divorce process.

Williams, T., and Kornblum, W. *Growing Up Poor.* San Francisco: Jossey-Bass, 1995. A gripping study of poverty-stricken neighborhoods and teenage accounts of their lives.

*Wolf, A. E. *Get Out of My Life: But First Could You Drive Me and Cheryl to the Mall? A Parent's Guide to the New Teenager.* New York: Noonday Press, 1992. A rude awakening to successful parenting during the teenage years.

Parenting

Anthony, E. J., and Benedek, T. *Parenthood: Its Psychology and Psychopathology.* New York: Jason Aronson, 1996. An advanced reader with many points of view.

Cowan, P. E., and Hetherington, M. (eds.). *Family Transitions.* Hillsdale, N.J.: Erlbaum, 1991.

Furstenberg, F. F., Jr., Brooks-Gunn, J., and Morgan, P. A. *Adolescent Mothers in Later Life.* New York: Cambridge University Press, 1987.

Furstenberg, F. F., Jr., and Cherlin, A. J. *Divided Families: What Happens to Children When Parents Part.* Cambridge, Mass.: Harvard University Press, 1994.

Furstenberg, F. F., Jr., and Nord, C. W. "Parenting Apart: Patterns of Childbearing after Marital Disruption." *Journal of Marriage and the Family,* 1985, *47,* 893–912.

*Galinsky, E. *The Six Stages of Parenthood.* Reading, Mass.: Addison-Wesley, 1990. An outstanding overview of the parenting years.

Goodnow, J. J., and Collins, W. A. *Development According to Parents: The Nature, Sources, and Consequences of Parent's Ideas.* Hillsdale, N.J.: Erlbaum, 1990.

Gurian, M. *A Fine Young Man: What Parents, Mentors and Educators Can Do to Shape Adolescent Boys into Exceptional Men.* New York: Tarcher, 1998. Filled with stories and examples of what people working with adolescent boys can do to link adolescent boys to successful paths ahead.

Hibbs, E. (ed.). *Adoption: International Perspectives.* Madison, Conn.: International Universities Press, 1991. Provides a broad overview of adoption issues in several countries.

Jendrek, M. P. "Grandparents Who Parent their Grandchildren: Effects on Lifestyle." *Journal of Marriage and the Family,* 1993, *55,* 609–621.

Kabat-Zinn, M., and Kabat-Zinn, J. *Everyday Blessings: The Inner Work of Mindful Parenting.* New York: Hyperion, 1997.

Lifton, B. J. *Lost and Found: The Adoption Experience.* New York: Harper & Row, 1988.

McGillicuddy, A. V., and Goodnow, J. J. (eds.). *Parental Belief Systems: The Psychological Consequences for Children.* (2nd ed.) Hillsdale, N.J.: Erlbaum, 1992.

Unell, B. C., and Wyckoff, J. L. *Twenty Teachable Virtues: Practical Ways to Pass on Lessons of Virtue and Character to Your Children.* New York: Perigee, 1995. Simple ways to teach children how to care about others and themselves.

Wyckoff, J. L. *How to Discipline Your Six to Twelve Year Old . . . Without Losing Your Mind.* New York: Doubleday, 1991. Proven ways to solve discipline problems.

Wyckoff, J., and Unell, B. C. *Discipline Without Shouting or Spanking.* Minneapolis, Minn.: Meadowbrook, 1984. A highly practical guide to positive discipline solutions.

Mothering

*Blakely, M. K. *American Mom.* Chapel Hill, N.C.: Algonquin, 1994. One of the best books for describing motherhood with insight, humor, and power.

Burns, A., and Scott, C. *Mother-Headed Families and Why They Have Increased.* Hillsdale, N.J.: Erlbaum, 1994.

Coleman, B., and Coleman, L. *Laughter and Tears: The Emotional Life of New Mothers.* New York: Holt, 1997.

Lerner, H. *The Dance of Anger.* New York: HarperPerrenial, 1997.

*Lerner, H. *The Mother Dance: How Children Change Your Life.* New York: HarperCollins, 1998.

Lerner, J. V., and Galambos, N. L. (eds.). *Employed Mothers and Their Children.* New York: Garland, 1991.

*Levinson, D. J. *The Seasons of a Woman's Life.* New York: Knopf, 1996.

*Peters, J. K. *When Mothers Work: Loving Our Children Without Sacrificing Our Selves.* New York: Perseus, 1998. An outstanding analysis of the working mother's basic dilemma.

Rich, A. *Of Woman Born: Motherhood as Experience and Institution.* New York: Norton, 1995.

Roland, A., and Harris, B. *Career and Motherhood: Struggles for a New Identity.* New York: Human Science Press, 1979. More about struggle than contentment.

Fathering

Angel, R. J., and Angel, J. L. *Painful Inheritance: Health and the New Generation of Fatherless Families.* Madison: University of Wisconsin Press, 1994.

Arendell, T. *Fathers and Divorce.* Newbury Park, Calif.: Sage, 1995.

Berman, P. W., and Pedersen, F. A. (eds.). *Men's Transitions to Parenthood. Longitudinal Studies of Early Family Experience.* Hillsdale, N.J.: Erlbaum, 1987.

Blankenhorn, D. *Fatherless America: Confronting Our Most Urgent Social Problem.* New York: Basic Books, 1995.

Brayfield, A. A. "Juggling Jobs and Kids: The Impact of Employment Schedules on Fathers' Caring for Children." *Journal of Marriage and the Family,* 1995, *57,* 321–332.

Cosby, B. *Fatherhood.* New York: Berkley Publications, 1994. A popular book, easy to comprehend.

Cottle, T. J. *Like Fathers, Like Sons: Portraits of Intimacy and Strain.* Norwood, N.J.: ABLEX, 1981.

Gilbert, L. A. *Men in Dual-Career Families: Current Realities and Future Prospects.* Hillsdale, N.J.: Erlbaum, 1985. A brief, clear presentation.

Greif, G. L., DeMaris, A., and Hood, J. C. "Balancing Work and Single Fatherhood." In J. C. Hood (ed.), *Men, Work, and Family.* Newbury Park, Calif.: Sage, 1993.

*Lamb, M. F. (ed.). *The Role of the Father in Child Development.* (2nd ed.) New York: Wiley, 1996. A scholarly report on fatherhood in the early years.

Levenson, R. W., Carstensen, L. R., and Gottman, J. M. "Long-term Marriage: Age, Gender, and Satisfaction." *Psychology and Aging,* 1993, *8,* 301–313.

*Levine, J. A. *Working Fathers: New Strategies for Balancing Work and Family.* Reading, Mass.: Addison-Wesley, 1997.

Levinson, D. J. *The Seasons of a Man's Life.* New York: Ballantine, 1986.

Grandparenting

Jendrek, M. P. "Grandparents Who Parent their Grandchildren: Effects on Lifestyle." *Journal of Marriage and the Family,* 1993, *55,* 609–621.

*Kitzinger, S. *Becoming a Grandmother: A Life Transition.* New York: Simon and Schuster, 1997.

Adult Friendships

Adams, R. G., and Bleiszner, R. (eds.). *Older Adult Friendship.* Newbury Park, Calif.: Sage, 1989.

Berndt, T. J. "Friendships in Childhood and Adolescence." In W. Damon (ed.), *Child Development Today and Tomorrow.* San Francisco: Jossey-Bass, 1989.

Berndt, T. J., and Perry, T. B. "Distinguishing Features of Early Adolescent Friendship." In R. Montemeyer, G. R. Adams, and T. P. Gullota (eds.), *From Childhood to Adolescence: A Transitional Period?* Newbury Park, Calif.: Sage, 1990.

Berndt, T. J., and Savin-Williams, R. C. "Peer Relations and Friendships." In P. H. Tolan and B. J. Kohler (eds.), *Handbook of Clinical Research and Practice with Adolescents.* New York: Wiley, 1992.

*Blieszner, R., and Adams, R. G. *Adult Friendship.* Newbury Park: Sage, 1992. A concise summary of the current studies of adult friendships.

Gottman, J. M., and Parker, J. G. (eds.). *Conversations of Friends. Speculations on Affective Development.* Cambridge, England: Cambridge University Press, 1986.

Howes, C. "Patterns of Friendship." *Child Development,* 1987, *54,* 1041–1053.

O'Meara, J. J. "Cross-sex Friendship: Four Basic Challenges of an Ignored Relationship." *Sex-Roles,* 1989, *21,* 525–543.

Rubin, L. *Just Friends: The Role of Friendship in Our Lives.* New York: HarperCollins, 1993.

Work

*Bennis, W. *Organizing Genius: The Secrets of Creative Collaboration.* Reading, Mass.: Addison-Wesley, 1997. A good coaching guide for evoking greatness.

Davidson, C. *Staying Home Instead: Alternatives to the Two-Paycheck Family.* San Francisco: Jossey-Bass, 1995.

*Simonsen, P. *Promoting a Development Culture in Your Organization.* Palo Alto, Calif.: Davies-Black, 1997. Describes ways to develop people and organizational systems simultaneously.

*Weisbord, M. R. *Productive Workplaces: Organizing and Managing for Dignity, Meaning, and Community.* San Francisco: Jossey-Bass, 1991.

Whole Work Catalog, PO Box 339–A. J., Boulder, CO 80306. Published each year; resources for promoting careers, jobs, and work.

Organizational Culture

Atthreya, N. H. *Spiritual Culture in the Corporate Drama.* Bombay, India: The Indian Centre for Encouraging Excellence, 1997. A unique book, in the form of a long poem, seeking to evoke work role excellence from a spiritual place in each worker.

*Deal, T. E., and Kennedy, A. A. *Corporate Cultures: The Rites and Rituals of Corporate Life.* Reading, Mass.: Addison-Wesley, 1982. Useful book on understanding symbolic corporate functions.

Fritts, P. *The New Managerial Mentor.* Palo Alto, Calif.: Davies-Black, 1998. Views mentoring as a force for collaborative decision making.

*Gozdz, K. *Community Building: Renewing Spirit and Learning in Business.* San Francisco: Sterling and Stone, 1995. A book of essays, including chapters by John Gardner, Peter Senge, Amitai Etzioni, Beth Jarman and George Land, Marvin Weisbord, and John Nirenberg.

*Wilkins, A. L. *Developing Corporate Character: How to Successfully Change an Organization Without Destroying It.* San Francisco: Jossey-Bass, 1989. Proposes ways to change organizations without losing their character by developing a corporate vision, sustaining a distinctive corporate character, and helping the corporate character adapt to change.

Leadership Coaching

*Adams, J. (ed.). *Transforming Leadership: From Vision to Results.* Alexandria, Va.: Miles River, 1999. Outstanding essays on leadership.

*Badaracco, J. L. Jr., and Ellsworth, R. R. *Leadership and the Quest for Integrity.* Boston: Harvard Business School Press, 1993. A good book on the issues facing executives if they have integrity as a central issue.

*Barker, J. A. *Paradigms: The Business of Discovering the Future.* New York: HarperCollins, 1992. A book on understanding how paradigms lead to perceptions which lead to the way we lead and live.

Bennis, W. *Why Leaders Can't Lead: The Unconscious Conspiracy Continues.* San Francisco: Jossey-Bass, 1989. A sober analysis of a worsening leadership pool.

*Bennis, W. *Organizing Genius: The Secrets of Creative Collaboration.* Reading, Mass.: Addison-Wesley, 1997. A good coaching guide for evoking greatness.

Conner, D. R. *Managing at the Speed of Change.* New York: Villard, 1993. A positive outlook for new forms of management.

Covey, S. R. *Principle-Centered Leadership.* New York: Fireside, 1992. Discusses how to lead through relationships that have integrity and character.

*Davis, S., and Davidson, W. *2020 Vision: Transform Your Business Today to Succeed in Tomorrow's Economy.* New York: Fireside, 1991. Thesis that information management is central to future success.

Douglas, C. A. *Formal Mentoring Programs in Organizations: An Annotated Bibliography.* Greensboro, N.C.: Center for Creative Leadership, 1997.

Eastman, L. J. *Succession Planning: An Annotated Bibliography.* Greensboro, N.C.: Center for Creative Leadership, 1995.

Gardner, J. W. *Leadership Attributes and Context.* Leadership Papers. Washington, D.C.: Leadership Studies Program, Independent Sector, 1828 L Street N.W., Washington, DC 20036.

Gardner, J. W. *Leadership and Power.* Leadership Papers. Washington, D.C.: Leadership Study Program, Independent Sector, 1828 L Street N.W., Washington, DC 20036.

Gardner, J. W. *Leadership Development.* Leadership Papers. Washington, D.C.: Leadership Studies Program, Independent Sector, 1828 L Street N.W., Washington, DC 20036.

Gardner, J. W. *The Moral Aspect of Leadership.* Leadership Papers. Washington, D.C.: Leadership Studies Program, Independent Sector, 1828 L Street N.W., Washington, DC 20036.

Gates, W. (Bill). *The Road Ahead.* New York: Viking, 1996. Conveys a brilliant, futurist attitude from personal to family to corporate visions.

Greenleaf, R. K. *Servant Leadership: A Journey into the Nature of Legitimate Power and Greatness.* Mahwah, N.J.: Paulist, 1983. An important book for its original thoughts on what constitutes legitimate power and greatness.

*Hesselbein, F., Goldsmith, M., and Beckhard, R. *The Leader of the Future.* San Francisco: Jossey-Bass, 1996. Important because the essays provide characteristics of future leadership.

Hillman, J. *Kinds of Power: A Guide to Its Intelligent Uses.* New York: Doubleday, 1997. Explores the styles of power, the myths of power, and the power of myth.

Kinlaw, D. C. *Coaching for Commitment: Managerial Strategies for Obtaining Superior Performance.* San Francisco: Jossey-Bass, 1999. Good advice but thin on models and strategies.

Koestenbaum, P. *Leadership: The Inner Side of Greatness.* San Francisco: Jossey-Bass, 1991. Describes the inner strengths of vital leaders.

Kotter, J. P. *The New Rules: How to Succeed in Today's Post-Corporate World.* New York: Free Press, 1995. Discusses eight new rules for leadership, as corporate career paths wither and global opportunities for leadership expand.

Kouzes, J. M., and Posner, B. Z. *The Leadership Challenge: How to Get Extraordinary Things Done in Organizations.* San Francisco: Jossey-Bass, 1996. Based on research tools for measuring perceived leadership abilities.

Mahoney, M. J. *Human Change Processes.* New York: Basic Books, 1991.

Maxwell, J. C. *Developing the Leader Within You.* Nashville, Tenn.: Nelson, 1993. A popular, brief summary of the literature on leadership.

*McNally, D. *Even Eagles Need a Push: Learning to Soar in a Changing World.* New York: Delacorte, 1994. A positive and optimistic guide to leadership development.

Morgan, F. E. *Living the Martial Way: A Manual for the Way a Modern Warrior Should Think.* Fort Lee, N.J.: Barricade, 1992. Conveys the mind-set, goals, and strategies of the modern warrior.

Morrison, A. M. *The New Leaders: Guidelines on Leadership Diversity in America.* San Francisco: Jossey-Bass, 1992. Probably the best book available on leadership diversity issues.

Murphy, E. C. *Leadership IQ: A Personal Development Process Based on a Scientific Study of a New Generation of Leaders.* New York: Wiley, 1996. Identifies eight kinds of leaders with a simple questionnaire.

Oakley, E., and Krug, D. *Enlightened Leadership.* New York: Fireside, 1994. A five-step program for getting the keys to renewal and success from your own employees and leaders.

Pauchant, T., and Associates. *In Search of Meaning: Managing Our Organizations, Communities, and the Natural World.* San Francisco: Jossey-Bass, 1994. A classic book on organizational existentialism, filled with theory, stories, and original ideas.

*Peterson, D. B., and Hicks, M. D. *The Leader as Coach: Strategies for Coaching and Developing Others.* Minneapolis: Personnel Decisions, 1995. An outline for training leaders as coaches.

Peterson, D. B., and Hicks, M. D. *Development First: Strategies for Self-Development.* Minneapolis: Personnel Decisions International, 1996.

Posner, M. J. *Executive Essentials.* Olympic Marketing, 1987. Provides details on how to perform executive functions.

Sessa, V. I., and Campbell, R. J. *Selection at the Top: An Annotated Bibliography.* Greensboro, N.C.: Center for Creative Leadership, 1997.

Sonnenfeld, J. *The Hero's Farewell: What Happens When CEOs Retire.* New York: Oxford, 1988. Describes four styles CEOs use when they leave: the monarch, the general, the ambassador, and the governor.

*Stevenin, T. J. *People Power: Tapping the Spirit of Quality Performance and Service in Your Organization.* Northfield Publishing, 1996. An optimistic book about inspiring organizations by inspiring the lives of the employees.

Thompson, A. D. *A Formative Evaluation of an Individualized Coaching Program for Business Managers and Professionals.* (Doctoral dissertation, University of Minnesota, 1986). Dissertation Abstracts International, 1987, *47*(12–A. Pt. 1), 4339.

*Tichy, N. M., and Devanna, M. A. *The Transformational Leader.* New York: Wiley, 1997. Structured in the same order as a coach would approach the revitalization of an organization based on visioning.

Tucker, R. B. *Managing the Future: Essential Survival Tools for Business.* New York: Berkley, 1991. A down-to-earth book on how to move ahead with confidence as a manager.

Weinberg, G. M. *Becoming a Technical Leader: An Organic Problem-Solving Approach.* New York: Dorset House, 1986. Describes how technical leaders need to know how to understand problems, manage the flow of ideas, and maintain quality.

*Weisbord, M. R., and Janoff, S. *Future Search: An Action Guide to Finding Common Ground in Organizations and Communities.* San Francisco: Berrett-Koehler, 1995. A natural application of the Hudson concept of visioning within corporate and community settings.

Wheatley, M. J. *Leadership and the New Science: Learning about Organization from an Orderly Universe.* San Francisco: Berrett-Koehler, 1992. Uses scientific thinking as a model for understanding leadership.

White, R. P., Hodgson, P., and Crainer, S. *The Future of Leadership: Riding the Corporate Rapids into the 21st Century.* Lanham, Md.: Pitman, 1996. Promotes leaders who embrace learning, maximize energy, foster resonant simplicity, maintain a multiple focus, and master their inner sense.

Coaching for High Performance of Individuals and Teams

Bradford, D. L., and Cohen, A. R. *Managing for Excellence: The Guide to Developing High Performance in Contemporary Organizations.* New York: Wiley, 1984. Advocates a new kind of leader who is a technician or conductor.

Buchholz, S., and Roth, T. *Creating the High-Performance Team.* New York: John Wiley, 1987.

*Deeprose, D. *The Team Coach: Vital New Skills for Supervisors and Managers in a Team Environment.* New York: AMACOM, 1995.

*Dyer, W. G. *Team Building.* (3rd ed.) Reading, Mass.: Addison-Wesley, 1995.

Fournies, F. *Coaching for Improved Work Performance.* New York: McGraw-Hill, 1988.

Johansen, R., Sibbet, D., Benson, S., Martin, A., Mittman, R., and Saffo, P. *Leading Business Teams: How Teams Can Use Technology and Group Process Tools to Enhance Performance.* Reading, Mass.: Addison-Wesley, 1991.

Katzenbach, J. R., and Smith, D. K. *The Wisdom of Teams.* New York: HarperCollins, 1993.

Kinlaw, D. *Coaching for Commitment: Obtaining Superior Employee Performance.* San Francisco: Jossey-Bass, 1996. Suggests that managers achieve superior performance not through control but by coaching, mentoring, tutoring, counseling, and confronting their employees.

Larson, C. E., and LaFasto, F.M.J. *TeamWork: What Must Go Right/What Can Go Wrong.* Newbury Park, Calif.: Sage, 1989. Strategies for success.

Martin, D. *TeamThink: Using the Sports Connection to Develop, Motivate, and Manage a Winning Business Team.* New York: Penguin, 1993.

Porter, M. *Competitive Advantage: Creating and Sustaining Superior Performance.* New York: Free Press, 1998. A guide for coaches working on improving performance in the workplace.

*Ray, D., and Bronstein, H. *Teaming Up: Making the Transition to a Self-Directed Team-Based Organization.* New York: McGraw-Hill, 1994.

Rees, F. *Teamwork from Start to Finish.* San Francisco: Jossey-Bass, 1998.

Whitmore, J. *Coaching for Performance.* New York: Atrium, 1996.

Wilson, J. M., and George, J. A. *Team Leader's Survival Guide.* New York: McGraw-Hill, 1997.

Organizational Learning

*Argyris, C. *Knowledge for Action.* San Francisco: Jossey-Bass, 1993. Shows connection between theory and action.

*Argyris, C. *On Organizational Learning.* Cambridge, Mass.: Blackwell, 1996. An outstanding book on learning within organization environments by a leading thinker in the field.

*Chawla, S., and Renesch, J. *Learning Organizations: Developing Cultures for Tomorrow's Workplace.* Portland, Ore.: Productivity, 1995. Outstanding readings on theories and applications of learning.

de Pree, M. *Leadership Is an Art.* New York: Doubleday, 1989. A reliable book on leadership.

Kline, P., and Saunders, B. *Ten Steps to a Learning Organization.* Arlington, Va.: Great Ocean, 1998. A simple, practical, down-to-earth book on creating learning organizations.

*Schön, D. *The Reflective Practitioner: How Professionals Think in Action.* New York: Basic Books, 1983.

*Senge, P. M. *The Fifth Discipline Fieldbook: Strategies and Tools for Building a Learning Organization.* New York: Doubleday, 1994. Models for connecting learning to personal mastery, shared vision, team learning, policymaking, organizational development.

Stata, R. "Organizational Learning: The Key to Management Innovation." *Sloan Management Review,* Spring 1989, 63–64.

*Tobin, D. R. *Transformational Learning: Renewing Your Company Through Knowledge and Skills.* New York: Wiley, 1996. A how-to book for creating continuous learning programs within organizations.

Career Coaching

*Bolles, R. *The 1997 What Color Is Your Parachute?* Berkeley, Calif.: Ten Speed Press, 1997. The most complete book on how to conduct a successful job hunt.

Booher, D. *Get Life Without Sacrificing Your Career.* New York: McGraw-Hill, 1997.

*Borchard, D., Kelly, J. J., and Weaver, N.-P. *Your Career: Choices and Changes.* (7th ed.) Dubuque, Iowa: Kendall/Hunt, 1998. An outstanding book for choosing or redesigning a career.

Bridges, W. *Jobshift: How to Prosper in a Workplace Without Jobs.* Reading, Mass.: Addison-Wesley, 1994.

*Brown, D., Brooks, L., and Associates. *Career Choice and Development.* (3rd ed.) San Francisco: Jossey-Bass, 1997. A useful book on career choice, career and life development, and midlife career change.

Career Planning and Adult Development Journal, 4965 Sierra Road, San Jose, CA 95132. A new journal covering a wide range of career development issues; aimed at human resources professionals and career counselors.

Dalton, G., Thompson, P., and Price, R. "The Four Stages of Professional Careers." *Organizational Dynamics,* Summer 1977, *6,* 19–42.

*Deeprose, D. *The Team Coach: Vital New Skills for Supervisors and Managers in a Team Environment.* New York: AMACOM, 1995. The best book on team coaching.

*Feller, R., and Walz, G. (eds.). *Career Transitions in Turbulent Times: Exploring Work, Learning and Careers.* Brief chapters by the giants of the field: Krumboltz, Gyspers, Osipow, Tiedeman, Schlossberg, Gelatt, Campbell, and Hudson (1996). An ERIC book to order at 800-414-9769.

Fox, M. *The Reinvention of Work: A New Vision of Livelihood for Our Time.* New York: HarperCollins, 1994. A spiritual, value-based interpretation of finding a "work" in balance with the rest of life.

Greif, G. L., DeMaris, A., and Hood, J. C. "Balancing Work and Single Fatherhood." In J. C. Hood (ed.), *Men, Work, and Family.* Newbury Park, Calif.: Sage, 1993.

*Gysbers, N. C., and Associates. *Designing Careers.* San Francisco: Jossey-Bass, 1984. Probably the best single book on how to design a career.

Hall, D. T., and Associates. *Career Development in Organizations.* San Francisco: Jossey-Bass, 1986. A scholarly book on promoting career development within organizations.

Herr, E. L., and Cramer, S. H. *Career Guidance and Counseling Through the Lifespan: Systematic Approaches.* Reading, Mass.: Addison-Wesley, 1995.

Higgins, C., Duxbury, L., and Lee, C. "Impact of Life-cycle Stage and Gender on the Ability to Balance Work and Family Responsibilities." *Family Relations,* 1994, *43,* 144–150.

Holland, J. "A Theory of Vocational Choice." *Journal of Counseling Psychology,* 1959, *6,* 35–45.

Holland, J. "A Theory-Ridden, Computerless, Impersonal, Vocational Guidance System." *Journal of Vocational Behavior,* 1971, *1,* 167–176.

Isaacson, L. E. *Career Information in Counseling and Career Development.* (4th ed.) Boston: Allyn & Bacon, 1996.

Kimeldorf, M. *Portfolio Power: The New Way to Showcase All Your Job Skills and Experiences.* Princeton, N.J.: Peterson's Guides, 1997.

Leibowitz, Z., and Lea, D. (eds.). *Adult Career Development.* Washington, D.C.: National Career Development Association, 1992. Provides an overview of adult life cycle change and career issues.

Leong, F.T.L. *Career Development and Vocational Behavior of Racial and Ethnic Minorities.* Hillsdale, N.J.: Erlbaum, 1995.

McKenna, E. *When Work Doesn't Work Anymore: Women, Work, and Identity.* New York: Delacorte, 1997.

Moses, B. *Career Intelligence: Mastering the New Work and Personal Realities.* Toronto: Stoddard, 1997. Distributed by General Distribution Services; describes the new employment contract and how workers can prepare for the future.

*Newman, B. K. *Now That You're All Grown Up, What Do You Want to Be?: A Career Transition Guide.* Dubuque, Iowa: Kendall/Hunt, 1996. Useful exercises for career coaching.

*Osipow, S. H. *Theories of Career Development.* (3rd ed.) Boston: Allyn & Bacon, 1995. The bible on theories of career development.

Peters, T., and Austin, N. *A Passion for Excellence.* New York: Warner, 1989. Contains a chapter on coaching.

Porter, S., Porter, K., and Bennett, C. *Me, Myself, and I, Inc.* Manassas Park, Va.: Impact, 1998. Describes ten steps to career independence, using an individualized portfolio development plan.

Rechtschaffen, S. *Time Shifting: Creating More Time for Your Life.* New York: Doubleday, 1996.

Roe, A., and Lunnenborg, P. W. "Personality Development and Career Choice." *Career Choice and Development.* D. Brown, L. Brooks, and Associates (eds.). San Francisco: Jossey-Bass, 1984. A good source for the theories of Anne Roe.

Savickas, M. L., and Lent, R. W. *Convergence in Career Development Theories.* Palo Alto, Calif.: Consulting Psychologists Press, 1994.

Schein, E. H. *Career Dynamics: Matching Individual and Organizational Needs.* New York: Addison-Wesley, 1978. Important for coaching, as are all of Schein's writings.

Simonsen, P. *Promoting a Development Culture in Your Organization: Using Career Development as a Change Agent.* Palo Alto, Calif.: Davies-Black, 1997. Explains how to generate a development culture into an organization.

Super, D. "A Theory of Vocational Development." *American Psychologist,* 1953, *8,* 185–190. Basic career theory.

*Super, D. "Career and Life Development." In D. Brown and L. Brooks (eds.), *Career Choice and Development* (pp. 192–234). San Francisco: Jossey-Bass, 1984. Career theory using life cycle information in the model.

Super, D. E. "A Life-span, Life-space Approach to Career Development." *Journal of Vocational Behavior, 16,* 1980, 282–298.

*Super, D. E., and Sverko, B. (eds.). *Life Roles, Values, and Careers.* San Francisco: Jossey-Bass, 1995. Reports how values, roles, and careers combine to forge the process of human development across the lifespan; includes good instruments that coaches can use.

Walsh, W. B., and Osipow, S. H. (eds.). *Handbook of Vocational Psychology.* Hillsdale, N.J.: Erlbaum, 1983. A reference guide.

*Waterman, R., Jr., Waterman, J. A., and Collard, B. A. "Toward a Career-Resilient Workforce." *Harvard Business Review,* Jul./Aug. 1994, 87–95.

Yost, E., and Corbishley, M. A. *Career Counseling.* San Francisco: Jossey-Bass, 1992. A solid guide to the art of career counseling.

*Zunker, B. G. *Career Counseling: Applied Concepts of Life Planning.* Monterey, Calif.: Brooks/Cole, 1997.

Coaching Corporate Managers

*Bolman, L. G., and Deal, T. E. *Modern Approaches to Understanding and Managing Organizations.* San Francisco: Jossey-Bass, 1986. Presents a master plan for the necessary developmental phases for building a successful company from stability to transition.

Bryson, J. M. *Strategic Planning for Public and Nonprofit Organizations: A*

Guide to Strengthening and Sustaining Organizational Achievement. San Francisco: Jossey-Bass, 1995.

Case, J. *Open-Book Management.* New York: HarperBusiness, 1995. A clearly written argument that workers are happiest and most productive when they have a stake in the success of the company.

*Davidson, M. *The Transformation of Management.* Boston: Butterworth-Heinemann, 1996. A good and concise book about future management issues and strategies.

Davis, S. M. *Future Perfect.* Reading, Mass.: Addison-Wesley, 1987. Describes management policies that will deliver.

Dixon, N. M. "Organizational Learning: A Review of the Literature with Implications for HRD Professionals." *Human Resource Quarterly,* Spring, 1992.

*Gilley, J. W., and Boughton, N. W. *Stop Managing, Start Coaching!* Chicago: Irwin, 1996. A reliable book on coaching with managers.

*Maynard, H. B., Jr., and Mehrtens, S. E. *The Fourth Wave.* San Francisco, Calif.: Berrett-Koehler, 1996. Predicts that business leaders of the future will be the shapers of the world community, models of environmental sustainability, advocates of continuous learning.

Nash, M. *Managing Organizational Performance.* San Francisco: Jossey-Bass, 1983. A practical guide to planning, getting consensus, and creating strategies for the future.

*Peters, T. *The Tom Peters Seminar: Crazy Times Call for Crazy Organizations.* New York: Vintage, 1994. Describes what organizational coaches do superbly.

Peters, T., and Austin, N. *A Passion for Excellence: The Leadership Difference.* New York: Warner, 1989. Contains a valuable chapter for coaches: Chapter Eighteen.

Peters, T. J., and Waterman, R. H. *In Search of Excellence: Lessons from America's Best-Run Companies.* New York: Harper & Row, 1988. Explains quite clearly through its excellent examples how to coach toward excellence in corporate settings.

Entrepreneurism

Brandt, S. C. *Entrepreneuring: The Ten Commandments for Building a Growth Company.* New York: Archipelgo, 1997. A paperback with solid information for first-time business people.

Hawken, P. *Growing a Business.* New York: Fireside, 1987. Highly readable book about succeeding as an entrepreneur and loving it.

*Hiam, A. W., and Olander, K. W. *The Entrepreneur's Complete Sourcebook.* Englewood Cliffs, N.J.: Prentice Hall, 1996. Easily the most comprehensive and usable advice for a new entrepreneur.

Lonier, T. *Working Solo: The Real Guide to Freedom and Financial Success with Your Own Business.* New York: Portico, 1994.

Montgomery, V. L. *The Smart Woman's Guide to Starting a Business.* Hawthorne, N.J.: Career Press, 1998.

*Rice, C. S. *Strategic Planning for the Small Business: Situations, Weapons, Objectives, and Tactics.* Holbrook, Mass.: Bob Adams, 1990. A guide to every step of the way into a successful small business.

Sitterly, C. *The Female Entrepreneur: Overcoming Challenges in the Business World.* Menlo Park, Calif.: Crisp, 1994. A popular treatment of how businesswomen can succeed.

*Sonnenfeld, J. *The Hero's Farewell: What Happens When CEOs Retire.* New York: Oxford, 1988.

*Wesman, J. *Dive Right In, The Sharks Won't Bite: The Entrepreneurial Woman's Guide to Success.* New York: Dearborn Financial Publishing, 1995. A street-smart guide to women who want to run their own business and succeed.

Organizational Development

Ambrose, D. *Healing the Downsized Organization.* New York: Harmony, 1996.

Bolman, L. G., and Deal, T. E. *Leading with Soul: An Uncommon Journey of Spirit.* San Francisco: Jossey-Bass, 1995. A simple narration of corporate discovery of profound meaning.

Cox, A. *Redefining Corporate Soul: Linking Purpose and People.* Chicago: Irwin, 1996. A simple and profound book.

*French, W. L., and Bell, C. H., Jr. *Organization Development: Behavioral Science Interventions for Organization Improvement.* (3rd ed.) Englewood Cliffs, N.J.: Prentice Hall. 1999. A useful manual for developing strategies within organizations.

*Galpin, T. J. *The Human Side of Change: A Practical Guide to Organization Redesign.* San Francisco: Jossey-Bass, 1996. A good book for corporate coaches.

*Gozdz, K. *Community Building: Renewing Spirit and Learning in Business.* San Francisco: Sterling and Stone, 1995. A book of essays, including chapters by John Gardner, Peter Senge, Amitai Etzioni, Beth Jarman and George Land, Marvin Weisbord, and John Nirenberg.

Hendricks, W. (ed.). *Coaching, Mentoring and Managing.* New York: Career Press, 1996.

*Hesselbein, F., Goldsmith, M., and Beckhard, R. *The Organization of the Future.* San Francisco: Jossey-Bass, 1997. Key readings by leading experts on how organizations will evolve into the twenty-first century.

Jarillo, J. C. *Strategic Networks: Creating the Borderless Organization.* Oxford, England: Butterworth-Heinemann, 1995. Presents the idea of strategic networking: working with and through other organizations.

Killinger, B. *Workaholics: The Respectable Addicts: A Family Survival Guide.* New York: Fireside, 1992. Argues that workaholics—to make themselves feel powerful and useful—reduce their focus of energy to their "work."

*Kilmann, R. H. *Beyond the Quick Fix: Managing Five Tracks to Organizational Success.* San Francisco: Jossey-Bass, 1989. Theorizes that theory, practice, culture, management skills, team-building, and strategy/structure must be changed if true reform is to occur.

Koestenbaum, P. *Managing Anxiety: The Power of Knowing Who You Are.* Englewood Cliffs, N.J.: Prentice Hall, 1974. A philosophical book about being conscious.

London, M. *Change Agents: New Roles and Innovation Strategies for Human Resource Professionals.* San Francisco: Jossey-Bass, 1988. A sound book for human resources people to understand ways of coaching for change within the system.

*Miller, J., and Brown, P. *The Corporate Coach: How to Build a Team of Loyal Customers and Happy Employees.* New York: HarperBusiness, 1994.

*Noer, D. M. *Breaking Free: A Prescription for Personal and Organizational Change.* San Francisco: Jossey-Bass, 1997. Describes how to interpret workforce behaviors and lead a company toward shared learning for future effectiveness.

Shore, L. M., and Bloom, A. J. "Developing Employees Through Coaching and Career Management." *Personnel,* 1986, *63,* 34–38.

*Whyte, D. *The Heart Aroused.* New York: Doubleday, 1994. A beautiful book by an English poet on the meaning of work in post-modern America.

*Wilkins, A. L. *Developing Corporate Character: How to Successfully Change an Organization Without Destroying It.* San Francisco: Jossey-Bass, 1989. Proposes ways to change organizations without losing their character by developing a corporate vision, sustaining a distinctive corporate character, and helping the corporate character adapt to change.

Coaching for Corporate Change

Adizes, I. *Corporate Life Cycles: How and Why Corporations Grow and Die and What to Do About It.* Englewood Cliffs, N.J.: Prentice Hall, 1988. A cyclical view of corporate development that is overtaxed, too complicated, and ultimately inflexible.

Adizes, I. *Mastering Change: The Power of Mutual Trust and Respect.* Santa Monica, Calif.: Adizes Institute, 1992.

Beckhard, R., and Pritchard, W. *Changing the Essence: The Art of Creating and Leading Fundamental Change in Organizations.* San Francisco: Jossey-Bass, 1992. Book about designing a strategic plan, training the leaders, and punting.

Bergquist, W. *The Postmodern Organization: Mastering the Art of Irreversible Change.* San Francisco: Jossey-Bass, 1993.

Bixler, S., and Bixler, S. *Take Action: 18 Proven Strategies.* New York: Fawcett, 1996. Simple, clear steps to consider, including the development of mentors and coaches.

Eccles, T. *Succeeding with Change: Implementing Action-Driven Strategies.* New York: McGraw-Hill, 1996. A very sound blueprint toward a successful future.

*Handy, C. *The Age of Unreason.* Boston: Harvard Business School, 1989. A prophetic book about our cultural shift from managing continuities to managing discontinuities.

*Handy, C. *The Age of Paradox.* Boston: Harvard Business School, 1994. Written by a prophet for our times, who has sound perceptions and a caring heart.

*Handy, C. *Beyond Certainty: The Changing Worlds of Organizations.* Boston: Harvard Business School Press, 1998. Thirty-five brief essays on organizational change, peppered with Handy's original wit.

*Jaffe, D. T., Scott, C. D., and Tobe, G. R. *Rekindling Commitment: How to Revitalize Yourself, Your Work, and Your Organization.* San Francisco: Jossey-Bass, 1994.

Coaching Organizational Transitions

*Beckhard, R., and Harris, R. T. *Organizational Transitions: Managing Complex Change.* (2nd ed.) Reading, Mass.: Addison-Wesley, 1987. A technical bible on organizational transitions.

Gersick, K. E., and Associates. *Generation to Generation: Life Cycles of the Family Business.* Cambridge, Mass.: Harvard Business School, 1997. A must book for any coach working with succession planning in a family business; contains sound theory along with practical savvy.

*O'Neil, J. R. *The Paradox of Success: When Winning at Work Means Losing at Life, A Book of Renewal for Leaders.* Los Angeles: Tarcher, 1993. A great book on the need for leaders to have a rich interiority.

Restructuring, Downsizing, and Outplacement

Ambrose, D. *Healing the Downsized Organization.* New York: Harmony, 1996. Focuses on restoring trust with the survivors of downsizing.

Caplan, G., and Teese, M. *Survivors: How to Keep Your Best People on Board After Downsizing.* Palo Alto, Calif.: Davies-Black, 1997.

Johansen, R., and Swigart, R. *Upsizing the Individual in the Downsized Organization: Managing in the Wake of Reengineering, Globalization, and Overwhelming Technological Change.* Reading, Mass.: Addison-Wesley, 1996. A positive approach to downsizing, viewing it as an opportunity to reconnect employees in more flexible ways.

Knowdell, R. L, Branstead, E., and Moravec, M. *From Downsizing to Recovery: Strategic Transition Options for Organizations and Individuals.* Palo Alto, Calif.: CPP Books, 1994. A practical book to understanding options to outplacement.

Marks, M. L., and Mirvis, P. "Rebuilding After the Merger: Dealing with Survivor Sickness." *Organizational Dynamics,* 1992, *2*(21), 18–32.

Noer, D. M. *Healing the Wounds: Overcoming the Trauma of Layoffs and Revitalizing Downsized Organizations.* San Francisco: Jossey-Bass, 1993. Challenges the basic philosophy of downsizing and outplacement.

*Noer, D. M. *Breaking Free: A Prescription for Personal and Organizational Change.* San Francisco: Jossey-Bass, 1997. Describes how to interpret workforce behaviors and lead a company toward shared learning for future effectiveness.

*Pickman, A. J. *The Complete Guide to Outplacement Counseling.* Hillsdale, N.J.: Erlbaum, 1995. Concise listing of the steps to take and the skills required.

Price, R. H. "Psychological Impact of Job Loss on Individuals and Families." *Current Directions in Psychological Science,* 1992, *1,* 9–11.

Coaching Organizational Transformation

*Adams, J. D. (ed.). *Transforming Work.* Alexandria, Va.: Miles River Press, 1999. A spiritual interpretation of the meaning of work and work system.

Beck, D. E., and Cowan, C. C. *Spiral Dynamics: Mastering Values, Leadership, and Change.* Cambridge, Mass.: Blackwell, 1996. A creative theory to understanding change as a flow of ever-deepening values and possibilities for the human adventure.

*Owen, H. *SPIRIT: Transformation and Development in Organizations.* Potomac, Md.: Abbott Publishing, 1987. A must read for anyone interested in one person's opinion about how spirit broods over and inspires work organizations.

Pinchot, G., and Pinchot, E. *The End of Bureaucracy and the Rise of the Intelligent Organization.* San Francisco: Berrett-Koehler, 1994. Shows how to facilitate moving the corporate culture away from bureaucratic constraints toward its own workforce intelligence through open systems.

Ray, M., and Rinzler, A. (eds.). *The New Paradigm in Business: Emerging Strategies for Leadership and Organizational Change.* New York: Tarcher, 1993. Bright chapters by noetic challengers of the status quo, organized into the World Business Academy.

Finding One's Own "Work"

*Adams, J. D. (ed.). *Transforming Work.* Alexandria, Va: Miles River Press, 1999. A book of readings on the theme of transformation through organizational work.

Boldt, L. G. *Zen and the Art of Making a Living.* New York: Penguin, 1993. Interesting in its format and style for finding a job that matches one's inner passion.

*Bridges, W. *Creating You & Co.: Learn to Think Like the CEO of Your Own Career.* Reading, Mass.: Addison-Wesley, 1997. An excellent book for understanding why and how to take personal responsibility for one's own work life.

Fox, M. *The Reinvention of Work: A New Vision of Livelihood for Our Time.* New York: HarperCollins, 1994. A book about reinventing work so that it adds meaning to life and contributes to a larger good.

Furniss, W. T. *The Self-Reliant Academic.* Washington, D.C.: American Council on Education, 1984. A pamphlet proposing that academic leaders—primarily professors—think like entrepreneurs, to take charge of their lives, money, and future.

*Hagberg, J., and Leider, R. *The Inventurers: Excursions in Life and Career Renewal.* (3rd ed.) Reading, Mass.: Addison-Wesley, 1988.

*Hakim, C. *We Are All Self-Employed: The New Social Contract for Working in a Changed World.* San Francisco: Berrett-Koehler, 1994.

Kimeldorf, M. *Portfolio Power: The New Way to Showcase All Your Job Skills and Experience.* Princeton, N.J.: Peterson's Guides, 1997.

*Leider, R. J. *The Power of Purpose: Discovering Your Calling for the 21st Century.* (rev. ed.) San Francisco: Berrett-Koehler, 1997. A detailed scheme for moving from questioning life to having life question you.

Miller, J. V., and Musgrove, M. L. (eds.). *Issues in Adult Career Counseling.* San Francisco: Jossey-Bass, 1986. Good ideas for deeper coaching.

*Moses, B. *Career Intelligence: Mastering the New Work and Personal Realities.* Buffalo, N.Y.: Stoddart Publishers, 1997. Distributed by General Distribution Services, Buffalo, N.Y. Describes how to evolve the career you want.

Owen, H. *SPIRIT: Transformation and Development in Organizations.* Abbott Pub. A brilliant book on how to find your soulful work.

*Porter, S. *Me, Myself, & I, Inc.: Ten Steps to Career Independence.* Manassas Park, Va.: Impact, 1998.

*Pozzi, D., and Williams, S. *Success with Soul.* Seattle, Wa.: Dorian-Welles, 1997. Describes how to build a career from the inside out.

Rechtschaffen, S. *Time Shifting: Creating More for Your Life.* New York: Doubleday, 1996.

*Schein, E. H. *Career Anchors: Discovering Your Real Values.* San Diego, Calif.: University Associates, 1985. One of the simplest and most profound books linking inner values to outer work.

Sitterly, C. *The Female Entrepreneur: Overcoming Challenges in the Business World.* Menlo Park, Calif.: Crisp, 1994. A popular treatment of how businesswomen can succeed.

*Whyte, D. *The Heart Aroused.* New York: Doubleday, 1994. An invitation to find your path into an enchanted future, where your concerns define your work.

Finding Financial Rewards Through Work

Bolles, R. N. *The New Quick Job-Hunting Map.* Berkeley, Calif.: Ten Speed Press, 1990. A check-list and set of directions in a thin, easy-to-carry journal-like paperback.

*Bolles, R. N. *The 1997 What Color Is Your Parachute? A Practical Manual for Job-Hunters and Career-Changers.* Berkeley, Calif.: Ten Speed Press, 1997. For twenty-five years the best-seller among job-hunting books; both practical and mission-driven.

*Borchard, D., and Associates. *Your Career: Choices, Chances, Changes.* (5th ed.) Dubuque, Iowa: Kendall/Hunt, 1998. The best career search guide in print.

Coaching for Community

Arrendondo-Dowd, P., and Consalves, J. "Preparing Culturally Effective Counselors." *Personnel and Guidance Journal,* 1980, *58,* 657–660.

Atkinson, D. R., Morton, G., and Sue, D. W. (eds.). *Counseling American Minorities: A Cross-Cultural Perspective.* (3rd ed.) Dubuque, Iowa: William C. Brown, 1993.

*Bellah, R., and Associates. *Habits of the Heart: Individualism and Commitment in American Life.* Berkeley: University of California Press, 1996. A groundbreaking book for debating individualism and social commitment.

Cross, E., Katz, J., Miller, F., and Seashore, E. *The Promise of Diversity.* Washington, D.C.: NTL Institute, 1994.

Elgin, D. *Awakening Earth: Exploring the Evolution of Human Culture and Consciousness.* New York: Morrow, 1993.

*Etzioni, A. *The Spirit of Community: The Reinvention of American Society.* New York: Simon and Schuster, 1993. An important book for understanding the social consequences of community spirit.

*Gozdz, K. *Community Building: Renewing Spirit and Learning.* San Francisco: Sterling and Stone, 1995. Contains chapters on global, corporate, and interpersonal community building, along with a section on the dimensions of a sustainable, regenerative community.

Katz, J. H. "Leveraging Diversity: The Business Imperative." *Cultural Diversity at Work,* 1995, *8,* 4.

Katz, J. H., and Miller, F. A. "Cultural Diversity as a Developmental Process: The Path from a Monocultural Club to an Inclusive Organization." In W. Pfeiffer (ed.), *The 1995 Annual* (Vol. 2), San Diego, 267–281.

Lopez, S. R., and Associates. "Development of Culturally Sensitive Psychotherapists." *Professional Psychology: Research and Practice,* 1989, *20,* 369–376.

Mecca, A. M., Smelser, N. J., and Vasconcellos, J. *The Social Importance of Self-Esteem.* Berkeley: University of California Press, 1989. A groundbreaking book linking self-esteem to social problems and issues, such as child maltreatment, school performance, teenage pregnancy, crime and violence, and drugs.

*Mindell, A. *The Leader as Martial Artist: Techniques and Strategies for Resolving Conflict and Creating Community.* New York: HarperCollins, 1993. Proposes the metaskills of leadership, combining deep democracy and inner work.

*Peck, M. S. *The Different Drum: Community Making and Peace.* New York: Touchstone, 1987.

Peck, M. S. *A World Waiting to Be Born: Rediscovering Civility.* New York: Bantam, 1993.

*Suzukie, D. *The Sacred Balance: Rediscovering Our Place in Nature.* New York: Prometheus, 1998. Urges thinking of the planet as sacred.

Toulmin, S. *Cosmopolis: The Hidden Agenda of Modernity.* Chicago: University of Chicago Press, 1992. A brilliant introduction to the post-modern world.

*Weisbord, M. R. *Discovering Common Ground: How Future Search Conferences Bring People Together to Achieve Breakthrough Innovation, Empowerment, Shared Vision, and Collaborative Action.* San Francisco: Berrett-Koehler, 1992. An application of Weisbord's concept of "future vision."

Leisure Coaching

Anderson, N. *Man's Work and Leisure.* Leiden, Netherlands: E. J. Brill, 1997.

Csikszentmihalyi, M. *Beyond Boredom and Anxiety: The Experience of Play in Work and Games.* San Francisco: Jossey-Bass, 1975.

EPM Communications. *At Our Leisure.* Ithaca, N.Y.: American Demographics, 1997. Describes how Americans are engaged in leisure at the present time.

Foster, S. *The Book of the Vision Quest: Personal Transformation in the Wilderness.* New York: Simon and Schuster, 1992. Converts an old Indian custom into a contemporary, adult ritual.

Huizinga, J. *Homo Ludens: A Study of the Play Element in Culture.* New York: Beacon Press, 1986. A scholarly writing on the importance of play in the resilience and creativity of a culture.

*Kelly, J. R. *Leisure.* Boston: Allyn & Bacon, 1995. An early study of the importance of leisure in adult lives.

*Kottler, J. A. *Travel That Can Change Your Life: How to Create a Transformative Experience.* San Francisco: Jossey-Bass, 1998. A beautifully written book about how to turn a vacation into journeys and adventures.

*Lederman, E. *Vacations That Can Change Your Life: Adventures, Retreats and Workshops for the Mind, Body and Spirit.* Naperville, Ill.: Sourcebooks,

1998. An outstanding collection of resources for renewal and learning.

Newlinger, J. *The Psychology of Leisure.* Springfield, Ill.: Charles C. Thomas, 1976. An original theory of leisure.

Rapoport, R., and Rapoport, R. *Leisure and Family Life Cycles.* London: Routledge and Kegan Paul, 1975. One of the first thorough studies of the importance of leisure in adult and family life.

Coaching for Society-at-Large Roles

Brown, L. R. *State of the World: A Report on Progress Toward a Sustainable Society.* New York: Norton, 1999.

Edelman, M. W. *The Measure of Our Success.* Boston: Beacon, 1992. A letter written to her children about what success really means in America today.

*Greenleaf, R. K. *Servant Leadership: A Journey into the Nature of Legitimate Power and Greatness.* Mahwah, N.J.: Paulist Press, 1983. An important book for its original thoughts on what constitutes legitimate power and greatness.

Masten, A. S. "Homeless Children in the United States: Mark of a Nation at Risk." *Current Directions in Psychological Science,* 1992, *1,* 41–43.

*Owen, H. *SPIRIT: Transformation and Development in Organizations.* Potomac, Md.: Abbott Publishing, 1987.

*Weisbord, M. R., and Janoff, S. *Future Search: An Action Guide to Finding Common Ground in Organizations and Communities.* San Francisco: Berrett-Koehler, 1995. A natural application of the concept of visioning within corporate and community settings.

 CHAPTER NINE 

Coaching for Visioning and Purpose

The ultimate function of coaches, no matter what their particular specialty or immediate issue, is to help persons and organizations find their purpose and vision and plans for the immediate future. *Purpose* is of ultimate concern. Purpose is a deep source of meaning, the reason we are alive; it generates energy and life direction. *Vision* is the way we see our lives or organizations being at some future time; it is a visual snapshot we can pursue. *Scenario development* incorporates purpose, vision, and planning into a living framework for inventing the future. *Planning* is a day-by-day measuring stick for linking today to a visionary tomorrow. Coaches help clients plan ways get to their future vision, with a high probability of success, all the while honoring their clients' purpose.

Four concepts—purpose, vision, scenario development, and planning—are equally important and they work together. Coaches weave these themes in and around each other as they work with their clients, mostly by way of asking probing questions that invite clients to envision their own future. To create a future, the purpose must become a dream, and the dream must become a plan. The dreamer becomes a planner. But planning is more than a bunch of skills; it is an inner force, a felt competence, a strength within. The planner pushes forward with logical, informed steps, like choosing reliable stepping stones to cross a stream. Through strategic thinking, the planner embroiders the dreamer's vision with the complexity of the world, weaving together technical and human resources that are required to bring the life structure into reality. The possible dream becomes a probable plan.

FINDING PURPOSE

Finding purpose is more than pursuing a goal. A person with purpose has a compelling reason for being alive, a raison d'être—an ontological pull, a motivational push, a calling. Purpose is the most important quality for every life to possess, experientially, consciously, and with words. It tells us what we want most to be about. At different times in the life cycle we reformulate our sense of purpose. Quite often, our sense of purpose changes as we mature. Most often it evolves from *ways to be successful* to *ways to be.*

Purpose produces passion or positive energy. On-purpose people have passion in their lives, and tapping the passion a client has for constructing a future direction is a coaching challenge. A coach should ask, What emotional resources does my client have for generating sustained motivation for inventing the future he or she wants?

VISIONING

A vision is a snapshot in our mind's eye of how we want to be, look, act, achieve, and interface with others at some given date in the future. It is more than visual. It includes hearing, sensing, feeling, and being. The more we can feel viscerally the excellence we are pursuing, the more likely we are to approximate it.

And what is the future? It is not something waiting for us but is something we create. The future is time and potential resources waiting for form, the not-yet waiting to be programmed. And if we don't create our own future, someone else will fit us into theirs. Life is a series of collisions with the future, said one Spanish writer. Tomorrow is either the sum of our pasts or the sum of our yearnings for what we may become. If we are creating our own future, we almost always begin with a dream. "I have a dream," yearned Martin Luther King in Washington, D.C., as he painted a picture of equality and fairness in America. The dream comes first. Reality chases after the dream, to make it happen.

A vision or dream, then, is

- *A simple picture of what the future means.* It declares what is important, purposive, and valuable for our lives ahead.
- *A poetic picture,* not a literal statement.
- *A visceral yearning,* not a wish list. It is not a vision or dream to want a new car, an exotic vacation, or even a new career. A vision is an all-

encompassing picture for our lives, not a simple wanting of something that would be nice to have.

- *A spiritual promise of a new quality of life,* a deeper sense of being. The vision within us is a yearning for an improved (not ideal or perfect) state of affairs, a promise for human betterment that is just beyond our reach, but worth reaching for and possible to approximate.
- *A promise that is convincing.* To think it is to go for it. It feels right, and it's going to happen. It's a Promise with a capital "P," and it pops into our minds frequently. It is a Promise happening. It feels that simple.
- *A pull toward it from without and a push toward it from within.* Its pull is the perception it gives to our priorities, and its push is high-level motivation within us.
- *Energy as much as anything else.* We know we have a vision when we get positive energy every time we think of it.
- *Like a haunting refrain.* We know we have a vision when it won't let us go and others are attracted to it. We know we have a vision when it is already guiding us ahead, and we instinctively trust it, and we don't feel we have to explain it to anyone.
- *An inspiration and motivation* that doesn't order us around. Human beings are the only creatures on earth capable of envisioning a future and then setting about to make it happen.

We dream and imagine; we expect and plan; we invent and create. Almost always, when we are alive and happy, we create our future to be different from the present. Then we set about to make it happen. This is how new companies get born, poems get conceived, Olympic races get won, music gets written, and better mouse traps get invented.

Much of the dreaming that humans do takes place in childhood and adolescence. We encourage children and young adults to dream and to launch plans to achieve those dreams. In the midlife and midcareer years, however, when life is complicated by many commitments and responsibilities, dreaming tends to diminish or to be limited and episodic. A midlife dream may be for a trip to Hawaii or a move into a new house.

Fundamentally, a vision or dream is holistic, encompassing all of life and unleashing enormous energy for a sense of personal mission. It feels deep and earth-shaking. The greatest power in our lives is our capacity to imagine, vision, or dream, not only when we are young but over and over again throughout the life cycle. It is an essential lifestyle ingredient for the self-renewing adult. The more we can create a sense of how we want the next few years to be, with continuities and change from the way we are today, the more we can and will make our futures happen.

DEVELOPING SCENARIOS

Guided by a sense of purpose and a vision, coaches help clients develop scenarios—show their pathway to the future, to their own desired reality. Scenario development is a necessary part of a good planning process. Coaches help clients create their preferred scripts, which contain stories, plots, cast of characters, episodes, themes, and anticipated results. Sometimes more than one scenario is created to explore options for reaching the preferred future. And careful planning in time management guides the scenario. Invariably, those plans must be changed because of changes in us and in the world, and the discovery of new opportunities. A good scenario takes changes into account; it contains what has been called a long view, coupled with several short planning periods and evaluations.

PLANNING

If visioning is the picturing of new possibilities, planning is implementing the vision in the real world. Visioning is dreamy, imaginative, soft-headed, indefinite, motivating, and energy releasing. Planning is realistic, logical, hard-headed, definite, factual, and time-driven. When we plan, we take a dream or expectation and break it down into goals, objectives, action steps, and time lines. A good planner also scans the environment to see if forces are working against the plan, and if some forces might make the plan easier to implement. First, we vision, then we plan. We link action steps to objectives and goals so the flow of events can be rehearsed, fine-tuned, and implemented.

A plan is a living document, not a stone etching. Frequent evaluation is required, along with adaptation to new resources and opportunities as they are discovered. Yet the basic plan will remain, as a vehicle for making the dream happen. Plans need to be definite, anchored carefully into a sequence of events and a committed life with time management.

 BASIC LIBRARY FOR COACHES

Coaching for Purpose

Ardell, D. B. *The Book of Wellness: A Secular Approach to Spirituality, Meaning, & Purpose.* New York: New World Library, 1990. Physicians and health promoters urged to spend less energy promoting fitness, nutrition, and stress management and more time encouraging people to ponder the meaning and purpose of their lives.

*Baumeister, R. F. *Meanings of Life.* New York: Guilford Press, 1991. A fresh and rewarding new book on values, purpose, and the meanings of life.

Bruner, J. *Acts of Meaning.* Cambridge, Mass.: Harvard University Press, 1990. A well-known educator speaks out on how words and activities arrive at "meaning."

Carter, S. L. *Integrity.* New York: Basic Books, 1996. Blunt talk about the nature and importance of integrity.

Cousins, N. *Head First: The Biology of Hope.* New York: Dutton, 1989. An original inquiry into how hope and optimism are required by our bodies for life to continue.

Elgin, D. *Voluntary Simplicity.* (rev. ed.) New York: Quill, 1993. A trumpet for personal downsizing.

Kavanaugh, J. *Search: A Guide for Those Who Dare to Ask of Life Everything Good and Beautiful.* New York: Steven J. Nash, 1996. A poet's plea for passion and purpose above all else.

*Leider, R. J. *The Power of Purpose: Discovering Your Calling for the 21st Century.* (rev. ed.) New York: Fawcett, 1997. A detailed scheme for moving from questioning life to having life question you.

McCarthy, K. W. *The On-Purpose Person.* Colorado Springs, Colo.: Pinon Press, 1992.

Peck, M. S. *The Road Less Traveled.* New York: Simon and Schuster, 1998.

Seligman, M. *Learned Optimism.* New York: Pocket Books, 1998. Argues that pessimism and optimism are fundamentally choices and habits; optimism is the gateway to learning, future vision, and happiness.

Coaching for Visioning

*Davis, S., and Davidson, W. *2020 Vision: Transform Your Business Today to Succeed in Tomorrow's Economy.* New York: Fireside, 1991. Argues that information management is central to future success.

*Dilts, R. B. *Skills for the Future: Managing Creativity and Innovation.* Capitola, Calif.: Meta, 1993. Applies creativity to problem solving of all types.

Heilbroner, R. *Visions of the Future: The Distant Past, Yesterday, Today, and Tomorrow.* New York: Oxford University Press, 1995. An important book for understanding how the cultural future is critical to the evolution of personal and social futures.

*Land, G., and Jarman, B. *Breakpoint and Beyond: Mastering the Future, Today.* New York: HarperBusiness, 1992. Puts the present in perspective with the future.

Longfellow, L. *Earth Is Alive: Where We Gonna Live if We Wear it Out.* Lecture Theatre audiotape (2). PO Box 4317, Prescott, AZ. 602-778-6629.

Loye, D. *The Knowable Future: A Psychology of Forecasting and Prophecy.* New York: ToExcel, 1998. A proposal for pooling the consciousness of all by tapping the whole mind and its imaginal choices.

Coaching for Personal Vision

Bolles, R. N. *How to Find Your Mission in Life.* Berkeley, Calif.: Ten Speed Press, 1991. An Episcopal priest and guru of the career field speaks candidly on finding one's true path.

*Ellis, D. B. *Creating Your Future: A Guide to Long-Range Visioning.* Rapid City, S.D.: Breakthrough Enterprises, 1997. A down-to-earth, practical guide to generating a future scenario.

Fanning, P. *Visualization for Change.* Oakland, Calif.: New Harbinger, 1994. Uses a visioning process to strengthen the immune system.

FM–2030. *Are You a Transhuman?* New York: Warner, 1989. Contains surveys to use for determining readiness to enter the coming decades.

Foster, S. *The Book of the Vision Quest: Personal Transformation in the Wilderness.* Covelo, Calif.: Island Press, 1980. A guide for ritualizing the turning points of life.

*Marks, L. *Living with Vision.* Indianapolis: Knowledge Systems, 1989. A usable book for generating powerful personal visions of the future.

Zdenek, M. *Inventing the Future: Advances in Imagery That Can Change Your Life.* New York: Two Roads, 1996.

Coaching for Corporate and Community Visions

Collins, J. C., and Porras, J. L. "Organizational Vision and Visionary Organizations." *California Management Review,* 1991, *34*(1).

James, J. *Thinking in the Future Tense: A Workout for the Mind.* New York: Touchstone, 1997. A comprehensive, upbeat, unique book on sustaining future-oriented thinking.

*Kennedy, P. *Preparing for the Twenty-First Century.* New York: Random House, 1993. Presents an informed opinion about the key ingredients for shaping global life in the twenty-first century.

Kiefer, C., and Stroh, P. "A Paradigm for Developing Organizations." In J. Adams (ed.), *Transforming Work.* Alexandria, Va.: Miles River, 1984.

Liebig, J. E. *Merchants of Vision: People Bringing New Purpose and Values to Business.* San Francisco: Berrett-Koehler, 1994. Stories of leaders with visions to improve business, to address social issues, to protect life's contexts, and to unleash creativity.

*Maynard, H. B., Jr., and Mehrtens, S. E. *The Fourth Wave: Business in the 21st Century.* San Francisco: Berrett-Koehler, 1996.

O'Toole, J. *Leading Change: Overcoming the Ideology of Comfort and the Tyranny of Custom.* San Francisco: Jossey-Bass, 1995. A philosophical triumph for the concept of value-based leadership.

Ridker, R. G., and Watson, W. D. *To Choose a Future.* Baltimore, Md.: Johns Hopkins, 1980. A social-economic exploration of future options for the United States.

*Weisbord, M. R., and Janoff, S. *Future Search: An Action Guide to Finding Common Ground in Organizations and Communities.* San Francisco: Berrett-Koehler, 1995. A natural application of the concept of visioning within corporate and community settings.

Developing Scenarios

Egan, G. *Exercises in Helping Skills: A Manual to Accompany the Skilled Helper.* Belmont, Calif.: Wadsworth, 1994.

*Egan, G. *The Skilled Helper: A Problem-management Approach to Helping.* (6th ed.) Pacific Grove, Calif.: Brooks/Cole, 1998. A good beginning point for developing scenarios.

McRae, H. *The World in 2020: Power, Culture and Prosperity.* Cambridge, Mass.: Harvard Business School Press, 1994.

*Schwartz, P. *The Art of the Long View: Planning for the Future in an Uncertain World.* New York: Doubleday, 1996. An original treatise on scenario building.

Planning

Ellis, D. B. *Creating Your Future: A Guide to Long-Range Visioning.* Rapid City, S.D.: Breakthrough Enterprises, 1997. A down-to-earth, practical guide to generating a future scenario.

*Hagberg, J., and Leider, R. *The Inventurers: Excursions in Life and Career Renewal.* (3rd ed.) Reading, Mass.: Addison-Wesley, 1988.

Lakein, A. *How to Get Control of Your Time and Your Life.* New York: New American Library, 1996. One of the early time-management books.

*Morrisey, G. L. *Creating Your Future: Personal Strategic Planning for Professionals.* San Francisco: Berrett-Koehler, 1992. A clear and thorough guide to planning.

*Morrisey, G. L. *Morrisey on Planning: A Guide to Strategic Thinking, Building Your Planning Foundation.* San Francisco: Jossey-Bass, 1996. A sound planning guide that teaches "strategic thinking" as a skill set.

 CHAPTER TEN 

The Adult Learning Agenda

Continuous learning is the secret weapon of adult empowerment in our age of constant change. This is true, no matter which part of adulthood a person is in. Unfortunately, few use it to full advantage. It is all too easy to lock oneself into the assumptions born of youthful schooling as the world spins on with new paradigms and technologies. It is just as easy to lose the learning edge in a mellowed-out midlife, leaving leadership to others.

Adults at any age—even twenty- and thirtysomethings—who fail to keep up with the global acceleration of learning are at risk. Younger adults miss opportunities; older adults take on stereotypical "old" behaviors—they seem over the hill, passive, resigned. But adults who keep pushing into new learning of any type are questioning, imaginative, daring. Continuous learning keeps a person vital, awake, and forward-looking. As America becomes a grayer culture, it must also become a continuous learning society if it wants to remain a leader among nations.

People in their twenties haven't yet launched their first life chapter. Many are busy going to school to get ready for the great adventure ahead—the grown-up years: earning degrees, getting work experience, learning to manage in many settings, becoming experts in something. Many imagine settling down after all this for the long haul.

Those who are now older adults remember that early period well; training for their first adult life chapter took more than twenty years. When they launched their first dreams, they may have lacked experience but they didn't lack careful preparation and powerful determination. During the rest of their lives, they gained lots of experience but probably never again had such intense learning preparation. They now must invent whatever learning they need if they are to sustain the great adventure of adulthood. (See Basic Library: Adult Personal and Professional Learning.)

HOW COACHES FACILITATE ADULT LEARNING

How do coaches engage clients who want to learn more about themselves, their potentials, and their optimal choices for the years ahead? First, coaches should have profound relationships with clients. Adult learning is visceral, holistic, and experiential. Coaches must experience the reality of their clients, face to face, to evolve a learning agenda that is challenging, engaging, and focused. Malcolm Knowles, a leader of adult learning in the past forty years, would have us begin with a learning contract that the client proposes in the form of new competencies desired. Then, through dialogue with the client, a coach explores ways to connect the resources that are available to the client—anywhere in the world. Adult learning is not the same as adult schooling, although entering formal learning in adult education institutions is one way to proceed. Adults learn experientially, and this involves all the parts of the person: values, developmental issues, career development, relationships, social concerns, and dreams for the future. When clients experience what they want to learn more about, they begin reflecting on it, and then they seek out information in the form of existing knowledge. They look for learning environments, experts, mentors, libraries, and computer resources. Finally, they look for skills or actions to apply the knowledge to their lives and commitments. That's the process a coach guides.

Most coaching for adult learning is conducted informally with a client, giving full consideration to any learning source that would best serve the learning goals of the client. A few potential coaching topics include traveling, volunteering, using the Internet, getting involved in social causes, finding internships, getting started in a hobby, creating a business, and dealing with a degenerative disease.

Sometimes it is possible to have a group of clients engage in learning projects so they can benefit from each other's explorations, discoveries, and new competencies. It is very exciting to have a client who is committed to being responsible for his or her own learning and learning outcomes. Part of the coach's responsibility is to facilitate and process those learning outcomes in the form of competencies, as outlined in the learning contract. Adult learning is much more than training for a new career or obtaining technical skill. At its best, adult learning lights a fire within the learner, and that fire translates into motivation, self-esteem, self-responsibility, growth, and achievement.

QUESTIONS FOR COACHES: A CLIENT'S LEARNING AGENDA

Coaches should ask themselves these questions about a client who seems ready to undertake a new learning agenda:

- What does my client need to unlearn, and how can I help build this agenda into the follow-up plan? What must she unlearn if she is to master the future she truly wants? What patterns of thinking that served her well earlier in life are now in the way of what she really wants to do and become?
- What new information does my client need to learn, and how can I help build this agenda into a follow-up plan? What new information and knowledge does he need in order to be at his best? What new information and knowledge can be legitimately avoided to prevent overload and to facilitate focusing?
- How can I facilitate increased personal competence with my client, and how can I help build this agenda into the follow-up plan?
- What new technical skills does my client need, and how can I help build this agenda into the follow-up plan?
- How can my client deepen his or her awareness and adherence to core values in all that he or she does?
- How can I help my client find the best learning environments for the next chapter of life?
- How can I help my client identify the best teachers and mentors for this learning agenda?
- What can I do to enable my client to network successfully?
- Does my client have an adequate support group for launching the next chapter of life? If not, where can that support be found?

QUESTIONS FOR CLIENTS: CONSTRUCTING A LEARNING AGENDA

To begin discussion of a learning program with clients, a coach should ask, in one way or another, the following eight questions. By answering the questions, clients can begin constructing their own learning agenda: (1) What do I need to unlearn? (2) What new information do I need? (3) How do I increase my personal competence? (4) What new technical skills do I need? (5) How can I deepen and clarify my own values? (6) Where are my best learning environments? (7) Who are my real teachers and mentors? (8) How will I execute and evaluate my current learning program?

Because abundant learning resources are available, not only through recognized educational institutions but through informal learning groups and the Internet, it is possible for all adults to be committed to a continuous learning agenda that evolves and changes throughout the adult life cycle.

TYPES OF ADULT LEARNING

The essence of adult learning, for all ages, is contracting for learning outcomes; adults must propose their own learning objectives, find the best learning resources and environments, and initiate their own learning agenda. The two basic types of lifelong learning are (1) enriching and updating the learning a person already has and (2) returning to square one to begin again, in some radical way—to start over with a career, life direction, or relationship.

In our kind of world we have to keep up in the areas of our special concerns, and we have to filter out media, passive uses of time, and the noises of the world that have little to do with the paths we are on.

WHERE ADULTS LEARN

The whole global village is an adult's campus. We can choose our own learning environments and formats—seminars, mentors, conferences, books, study groups, certification programs, advanced degrees, and ways to get connected. There is no paucity of adult learning opportunities near and far.

Adults do not want to sit at the feet of mere knowledge experts; we want to learn from masters of our fields—persons who have applied the knowledge they are espousing to themselves and their professions. That is why so many conventional college professors do not appeal to midlife adults as appropriate teachers. The new adult teacher is a mentor, mensch, or master—someone who lives and breathes what the learner wants to learn. Many such experts are available around the world today. Each of us has to find them and hire them. We may not find them at conventional learning institutions, although some can be found there, too.

 BASIC LIBRARY FOR COACHES

Adult Personal and Professional Learning

Astin, A. W. *Four Critical Years.* San Francisco: Jossey-Bass, 1977. An ingenious and original study of the effects of different kinds of schools on the development of eighteen- to twenty-five-year-olds, ending up to be a defense of liberal arts schools.

*Brookfield, S. D. (ed.) *Self-Directed Learning: From Theory to Practice.* New Directions for Adult and Continuing Education, no. 25. San Francisco: Jossey-Bass, 1985. Excellent chapters on how to conduct self-directed learning.

*Brookfield, S. D. *Understanding and Facilitating Adult Learning.* San Francisco: Jossey-Bass, 1986. An outstanding review of the literature on adult learning.

*Brookfield, S. D. *Developing Critical Thinkers: Challenging Adults to Explore Alternative Ways of Thinking and Acting.* San Francisco: Jossey-Bass, 1987. The best book available for training clients to be more reflective and thereby more effective and innovative in every aspect of life and work.

Career Planning and Adult Development Journal, a publication of Career Planning and Adult Development Network, 4965 Sierra Road, San Jose, CA 95132. 408-559-4946. A journal devoted to applications of career theories.

*Chickering, A. W. *Education and Identity.* San Francisco: Jossey-Bass, 1969. A classic treatise on the learning needs of adults of all ages and the environments that best serve their learning.

Cross, K. P. *Adults as Learners: Increasing Participation and Facilitating Learning.* San Francisco: Jossey-Bass, 1981. Presents the foundations for understanding the adult learning process and institutional needs.

Freire, P. *Pedagogy of the Oppressed.* New York: Herder and Herder, 1972. A bold attack on traditional learning, along with a design for how to bring learning to the oppressed.

Freire, P. *Pedagogy in Process.* New York: Seabury Press, 1978. A prophetic book on designing learning systems outside of structures of formal education.

Gross, R. *The Lifelong Learner.* New York: Simon and Schuster, 1977. Talks about the adult learning agenda and how adults learn primarily through the invisible university—ad hoc, protean learning opportunities.

Houle, C. O. *The External Degree.* San Francisco: Jossey-Bass, 1973. Discusses external learning systems that offer nonresidential learning through computer, video, telephone, conferencing, and other means other than classrooms.

Houle, C. O. *Patterns of Learning.* San Francisco: Jossey-Bass, 1984. An examination of the learning patterns of notable leaders, including Thoreau, Montaigne, and Billy Graham.

Illich, I. *Celebration of Awareness.* New York: Doubleday, 1969.

Illich, I. *Deschooling Society.* New York: Harper & Row, 1970. A radical book on the difference between learning and schooling-teaching.

Illich, I. *Tools for Conviviality.* New York: Harper & Row, 1973. Suggests specific ways people can engage in real learning, for the celebration of life.

John, D. W., and Johnson, R. T. *Learning Together and Alone: Cooperative, Competitive, and Individualistic Learning.* (4th ed.). Boston: Allyn & Bacon, 1994.

John-Steiner, V. *Notebooks of the Mind: Explorations of Thinking.* Albuquerque: University of New Mexico Press, 1986.

Keeton, M. T., and Associates. *Experiential Learning.* San Francisco: Jossey-Bass, 1976. Book of readings by one of the major voices in the field of experiential learning, an area of strategic importance to coaches.

Kline, P., and Saunders, B. *Ten Steps to a Learning Organization.* Arlington, Va.: Great Ocean, 1993. A simple, practical, down-to-earth book on creating learning organizations.

Knowles, M. *The Modern Practice of Adult Education—Andragogy versus Pedagogy.* New York: Association Press, 1977. Argues that adults learn differently from children and need experiential learning laboratories, learning contracts, and facilitators for leaders; shows how to establish such a practice.

*Knowles, M. *The Adult Learner: A Neglected Species.* (2nd ed.) Houston, Tex.: Gulf, 1978. Knowles's theory of andragogy is explained here, including a model of lifelong education.

Knowles, M. *Using Learning Contracts.* San Francisco: Jossey-Bass, 1986. A basic text for understanding how to contract for learning outcomes.

Knowles, M. S., and Associates. *Andragogy in Action.* San Francisco: Jossey-Bass, 1984. Stories of successful applications of contract learning and discussions of self-directed learning principles.

Menson, B. *Building on Experiences in Adult Development.* San Francisco: Jossey-Bass, 1982. A little-known book of applied developmental strategies for higher education.

Patton, C. V. *Academia in Transition: Mid-Career Change or Early Retirement?* Cambridge, Mass.: Abi, 1979.

*Peterson, D. A. *Facilitating Education for Older Learners.* San Francisco: Jossey-Bass, 1983. About the needs of elders for learning, touching on retraining for extended employment, retirement preparation, and implementing effective educational programs.

Phenix, P. H. *Education and the Common Good: A Moral Philosophy of the Curriculum.* New York: Harper & Row, 1961. A concise description of the knowledge and values that people need to be joyous, effective, self-responsible, and socially valid.

*Sanford, N. *Learning After College.* Orinda, Calif.: Montaigne, Inc, 1979. A discourse on personality development after college, with an emphasis on action research and moral development.

*Senge, P. *The Fifth Discipline: The Art and Practice of the Learning Organization.* New York: Doubleday, 1990. A summary of Senge's concepts about the importance of learning as a central commitment in all of today's organizations (workbook available).

Smith, R. M. (ed.). *Helping Adults Learn How to Learn.* San Francisco: Jossey-Bass, 1983.

*Smith, R. M., and Associates. *Learning to Learn Across the Life Span.* San Francisco: Jossey-Bass, 1990. A thorough investigation by leading scholars on how people learn and how learning organizations can deliver learning programs across the life cycle in diverse ways.

Sork, T. J. *Designing and Implementing Effective Workshops.* San Francisco: Jossey-Bass, 1984. A practical book on how to create participatory, task-oriented learning environments through workshops.

*Thomas, A. M. *Beyond Education: A New Perspective on Society's Management of Learning.* San Francisco: Jossey-Bass, 1991. Examines when and why learning takes place throughout society and how creative people can supplement learning beyond the limits of formal education.

Tough, A. *Intentional Changes.* Chicago: Follett, 1982. An original approach to change, based on how to manage optimal choices.

*Vaill, P. B. *Learning as a Way of Being: Strategies for Survival in a World of Permanent White Water.* San Francisco: Jossey-Bass, 1996. A unique book on learning, in that it stresses the integration of learning into the being of the learner.

Van Aalst, F. D. (ed.). *Combining Career Development with Experiential Learning.* San Francisco: Jossey-Bass, 1979. Essays on ways to combine deep, experiential learning with career improvement.

Walter, G. A., and Marks, S. E. *Experiential Learning and Change.* New York: Wiley, 1981. Theory and application of adult learning principles.

PART FOUR

COACHING FOR MASTERY OF THE ADULT YEARS

CHAPTER ELEVEN 

Coaching Throughout the Adult Life Cycle

Young Adults

Most adults—even younger adults just starting out on their life journey—try to walk backward through time, studying ways in which they aren't who they used to be. They seldom try to make sense of the long-distance journey they are, in fact, taking. They imagine their lives staying about the way they have been, possibly with declines in old age. The truth is that we change throughout our years, and every change has trade-offs—advantages and disadvantages.

Coaches help clients look for both advantages and disadvantages in the changes that accompany the developmental aging process. Specifically, coaches watch for

- Emerging strengths and deficits of life throughout the adult life cycle
- The importance of nutrition, exercise, and financial planning
- The importance of social engagement, goals, friendships, and family
- The importance of social caring

Coaches can help demystify the cultural myth that getting older is a steady decline by presenting a growth model (human development) of the life cycle. Clients can then envision themselves growing into their fullness as they mature. Coaches should get specific data on the upper range of possibilities of persons in their fifties, sixties, seventies, eighties, and nineties and help clients anticipate options for making vital connections between their present and future plans.

The greatest dilemma in the lives of many adults is that they lose sight of legitimate expectations and fantastic possibilities for the years ahead. Time left is all we ever have, so coaches should learn to help clients lean into the wind, with their sails set and their hand on the rudder. Most adults have considerable flexibility in how they choose to design their lives and chart their ways through the life cycle. If they know approximately what to expect as they mature, they can plan ahead and enjoy the journey. (See Basic Library: Overviews of Adult Life.)

LONGEVITY COACHING

Longevity means to stay engaged with life, to take responsibility for designing the futures we want, to stay vitally connected to friends and loved ones and to society at large. A coach might help clients make the most important decision of all: the decision to change and become responsible for his or her own future.

Coaching for longevity can take place at any time. Features of this approach to coaching include facilitating more inner-driven behaviors and helping clients find ease with which to enjoy many things. The focus should be on the here and now rather than yesterday or tomorrow. Clients can be comforted with training in both assertiveness and compromise.

Clients often seek to broaden and deepen their expressions of intimacy or caring—to be close and affectionate with more people in appropriate ways. Friendships increase in importance; coaches can facilitate the building of connections.

A good suggestion coaches can propose to younger adult clients is to *join the 100 plan.* Tell clients that the sooner they commit to living to one hundred, the sooner they commit to having a vision and a plan for the rest of their life. The concept of longevity is something to be practiced during young and middle adulthood, so bodies and minds are prepared for the full journey of the normal life cycle. Not everyone who aims at one hundred will get there, but more and more people will, and the statistics point toward a marked increase in numbers of centenarians in the next century. Clients can assume that the odds are in their favor and seek to make that a self-fulfilling prophecy. Coaches should help clients of all ages look for both advantages and disadvantages in the changes that accompany developmental aging.

TIPS FOR CLIENTS OF ALL AGES

The following tips of a general nature can be helpful for clients of all ages. (Note that I'm calling these tips rather than pieces of advice!)

- Read, read, read. In our technical age, reading remains the number-one highway into the further reaches of the mind.
- Use your time management skills on your personal life, so you control the intrusions of television, radio, and consumerism. Make your reading schedule of newspapers, magazines, books of all sorts, professional journals, and computer-based materials the steady core of your learning agenda. If at all possible, join reading groups so you can discuss new ideas with others.
- Go to intensive seminars and workshops—not the one-day entertainment varieties but the three- to five-day group learning formats that engage you profoundly in basic learning.
- Travel alone, climb a mountain, take an adventure, conduct a vision quest, or join an adult education class in some new but intriguing subject. Jolt your routines to discover the ones that connect you better to the future.
- Sign up for an advanced certification or degree program. A large number of advanced learning programs for adults of all ages now exist; they can provide a rite of passage from one life chapter to another. These programs often provide not only intensive learning opportunities but the discovery of friends, networking contacts, and personal or professional renewal.
- Consider psychotherapy, if appropriate. It often performs the function of teaching personal life skills and can help you get anchored in your true abilities and values.
- Discover churches, adult education, and other community organizations that have learning programs, trips, and training for learning basic life skills. Some adults discover these skills through short-term commitments through volunteer service roles in the community or working with the Peace Corps or any of the many worldwide service organizations.
- Ask your boss and work friends for ways to pursue professional skills in your career field.
- Take advantage of the ongoing training and credentialing programs of the professional organizations in your specialized area.
- Join a computer network group working on cutting-edge issues in your field.
- Create a weekly or monthly meeting of "experts" like yourself from various companies in your geographic area to provide each other with updates and learning challenges.

COACHING YOUNG ADULTS

Some coaching tasks when working with young adults are to

- Help them develop a sense of self, or adult identity, with consistent behavioral patterns in intimate relationships, work settings, and social interactions.

- Help them learn to foster and sustain intimacy with peer friendships and in love or sexual relationships.
- Offer career coaching so they develop a work identity congruent with their personality and life goals.
- Mentor the basic human life skills, such as acquiring and managing money, managing time, sustaining personal hygiene, and maintaining leisure activities.

Possible coaching goals for people in this age group include searching for a college-client fit, finding meaningful work, avoiding alcoholism and other addictions, following dreams, experimenting with healthy relationships, planning adventure-leisure trips, taking up new sports activities, redefining relationships to parents and family of origin, and finding mentoring roles with younger children through community service.

COACHING ADULTS IN THEIR TWENTIES

People in their twenties are *staking out the adult world.* The first chapter of adult life begins to happen when adolescents leave their family of origin and begin to care for themselves. This is an experimental period lasting from late adolescence until about age twenty-eight; young people try on adulthood as if it were an infinite wardrobe of possibilities. They live out the expectations others had for their lives, particularly those of parents, siblings, teachers, peers, and childhood heroes. Twentysomethings also live out rebellion against those very expectations. They are sensitive to peer opinions and tend to be other-directed, not inner-directed. Twentysomethings attach themselves, tentatively, to their relationships, jobs, and other commitments. But they also have a propensity to get unattached when they feel like it and look at life as an experiment they are not fully within. (See Basic Library: Twentysomethings.)

COACHING ADULTS IN THEIR THIRTIES

Most adults spend their thirties trying to make it, to become full-fledged citizens of the adult world. This is the time for shaping careers toward successful plateaus, settling down into long-term intimate relationships, having babies, buying things, and eliciting a chorus of approval. This is a big decade for acquisitions: a home, furnishings, cars, investments, marriage, children, friends, adult toys, and equipment for leisure and recreation. The thirties is often the most exhausting decade in the life cycle.

This is a major adult period of high expectations and role demands, based largely on blueprints obtained from parents, peers, mentors, and society itself.

Thirtysomethings are often programmed and managed by a "committee in their head," implanted in their twenties or earlier. The committee gives a lot of commands: "hurry up," "don't do that," "lose weight," and "you should be further along toward success than you are."

Thirtysomethings are likely to view this decade as the last time period for reaching their major goals. They are racing against time, believing that "forty" is a metaphor for "as old as I can ever imagine myself in ascendancy." Their lives have both a sense of urgency and a sense of limitless time if something goes awry. They are driven by intense internal pressures to arrive at plateaued levels of success, recognition, and happiness—as if such plateaus existed.

Thirtysomethings usually find considerable gender diversity that they did not feel in their twenties. This is when career men and women typically over-identify with their jobs and careers. At the same time, many women find it difficult to balance all the life roles they feel they "should" have, including careers or work, household, mothering, and managing relationships. A woman's life often gets shaped more and more by activities and friends.

A coach can help clients avoid the excesses and pitfalls of the thirties by helping and encouraging clients to

- Increase their personal autonomy by developing self-confidence and self-esteem; stay connected to favorite activities; nurture themselves
- Deepen primary love relationships; grow marriage or intimate connections; spend quality time with children and friends
- Develop job or career paths; evaluate ways to enrich the meaning and rewards of work; consider the advantages and disadvantages of changing jobs; seek ways to use prized abilities while getting a funding mechanism for life
- Work on a financial plan; seek out a financial planner whom they can pay by the hour for services without having to buy specific forms of investments
- Examine the importance of friendships and leisure life

To reach their many goals, thirtysomething clients may have to postpone many aspects of personal development. A coach can help them get perspective on the many years ahead so they can enjoy the years they are in. (See Basic Library: Thirtysomethings.)

COACHING EARLY BLOOMERS AND LATE PEAKERS

Two patterns of development vary considerably from the life cycle flow described thus far: early bloomers and late peakers. In today's world—mostly thanks to the mass media—there are significant numbers of adults in each category.

Early bloomers are people who reach their peak during the early adult years. For example, actors, athletes, and people who inherit money might experience early success. Typically, early bloomers try to hold on to their fame and glory and have great difficulty managing transitions into the rest of their lives. Their ego becomes fused with their success, and when decline sets in, they feel their lives, along with their roles, fading into oblivion.

Early bloomers are often very dependent on recognition and approval from others, and when they can't command that, their behavior may deteriorate and even become dysfunctional. Even if they do make a transition into a new career, if their primary recognition in life is behind them rather than ahead, they often live as shadows of themselves. What they need is an understanding of life transitions and ways to let go of what they can no longer be so they can take on new purpose and direction.

The late peaker is typically someone who has struggled throughout life with low self-esteem and relatively low social performance, particularly in work settings. But at some time after the age of thirty-five, the person is propelled by internal and external forces into high-powered roles. Examples are politicians, entrepreneurs, and many women. Late peakers often have poise and style, as well as enough energy and commitment for winning. But linear social customs—careers, seniority in jobs, professions requiring credentialing or licensing—make it difficult for late peakers to reach the top. Fields that measure success by competency and performance attract these people. Ageism in the workplace and in society at large discourages late peakers from high leadership positions, but this is breaking down as many people who follow mainstream development also recycle themselves through many role identities and join the cadre of late peakers.

 BASIC LIBRARY FOR COACHES

Overviews of Adult Life

Arking, R. *Biology of Aging: Observations and Principles.* New York: Sinauer Associates, 1998.

Booth, W. (ed.). *The Art of Growing Older: Writers on Living and Aging.* Chicago: University of Chicago Press, 1996. Three hundred pages of poems and readings from throughout the ages.

*Colarusso, C. A., and Nemiroff, R. A. *Adult Development: A New Dimension in Psychodynamic Theory and Practice.* New York: Plenum, 1981. One of the best introductory texts on the adult years; well informed by psychoanalytic theories.

*Neugarten, D. A. (ed.). *The Meanings of Age: Selected Papers of Bernice L. Neugarten.* Chicago: University of Chicago Press, 1996. A reliable reference guide for coaches in the area of adult life.

*Rowe, J. W., and Kahn, R. L. *Successful Aging.* New York: Pantheon, 1998. Current information on promoting learning and development throughout the aging process.

Schuster, C. S., and Ashburn, S. S. *The Process of Human Development: A Holistic Approach.* New York: Lippincott-Raven, 1992. One of the most complete texts available on all age groups.

*Sze, W. C. *Human Life Cycle.* New York: Jason Aronson, 1975. A superb collection of readings on many topics.

Longevity Coaching

Adler, L. P. *Centenarians: The Bonus Years.* Santa Fe, N.M.: Health Press, 1995. One of the few books available describing healthy, active people over the age of one hundred.

Alexander, C. N., and Langer, E. J. (eds.). *Higher Stages of Human Development.* New York: Oxford University Press, 1990.

*Atchley, R. C. "Family, Friends, and Social Support." In *Social Forces and Aging.* Belmont, Calif.: Wadsworth, 1991.

Ausman, L. M., and Russell, R. M. "Nutrition in Aging." In *Handbook of the Biology of Aging.* (3rd ed.) San Diego, Calif.: Academic Press, 1990.

Baltes, P. B. "The Aging Mind: Potential and Limits." *Gerontologist,* 1993, *33,* 580–594. Summary of the ideas of a leading expert on this subject.

Baltes, P. B., and Baltes, M. M. "Psychological Perspectives on Successful Aging: The Model of Selective Optimization with Compensation." In P. B. Baltes and M. M. Baltes (eds.), *Successful Aging: Perspectives from the Behavioral Sciences.* Cambridge, England: Cambridge University Press, 1993.

*Baltes, P. B., and Baltes, M. M. (eds.). *Successful Aging: Perspectives from the Behavioral Sciences.* Cambridge, England: Cambridge University Press, 1993.

Baltes, P. B., and Smith, J. "Toward a Psychology of Wisdom and Its Ontogenesis." In R. J. Sternberg (ed.), *Wisdom: Its Nature, Origins, and Development.* Cambridge, England: Cambridge University Press, 1990.

Baltes, P. B., Smith, J., and Staudinger, U. M. "Wisdom and Successful Aging." In T. B. Sonderegger (ed.), *Nebraska Symposium on Motivation, 1991.* Lincoln: University of Nebraska Press, 1992.

Barusch, A. S. *Older Women in Poverty: Private Lives and Public Policies.* New York: Springer, 1994.

Bass, S. A. (ed.). *Older and Active: How Americans Over Age 55 Are Contributing to Society.* New Haven, Conn.: Yale University Press, 1995.

Bass, S. A., Caro, F. G., and Chen, Y.-P. (eds.). *Achieving a Productive Aging Society.* Westport, Conn.: Auburn House, 1993.

Bassuk, E. L. "Homelessness: A Growing American Tragedy." *Division of Child, Youth, and Family Services Newsletter,* 1989, *12,* 1–13.

Bayley, N., and Oden, M. "The Maintenance of Intellectual Ability in Gifted Adults." *Journal of Gerontology,* 1955, *10*(1), 91–107.

Beard, B. B. *Centenarians: The New Generation.* Westport, Conn.: Greenwood Press, 1991.

Bedford, V. H. "Sibling Relationships in Middle and Old Age." In R. Blieszner and V. H. Bedford (eds.), *Handbook of Aging and the Family.* Hillsdale, N.J.: Greenwood Press, 1995.

Beizer, J. L. "Medications and the Aging Body: Alteration as a Function of Age." *Generations,* 1994, *18,* 13–18.

Bengtson, V. L., Rosenthal, C., and Burton, L. M. "Paradoxes of Families and Aging." In J. E. Birren and K. W. Schaie (eds.), *Handbook of Aging and the Social Sciences.* San Diego, Calif.: Academic Press, 1996.

*Bengtson, V. L., and Schaie, K. W. (eds.). *The Course of Later Life.* New York: Springer, 1989.

Bengtson, V. L., Schaie, K. W., and Burton, L. M. (eds.). *Adult Intergenerational Relations: Effects of Societal Change.* New York: Springer, 1995.

Benoit, D., and Parker, K. C. "Stability and Transmission of Attachment Across Three Generations." *Child Development,* 1994, *65,* 1444–1456.

Berg, C. A., and Sternberg, R. J. "A Triarchic Theory of Intellectual Development During Adulthood." *Developmental Review,* 1985, *5,* 334–370.

*Berg, R. L., and Cassells, J. E. *The Second Fitfy Years: Promoting Health and Preventing Disability.* Washington, D.C.: National Academy Press, 1992.

*Bianchi, E. C. *Aging as a Spiritual Journey.* New York: Crossroad, 1987.

Binstock, R. H., and George, L. K. (eds.). *Handbook of Aging and the Social Sciences.* (2nd ed.) New York: Van Nostrand Reinhold, 1996.

Binstock, R. H., Post, S. G., and Whitehouse, P. J. (eds.). *Dementia and Aging: Ethics, Values, and Policy Choices.* Baltimore, Md.: Johns Hopkins University Press, 1992.

*Birren, J. E., and Schaie, K. W. (eds.). *Handbook of the Psychology of Aging.* (3rd ed.) San Diego, Calif.: Academic Press, 1996.

*Birren, J. E., and Sloane, R. B. (eds.). *Handbook of Mental Health and Aging.* (3rd ed.) Englewood Cliffs, N.J.: Prentice Hall, 1992. A priceless reference book on the aging process and current thinking in geriatric practices.

Booth, W. (ed.). *The Art of Growing Older: Writers on Living and Aging.* Chicago: University of Chicago Press, 1996.

Bornstein, M. H., and Lamb, M. E. (eds.). *Developmental Psychology: An Advanced Textbook.* Hillsdale, N.J.: Erlbaum, 1992.

Brandtstadter, J., and Greve, W. "The Aging Self: Stabilizing and Protective Processes." *Developmental Review,* 1994, *14,* 52–80.

Brubaker, T. H. *Later Life Families.* Newbury Park, Calif.: Sage, 1985.

Brubaker, T. H. (ed.). *Family Relationships in Later Life.* Newbury Park, Calif.: Sage, 1993. Essays on intra-family relationships, the effects of various social issues, and the evolution of social policy.

Busse, E. W. "Normal Aging: The Duke Longitudinal Studies." In M. Bergener, M. Ermini, and H. B. Stahelin (eds.), *Thresholds in Aging.* London: Academic Press, 1985.

Busse, E. W., and Pfeiffer, E. *Behavior and Adaptation in Late Life.* (2nd ed.) Boston: Little, Brown, 1977.

Butler, R. N., and Brody, J. A. (eds.). *Delaying the Onset of Later-Life Dysfunction.* New York: Springer, 1995.

Canetto, S. S. "Gender and Suicide in the Elderly." *Suicide and Life-Threatening Behavior,* 1992, *22,* 88–96.

*Cherlin, A., and Furstenberg, F. F., Jr. *The New American Grandparent: A Place in the Family, a Life Apart.* Harvard University Press, 1992.

Coke, M. M., and Twaite, J. A. *The Black Elderly: Satisfaction and Quality of Later Life.* New York: Hayworth Press, 1995.

*Cole, T. R., and Gadow, S. A. (eds.). *What Does It Mean to Grow Old?* Durham, N.C.: Duke University Press, 1987.

Cole, T. R., and Winkler, M. G. *The Oxford Book of Aging: Reflections on the Journey of Life.* New York: Oxford, 1994.

Crimmins, E. M., and Ingegneri, D. G. "Interaction and Living Arrangements of Older Parents and their Children: Past Trends, Present Determinants, Future Implications." *Research on Aging,* 1990, *2,* 3–35.

Datan, N., Greene, A., and Reese, H. W. (eds.). *Life-span Developmental Psychology: Intergenerational Relations.* Hillsdale, N.J.: Erlbaum, 1986.

Dixon, R. A., and Baltes, P. B. "Toward Life-span Research on the Functions and Pragmatics of Intelligence." In R. J. Sternberg and R. K. Wagner (eds.), *Practical Intelligence.* Cambridge, England: Cambridge University Press, 1986.

Dixon, R. A., Kramer, D. A., and Baltes, P. B. "Intelligence: A Life-Span Developmental Perspective." In B. B. Wolman (ed.), *Handbook of Intelligence: Theories, Measurements, and Applications.* New York: Wiley, 1985.

Dreher, G., and Ash, R. "A Comparative Study of Mentoring Among Men and Women in Managerial, Professional and Technical Positions." *Journal of Applied Psychology,* 1990, *75,* 525–535.

*Dychtwald, K. *Age Wave: The Challenges and Opportunities of an Aging*

America. Los Angeles: Tarcher, 1989. A popular overview of the population shift from young to old.

Edelman, M. W. *The Measure of Our Success.* Boston: Beacon, 1992.

Edwards, A. J. *Dementia.* New York: Plenum, 1993.

Egeland, B., Carlson, E., and Sroufe, L. A. "Resilience as Process." *Development and Psychopathology,* 1993, *5,* 517–528.

Elderhostel: United States Catalog. Summer, 1998. Boston: Elderhostel, Inc.

Ericsson, K. A. "Peak Performance and Age: An Examination of Peak Performance in Sports." In P. B. Baltes and M. M. Baltes (eds.), *Successful Aging: Perspectives from the Behavioral Sciences.* Cambridge, England: Cambridge University Press, 1990.

Erikson, E. H., Erikson, J. M., and Kivnick, H. Q. *Vital Involvement in Old Age.* New York: Norton, 1986.

Field, T. M., McCabe, P. M., and Schneiderman, N. (eds.). *Stress and Coping Across Development.* Hillsdale, N.J.: Erlbaum, 1988.

Fingerman, K. L. "Sources of Tension in the Aging Mother and Adult Daughter Relationship." *Psychology and Aging,* 1996, *11,* 591–606.

Fozard, J. L. "Vision and Hearing in Aging." In J. E. Birren and K. W. Schaie (eds.), *Handbook of the Psychology of Aging.* (3rd ed.) San Diego, Calif.: Academic Press, 1990.

*Friedan, B. *The Fountain of Age.* New York: Simon and Schuster, 1993. An informed introduction to the themes of aging and development.

Friedman, H. S., Hawley, P. H., and Tucker, J. S. "Personality, Health, and Longevity." *Current Directions in Psychological Science,* 1994, *3,* 37–41.

Fries, J. F. *Living Well: Taking Care of Your Health in the Middle and Later Years.* Reading, Mass.: Addison-Wesley, 1994.

Funder, D. C., Parke, R. D., Tomlinson-Keasy, C., and Widaman, K. (eds.), *Studying Lives Through Time.* Washington, D.C.: American Psychological Association, 1997.

Glendenning, F. "Education for Older Adults: Lifelong Learning, Empowerment, and Social Change." In J. F. Nussbaum and J. Coupland (eds.), *Handbook of Communication and Aging Research.* Mahway, N.J.: Erlbaum, 1995.

Goetting, A. "The Developmental Tasks of Siblingship Over the Life Cycle." *Journal of Marriage and the Family,* 1986, *48,* 737–747.

Goldman, C. "Late Bloomers: Growing Older or Still Growing?" *Generations,* 1991, *15,* 41–44.

Goodman, N. C. "Girls with Learning Disabilities and Their Sisters: How are

They Faring in Adulthood?" *Journal of Clinical Child Psychology,* 1987, *16,* 290–300.

Gordon, G. K., and Stryker, R. *Creative Long-term Care Administration.* Springfield, Ill.: Thomas, 1994.

Gratton, B., and Haber, C. "Three Phases in the History of American Grandparents: Authority, Burden, Companion." *Generations,* 1966, *20,* 7–12.

Guralnik, J. M., and Simonsick, E. M. "Physical Disability in Older Americans." (Special issue). *Journal of Gerontology,* 1993, *48,* 3–10.

Hawkins, H. L., Kramer, A. F., and Capaldi, D. "Aging, Exercise, and Attention." *Psychology and Aging,* 1992, *7,* 643–653.

Hayflick, L. "Origins of Longevity." *Aging,* 1987, *31,* 21–34.

*Hayflick, L. *How and Why We Age.* New York: Ballantine, 1996. Accurate information about the aging process provided by a gerontologist, who dispels many myths and cultural rumors.

Hayward, M. D. "Race Inequities in Men's Retirement." *Journal of Gerontology,* 1996, *51B,* S1–S10.

Hayward, M. D., and Hardy, M. A. "Early Retirement Processes Among Older Men: Occupational Differences." *Research on Aging,* 1985, *7,* 491–518.

*Heikkinen, E., Kuusinen, J., and Ruoppila, I. (eds.). *Preparation for Aging.* New York: Plenum Press, 1995.

*Heilbrun, C. G. *The Last Gift of Time: Life Beyond 60.* New York: Dial, 1997. An original approach to prizing elderhood.

Herzog, A. R., and House, J. S. "Productive Activities and Aging Well." *Generations,* 1991, *15*(1), 49–54.

Herzog, A. R., House, J. S., and Morgan, J. N. "Relation of Work and Retirement to Health and Well-being in Older Age." *Psychology and Aging,* 1991, *6,* 202–211.

*Hess, B. B., and Markson, E. W. *Growing Old in America.* (4th ed.) New Brunswick, N.J.: Transaction, 1995.

Heston, L. L., and White, J. A. *The Vanishing Mind. A Practical Guide to Alzheimer's Disease and Other Dementias.* New York: Freeman, 1991. A leading reference book on this topic.

Hill, R. D., Storandt, M., and Malley, M. "The Impact of Long-term Exercise Training on Psychological Function in Older Adults." *Journal of Gerontology: Psychological Sciences,* 1993, *48,* 12–17.

Hodgson, J. L., and Buskirk, E. R. "The Role of Exercise in Aging." In D. Danon, N. W. Schock, and M. Marios (eds.), *Aging: A Challenge to Science and Society.* London: Oxford University Press, 1981.

Holliday, R. *Understanding Aging.* Cambridge, England: Cambridge University Press, 1995.

Holmes, E. R., and Holmes, L. D. *Other Cultures, Elder Years.* Newbury Park, Calif.: Sage, 1995.

Horn, J. L., and Hofer, S. M. "Major Abilities and Development in the Adult Period." In R. J. Sternberg and C. A. Berg (eds.), *Intellectual Development.* New York: Cambridge University Press, 1992.

Horwitz, A., Macfadyen, D. M., Nunro, H., Scrimshaw, N. S., Steen, B., and Williams, T. F. (eds.). *Nutrition in the Elderly.* Oxford, England: Oxford University Press, 1989.

Howe, N. "Why the Graying of the Welfare State Threatens to Flatten the American Dream: or Worse: Age-Based Benefits as Our Downfall." *Generations, 19,* 15–19, 1995.

*Hudson, F. M. *LifeLaunch: A Passionate Guide to the Rest of Your Life.* Santa Barbara, Calif.: Hudson Institute Press, 1996. A workbook for composing chapters and life transitions of adult lives throughout the life cycle.

*Hudson, F. M. *The Adult Years: Mastering the Art of Self Renewal.* (rev. ed.) San Francisco: Jossey-Bass, 1999. Describes the maturation process and human potential of adults.

Hulbert, K. D., and Schuster, D. T. (eds.). *Women's Lives Through Time: Educated American Women of the Twentieth Century.* San Francisco: Jossey-Bass, 1993.

Hunsberger, B. "Religion, Age, Life Satisfaction, and Perceived Sources of Religiousness: A Study of Older Persons." *Journal of Gerontology,* 1985, *40,* 615–620.

Hunt, E. "What Do We Need to Know About Aging?" In J. Rybash, W. Hoyer, and M. L. Commons (eds.), *Adult Information Processing: Limits on Loss.* San Diego, Calif.: Academic Press, 1993.

Ingersol-Dayton, B., and Starrels, M. E. "Caregiving for Parents and Parents in Law: Is Gender Important?" *Gerontologist,* 1996, *36,* 438–491.

Johnson, C. I., and Baer, B. M. "Coping and a Sense of Control Among the Oldest Old." *Journal of Aging Studies,* 1991, *7,* 67–80.

Jones, C. J., and Meredith, W. "Patterns of Personality Change Across the Life Span." *Psychology of Aging,* 1996, *11,* 57–65.

Kalish, R. A. *"Late Adulthood: Perspectives on Human Development."* Monterey, Calif.: Brooks/Cole, 1975. A book about successful aging and what it will be like.

Khachaturian, Z. S., and Radebaugh, T. S. *Alzheimer's Disease: Causes, Diagnosis, Treatment, and Care.* Boca Raton, Fla.: CRC Press, 1997.

Klatz, R. *Grow Young with HGH.* New York: HarperCollins, 1997. A book on ways to reverse the effects of aging and promote youthful performance in midlife and elderhood; recommended for information, not advice.

Lesnoff-Caravaglia, G. *The World of the Older Woman: Conflicts & Resolutions.* New York: Human Sciences, 1994.

Lovelace, E. A. (ed.). *Aging and Cognition: Mental Processes, Self-awareness and Interventions.* Amsterdam: North-Holland/Elsevier, 1990.

Luke, H. M. *Old Age.* New York: Parabola, 1987. A Jungian interpretation.

*Mahoney, D., and Restak, R. *The Longevity Strategy.* New York: Wiley, 1998. Recommends twenty-three ways adults can proactively promote healthy and conscious living; based on current research.

Mangen, D. J., Bengston, V. L., and Landry, P. H. *Measurement of Intergenerational Relations.* Newbury Park, Calif.: Sage, 1998.

Mann, D. *Moderate Exercise Promotes Longevity.* Medical Tribune News Service, 1996.

Markides, K. S., and Mindel, C. H. *Aging and Ethnicity.* Newbury Park, Calif.: Sage, 1987.

McAdams, D. P., de St. Aubin, E., and Logan, R. L. "Generativity Among Young, Midlife, and Older Adults." *Psychology and Aging,* 1993, *8,* 221–230.

McCrae, R. R., and Costa, P. T., Jr. "Psychological Maturity and Subjective Well-Being: Toward a New Synthesis." *Developmental Psychology,* 1983, *19,* 243–248.

McGraw, P. C. Life Strategies: *Doing What Works, Doing What Matters.* New York: Hyperion, 1999. Popular advice for living, including clues for effective coaching.

McIntosh, J. L., and Associates. *Elder Suicide: Research, Theory, and Treatment.* San Antonio, Tex.: The Psychological Corporation, 1994.

McLaughlin, D. K., and Jensen, L. "Poverty Among Older Americans: The Plight of Nonmetropolitan Elders." *Journal of Gerontology: Social Sciences,* 1993, *48,* S44–S54.

Menken, J., Trussell, J., and Larsen, U. "Age and Infertility." *Science,* 1986, *233,* 1389–1394.

Midlarsky, E., and Hannah, M. E. "The Generous Elderly: Naturalistic Studies of Donations Across the Life Span." *Psychology and Aging,* 1989, *4,* 346–351.

*Monk, A. (ed.). *The Age of Aging: A Reader in Social Gerontology.* New York: Prometheus, 1993.

Montada, L. F., and Lerner, M. J. (eds.). *Life Crises and Experiences of Loss in Adulthood.* Hillsdale, N.J.: Erlbaum, 1992.

Moody, H. R. "A Strategy for Productive Aging: Education in Later Life." In S. A. Bass, F. G. Caro, and J-P. Chen (eds.), *Achieving a Productive Aging Society.* Westport, Conn.: Auburn House, 1993.

*Moody, H. R. "Meaning and Late Life Learning." In E. Heikkinen, J. Kuusinen, and I. Ruoppila (eds.), *Preparation for Aging.* New York: Plenum, 1995.

*Morris, V. *How to Care for Aging Parents.* New York: Workman, 1996.

Moyer, M. S. "Sibling Relationships Among Older Adults." *Generations,* 1992, *27*(3), 55–60.

Murphy, J. S., and Hudson, F. M. *The Joy of Old: A Guide to Successful Elderhood.* Altadena, Calif.: Geode Press, 1998.

Neisser, U., Boodoo, G., Bouchard, T. J., and Associates. "Intelligence: Knowns and Unknowns." *American Psychologist,* 1996, *51,* 77–101.

*Nemiroff, R., and Colarusso, C. *The Race Against Time.* New York: Plenum, 1985. An elegant study of midlife males and how they deal with their increasing sense of mortality.

Neugarten, D. A. (ed.). *The Meanings of Age: Selected Papers of Bernice L. Neugarten.* Chicago: University of Chicago Press, 1996.

Nussbaum, J. F., and Coupland, J. (eds.). *Handbook of Communication and Aging Research.* Mahwah, N.J.: Erlbaum, 1995.

O'Brien, M. "Never Married Older Women: The Life Experience." *Social Indicators Research,* 1991, *24,* 301–315.

Ostrow, A. C. *Physical Activity and the Older Adult.* Princeton, N.J.: Princeton Book Company, 1984. A good summary source on this topic.

Palmore, E. B. *Ageism: Negative and Positive.* New York: Springer, 1990.

Palmore, E. B. (ed.). *Developments and Research on Aging. An International Handbook.* Westport, Conn.: Greenwood Press, 1993.

Palus, C. J. "Transformative Experiences of Adulthood: A New Look at the Seasons of Life." In J. Demick, K. Bursik, and R. DiBiase (eds.), *Parental Development.* Hillsdale, N.J.: Erlbaum, 1993.

Parkes, C. M., Stevenson-Hinde, J., and Marris, P. (eds.). *Attachment Across the Life Cycle.* London: Routledge, 1993.

Peterson, B. E., and Stewart, A. J. "Antecedents and Contexts of Generativity Motivation at Midlife." *Psychology and Aging,* 1996, *11,* 21–33.

*Pifer, A., and Bronte, L. (eds.). *Our Aging Society: Paradox and Promise.* New York: Norton, 1986.

Pillemer, K., and McCartney, K. (eds.). *Parent-child Relations Throughout Life.* Hillsdale, N.J.: Erlbaum, 1991.

*Pollock, G. H., and Greenspan, S. L. *The Course of Life, Vol. VI: Late Adulthood.* Madison, Conn.: International Universities Press, 1995.

Poon, L. W., Rubin, D. C., and Wilson, B. A. (eds.). *Everyday Cognition in Adulthood and Later Life.* Cambridge, England: Cambridge University Press, 1992.

*Posner, R. A. *Aging and Old Age.* Chicago: University of Chicago Press, 1995.

Powell, D. *Profiles in Cognitive Aging.* Cambridge, Mass.: Harvard University Press, 1994.

Restak, R. M. *Older and Wiser: How to Maintain Peak Mental Ability for as Long as You Live.* New York: Berkley Books, 1997. A medical doctor writes on research knowledge that will keep the mind active and effective throughout old age.

Riley, M. W., and Riley, J. W., Jr. "Age Integration and the Lives of Older People." *Gerontologist,* 1994, *11,* 79–87.

Rodin, J., Schooler, C., and Schaie, K. W. (eds.). *Self-Directedness: Cause and Effects Throughout the Life Course.* Hillsdale, N.J.: Erlbaum, 1990.

Roizer, M. F. *Real Age: Are You as Young as You Can Be?* New York: HarperCollins, 1999. Sound advice for taking care of your mind and body as you age.

Rosen, E. J. *Families Facing Death: Family Dynamics of Terminal Illness, A Guide for Health-care Professionals and Volunteers.* San Francisco: Jossey-Bass, 1996.

Rossi, A. S. (ed.). *Sexuality Across the Life Course.* Chicago: University of Chicago Press, 1994.

Rutter, M., and Rutter, M. *Developing Minds: Challenge and Continuity across the Life Span.* New York: Basic Books, 1993.

Sable, P. "Attachment, Loss of Spouse, and Grief in Elderly Adults." *Omega,* 1991, *23,* 587–596.

Sanders, C. M. *Grief: The Mourning After.* New York: Wiley, 1998.

Sarason, B. R., Sarason, I. G., and Pierce, G. R. (eds.). *Social Support: An Interactional View.* New York: Wiley, 1990.

Sarton, M. *Encore: Journal of the 80th Year.* New York: Norton, 1995. Journals like this can open the gates ahead.

Saunders, C. M. *The Management of Terminal Disease.* London: Edward Arnold, 1993.

Schaie, K. W. "The Course of Adult Intellectual Development." *American Psychologist,* 1994, *49,* 304–313.

*Schaie, K. W. *Handbook of the Psychology of Aging.* (3rd ed.) San Diego, Calif.: Academic Press, 1996. An essential reference book for coaching elders.

Schaie, K. W. (ed.). *Annual Review of Gerontology and Geriatrics* (Vol. 7). New York: Springer, 1997. Outstanding chapters on intellectual change in adults and the effects of training on the maintenance or increase in intellectual functioning in old age.

Schaie, K. W., Blazer, D., and House, J. S. *Aging, Health Behaviors, and Health Outcomes.* Hillsdale, N.J.: Erlbaum, 1992.

*Schaie, K. W., and Willis, S. L. *Adult Development and Aging.* New York: HarperCollins, 1996.

Schulz, J. H. *The Economics of Aging.* (5th ed.) Dover, Mass.: Auburn House, 1992.

*Scott, L., with K. Schremp, B. Soldz, and B. Weiss. *Wise Choices Beyond Midlife: Women Mapping the Journey Ahead.* Watsonville, Calif.: Papier-Mache Press, 1997. A practical book for women over sixty who want to plan their lives proactively: relationships, money, health, and more.

*Seltzer, M. M. *The Impact of Increased Life Expectancy: Beyond the Gray Horizon.* New York: Springer, 1995.

*Smelser, N. J., and Erikson, E. H. *Themes of Work and Love in Adulthood.* Cambridge, Mass.: Harvard University Press, 1980. A collection of masterful writings by Erikson, Gould, Levinson, and others.

Solomon, M. Z., O'Donnell, L., and Associates. "Decisions Near the End of Life: Professional Views on Life-Sustaining Treatments." *American Journal of Public Health,* 1993, *83,* 14–23.

Sperling, M. B., and Berman, W. H. (eds.). *Attachment in Adults: Clinical and Developmental Perspectives.* New York: Guilford Press, 1994.

Sze, W. C. *Human Life Cycle.* New York: Jason Aronson, 1975. Excellent essays on aging.

*Thomasma, D. C., and Kushner, T. (eds.). *Preparation for Aging.* Cambridge, England: Cambridge University Press, 1996.

Thorson, J. A. *Aging in a Changing Society.* Belmont, Calif.: Wadsworth, 1995.

Timiras, P. S. (ed.). *Physiological Basis of Aging and Geriatrics.* (2nd ed.) Boca Raton, Fla.: CRC Press, 1994.

Torres-Gil, F. M. *The New Aging.* New York: Auburn House, 1992.

*Turner, B. F., and Troll, L. E. (eds.). *Women Growing Older: Psychological Perspectives.* Newbury Park: Sage, 1994. Examines the realistic and optimal developmental paths for women, as well as the realistic deficits to expect.

Turner, J. S., and Helms, D. B. *Lifespan Development.* Cambridge, Mass.: Harvard Business School, 1997.

Umberson, D. "Relationship Between Adult Children and Their Parents: Psychological Consequences for Both Generations." *Journal of Marriage and the Family,* 1992, *54,* 366–380.

Weaver, F. *The Girls with the Grandmother Faces: Single and Sixty Is Not for Sissies.* New York: Hyperion Press, 1996. Delightful reading on widowhood, moving, finding men, traveling, support groups, and Elderhostel.

Whitbourne, S. K. *The Aging Body.* New York: Springer-Verlag, 1985.

Winnicott, D. W. *The Maturational Processes and the Facilitating Environment.* London: Hogarth Press; Toronto: Clarke, Irwin, and Company, 1965.

Winnicott, D. W. *Playing and Reality.* New York: Routledge, 1982.

Winnicott, D. W. *Home Is Where We Start From.* New York: Norton, 1990.

Twentysomethings

*Bradford, L. J., and Raines, C. *Twenty-Something: Managing and Motivating Today's New Work Force.* New York: MasterMedia Limited, 1992. Good book for understanding Generation X or Generation Next in relation to corporate thinking.

*Cairns, R. B., and Cairns, B. D. *Lifelines and Risks: Pathways of Youth in Our Time.* Cambridge, England: Cambridge University Press, 1994.

Carnegie Council on Adolescent Development. *Turning Points: Preparing American Youth for the 21st Century.* New York: Carnegie Corporation, 1989.

Clemens, A. W., and Axelson, L. J. "The Not-so-Empty Nest: The Return of the Fledgling Adult." *Family Relations,* 1985, *34,* 259–264.

Coleman, J. C., and Hendry, L. *The Nature of Adolescence.* (2nd ed.) London: Routledge, 1990.

*Csikszentmihalyi, M. *Being Adolescent.* New York: Basic Books, 1996.

D'Augelli, A. R., and Hershberger, S. L. "Lesbian, Gay, and Bisexual Youth in Community Settings: Personal Challenges and Mental Health Problems." *American Journal of Community Psychology,* 1993, *21,* 421–448.

Eccles, J. S., Midgley, C., Wigfield, A., Buchanan, C. M., Reuman, D., Flanagan, C., and MacIver, D. "Development During Adolescence: The Impact of Stage Environment Fit on Young Adolescents' Experiences in Schools and in Families." *American Psychologist,* 1993, *48,* 90–101.

Feldman, S. S., and Elliott, G. R. (eds.). *At the Threshold: The Developing Adolescent.* Cambridge, Mass.: Harvard University Press, 1990.

*Fenwick, E., and Smith, T. *Adolescence: The Survival Guide for Parents and Teenagers.* New York: Dorling Kindersley, 1996. A comprehensive text and a magnificent achievement.

Gaddis, A., and Brooks-Gunn, J. "The Male Experience of Pubertal Change." *Journal of Youth and Adolescence,* 1985, *4,* 61.

Galambos, N. L. "Parent-Adolescent Relations." *Current Directions in Psychological Science,* 1992, *1,* 146–149.

*Gilmore, D. D. *Manhood in the Making: Cultural Concepts of Masculinity.* New Haven, Conn.: Yale University Press, 1990. An outstanding read for young men to ponder as they choose for themselves what manhood is about.

Goldscheider, F. K., and Goldscheider, C. "Leaving and Returning Home in 20th Century America." *Population Bulletin,* 1993, *48*(4), 1–35.

Gordon, D. E. "Formal Operational Thinking: The Role of Cognitive-Developmental Processes in Adolescent Decision-Making about Pregnancy and Contraception." *American Journal of Orthopsychiatry,* 1990, *60,* 346–356.

Gurian, M. *A Fine Young Man: What Parents, Mentors and Educators Can Do to Shape Adolescent Boys into Exceptional Men.* New York: Tarcher, 1998. Filled with stories and examples of what people working with adolescent boys can do to link adolescent boys to successful paths ahead.

Hacker, D. J. "An Existential View of Adolescence." *Journal of Early Adolescence,* 1994, *14,* 300–327.

Haley, J. *Leaving Home: The Therapy of Disturbed Young People.* New York: Brunner/Mazel, 1993. A classic book that underscores the importance of parenting throughout the leaving-home period of about ten years.

*Hudson, F. M. *LifeLaunch: A Passionate Guide to the Rest of Your Life.* Santa Barbara, Calif.: Hudson Institute Press, 1996. A workbook for composing chapters and life transitions of adult lives throughout the life cycle.

*Hudson, F. M. *The Adult Years: Mastering the Art of Self Renewal.* (rev. ed.) San Francisco: Jossey-Bass, 1999. Outlines the maturation process and human potential of adults and presents detailed descriptions of each adult decade.

Jessor, R. "Risk Behavior in Adolescence: A Psychosocial Framework for Understanding and Action." *Developmental Review,* 1992, *12,* 374–390.

Jessor, R., Donovan, J. E., and Costa, F. M. *Beyond Adolescence: Problem Behavior and Young Adult Development.* Cambridge, England: Cambridge University Press, 1991.

Mann, L., Harmoni, R., and Power, C. "Adolescent Decision-making: The Development of Competence." *Journal of Adolescence,* 1989, *12,* 265–278.

Miller, C. K. *Postmoderns: The Beliefs, Hopes, and Fears of Young Americans (1965–1981).* Ithaca, NY: American Demographics, 1996.

Millman, D. *Sacred Journey of the Peaceful Warrior.* Tiburon, Calif.: Kramer, 1991. Stories for inspiring greatness in young people.

Mitchell, S. *Generation X: The Young Adult Market.* Ithaca, NY: American Demographics, 1996.

Montemayor, R., Adams, G. R., and Gullotta, T. P. (eds.). *From Childhood to Adolescence: A Transitional Period?* Newbury Park, Calif.: Sage, 1996.

Murphy, P. A. "Parental Death in Childhood and Loneliness in Young Adults." *Omega,* 1986–1987, *17,* 219–228.

Pascarella, E. T., and Terenzini, P. T. *How College Affects Students: Findings and Insights from Twenty Years of Research.* San Francisco: Jossey-Bass, 1991.

Pollock, G. H., and Greenspan, S. L. *The Course of Life, Vol. V: Early Adulthood.* Madison, Conn.: International Universities Press, 1992.

*Raines, C. *Beyond Generation X: A Practical Guide for Managers.* Menlo Park, Calif.: Crisp, 1997. An application to corporate settings.

Robins, L. N., and Rutter, M. (eds.). *Straight and Devious Pathways from Childhood to Adulthood.* Cambridge, England: Cambridge University Press, 1992.

*Rushkoff, D. *Playing the Future: How Kids' Culture Can Teach Us to Thrive in an Age of Chaos.* New York: HarperCollins, 1996. A young man's proud interpretation of his own generation.

Rutter, M. (ed.). *Psychosocial Disturbances in Young People: Challenges for Prevention.* Cambridge, England: Cambridge University Press, 1997.

Rutter, M., and Rutter, M. *Developing Minds: Challenge and Continuity Across the Life Span.* New York: Basic Books, 1993.

Rutter, M., and Smith, D. J. (eds.). *Psychosocial Disorders in Young People: Time Trends and Their Causes.* New York: Wiley, 1995.

Shedler, J., and Block, J. "Adolescent Drug Use and Psychological Health: A Longitudinal Inquiry." *American Psychologist,* 1990, *45,* 612–630.

Stein, M. D., and Davis, J. K. *Therapies for Adolescents.* San Francisco: Jossey-Bass, 1992. Describes effective techniques for treating a wide range of adolescent problems and dysfunctions.

*Tapscott, D. *Growing up Digital: The Rise of the Net Generation.* New York: McGraw-Hill, 1998. Indicates the impact of computer technology on the consciousness, careers, and values of the net-generation.

Troll, L. E. *Early and Middle Adulthood.* Belmont, Calif.: Wadsworth, 1984.

*Tulgan, B. *Managing Generation X: How to Bring Out the Best in Young Talent.* Santa Monica, Calif.: Merritt Publishing, 1997. Describes a generation of people who value individualism and personal empowerment who have entrepreneurial skills for big-time success.

Youth and the Needs of the Nation. Washington, D.C.: Potomac Institute, 1979. Recommends ways that "service" can be restored as a valuable part of the young adult years.

Thirtysomethings

Eichorn, D., Hunt, J. V., and Honzik, M. P. "Experience, Personality, and IQ: Adolescence to Middle Age." In D. H. Eichorn, J. A. Clausen, N. Haan, M. P. Honzik, and P. H. Mussen (eds.), *Present and Past in Middle Life,* New York: Academic Press, 1981.

*Hudson, F. M. *LifeLaunch: A Passionate Guide to the Rest of Your Life.* Santa Barbara, Calif.: Hudson Institute Press, 1996. A workbook for composing chapters and life transitions of adult lives throughout the life cycle.

*Hudson, F. M. *The Adult Years: Mastering the Art of Self Renewal.* (rev. ed.) San Francisco: Jossey-Bass, 1999. The maturation process and human potential of adults is outlined along with detailed descriptions of each adult decade.

Naelson, C. C. "Issues in the Analyses of Single Women in Their Thirties and Forties." In J. M. Oldham and R. S. Liebert (eds.), *The Middle Years.* New Haven, Conn.: Yale University Press, 1989.

Troll, L. E. *Early and Middle Adulthood.* Belmont, Calif.: Wadsworth, 1984.

CHAPTER TWELVE 

Coaching Throughout the Adult Life Cycle

Older Adults

The midlife transition occurs sometime between the ages of thirty-five and fifty, representing the first major transition after adolescence for most adults. This is the likely time for a midlife crisis. As Joseph Campbell often said, "Just when you get to the top of your ladder, you realize it is up against the wrong wall." Major reevaluation of everything takes place. People in a midlife transition are looking for some fundamental changes in life. They want to move

- From expansiveness and acquisitions toward self-reliance and simplicity
- From external goals toward internal enrichment; from relationship maintenance toward external goals
- From infinite time toward time left
- From parental scripts toward internal ones
- From body issues toward spiritual themes

In a midlife transition, people yearn for a private life beyond success and beyond parenting. They tap a gradual change of consciousness. They often seek to renew their marriages or intimate life. Some divorce, make a career change, move to another part of the country, or make other major decisions. Most often it is a quieter and almost imperceptible change of attitudes and perspective. Almost always, they move from early adult thinking to midlife thinking, beginning with adopting a long view of their life and possibilities. Spirituality often becomes of intense interest. They seek new information from those older than they are.

MIDLIFE COACHING

Possible coaching goals for clients in or approaching midlife include becoming renewed as a couple, changing careers, finding lasting friendships, traveling as an adventure, finding a meaningful hobby, working on life balance, deepening friendships, moving to another location, learning more about parenting, and maturing as a person. People in midlife are beginning to understand the importance of life transitions, developmental crises, and evolving. They are facing the fact that they are going to die, and they feel in a hurry to invest in living. (See Basic Library: Midlife Development.)

Other features of clients' lives that coaches should be aware of include

- A changing leadership style—a shift from active mastery to passive mastery. A client might be exerting influence through policies, supervisory roles, episodic events, symbolic actions, and episodic work instead of daily, hands-on roles. He or she may want coaching on how to succeed at this shift.
- A need to explore outlets for increased social caring, which may lead to new leadership roles in the post-parental years.
- A new way to look at travel and leisure. Sometimes "play" becomes as important a feature in life as "work."
- A need to create a simpler yet more profound time schedule.
- A wish to deepen spiritual sensitivity.

Following are several tips (not advice!) a coach might offer an older client:

• *Challenge all the stereotyped ideas about aging.* Plan to get older and better, even as your body may get worse in many ways. Take a long view of life, and pace yourself daily and weekly with shorter views. Learn to live into a future vision, and your brain (frontal lobes) will actually be stimulated to help you reach your vision through daily actions. Take executive control of yourself and your choices on the road ahead.

• *Manage aging; reject becoming old.* There is a difference between aging and getting old. Aging is finding ways to manage life changes in order to be optimally alive, active, and engaged. You'll find advantages and disadvantages to every age, and positive aging means to employ the advantages while managing the disadvantages. In the elder years the advantages have to do with spiritual concerns: soulful dialogues, transformative mentoring, and legacy planning. The disadvantages have to do with the body, which is experiencing a weaker immune system and declining in bodily functions.

"Getting old" means taking on the characteristics that society expects old people to have: losing interest in life, accepting the notion that it's too late to change, becoming dependent on others for self-care and motivation, failing to set goals and commitments, losing a sense of surprise, and giving in to passivity and boredom. Most jokes about old people are about negative stereotypes that do not represent the way most old people really are.

Aging is not a spectator sport. Step out of the stands and do something now to increase your chances for a long life. You will experience vitality and hope that most previous generations never imagined. None of us can stop aging, but we don't have to grow old.

- *Promote positive aging in yourself.* The formula includes basic optimism, healthy self-esteem, a willingness to adapt to new situations, a sense of personal power and readiness to take responsibility, self-motivation for continued resilience and staying power, involvement in meaningful projects and relationships. Healthy aging includes a positive attitude toward life, good stress-coping skills and health-promoting behaviors, skills to deal with everyday problems of living, and the ability to avoid passivity, reminiscence, self-pity, infectious diseases, and serious injuries. Centenarians score high on optimism; they are rarely depressed.
- *Know how to manage stress.* When your brain is healthy, your body does a better job of resisting illness. When your body functions at its best, your brain is stimulated and feelings are more positive. It is essential to manage information overload and not be overwhelmed by media invasion and its consequent feelings of helplessness. A key to stress management is learning to let go of things that are outside your control or influence. The opposite of feeling stressed is a feeling of well-being. Stay connected to friends, networks, and other people. Don't withdraw into self-pity or into dependence on spouse, friends, or physicians. Lack of trust has great mental health consequences. Practice trustful optimism along with self-talk. Sustain a healthy sense of humor.
- *Genes aren't as important as we used to think.* It does no good to blame our genes; better to invest in your best choices. Heredity accounts for only one-fourth of the variation in human life spans. Gerontologists have found that nutrition, exercise, and social relationships are more important than genetic structures.
- *Strive to keep up, mentally, with your field of expertise.* Try to gain new knowledge and skills in areas of emerging interest. Neglecting talents and skills that were once essential to life means that those talents begin to wane. The well-known phrase "Use it or lose it" applies to every part of your body, mind, and social life. If new skills and directions appeal more than former talents, that's

fine. The point is to be actively engaged through learning. Learning is a central feature of creative aging. By keeping your life engaged in purposive living, your neurons will remain active unless some kind of brain atrophy takes place. Resilience will be sustained best if you make small, consistently applied efforts at sustaining competence and skills.

Our brains are the most important organ to invest in for positive aging. If we use them regularly, we are less likely to lose the use of them. We can tweak the high-performing parts of our brains through reading, reflection, and discussions with others of all ages. We should relax about normal slips and slowings of brain functions as we get older. Our reservoir is huge from all the experience we have had, so respect the slower speed of our internal CPUs. If we give our brains smaller assignments as we age, we can keep them on duty at all times. It is very important that we understand the degenerative diseases of the brain and what we can do to stay healthy and able to do our best to avoid Alzheimer's, Parkinson's, schizophrenia, depression, cancer, heart attacks, and strokes.

- *Be physically active.* At every age we need to maintain a high level of physical fitness: muscle strength, agility, and endurance to sustain vigorous exercise. The object is not to prove we are young but to sustain our bodies to be the best they can be at the age we are.
- *Follow the Rule of Ten.* Each month for the next six months, introduce a 10 percent increase in the following life areas: physical activity, dietary complex carbohydrates, fiber intake, sleep or naps, and reading and other mind-expanding, intellectually stimulating activities. Each month, *decrease* by 10 percent the following: calories, fat, alcohol (no more than two to three ounces per day), and stress. Eliminate all smoking (including breathing secondhand smoke), TV watching, and other passive pastimes.
- *Stay in continuous learning.* Continuous learning tops the list of factors that scientists have found to promote longevity and the retention of mental acuity. We need to stay curious about something, preferably something that evokes a sense of purpose. Enthusiasm and zest are natural byproducts of new learning.
- *Invest in your family and friends.* We age better if we stay connected to the concerns of our extended families and friends. The goal here is to be an intimate player with others to the very end, investing in family and friends as our most precious assets and legacies.
- *Maintain a broad portfolio of skills and activities.* Longevity scholars recommend that we maintain several task areas in parallel—areas of commitment and rewards for our lives: Some may be work related. Others are avocations. We should learn to schedule ourselves into multiple areas of interest, such as training, consultation, careering, and leisure.
- *Live on the edge of your possibilities but be able to lose and adapt.* As we age, we become freer and freer to have our own voices, our own projects, our

own impact. Therefore, we need to pace ourselves with balance yet spice up our lives with risks.

- *Keep up with longevity research.* The twenty-first century will be the century of increasing numbers of elders. Scientific research that relates to longevity is appearing daily. It may well apply to us. The idea is not to live forever but to live fully as long as we can, or to help us die young, as late as possible.

Fortysomethings

People in their forties are taking charge. This is the decade when people individuate and seek autonomy and personal clarity. Although they want to live out of their deep inner resources and reach the profound levels of their maturity, they often feel compromised by their roles and commitments: jobs, debts, marriages, children, and the been-there-did-that feeling.

Persons entering individuation are likely to benefit if their coach helps them

- Conduct an audit of their personal commitments, relationships, financial plans, and careers
- Lower expectations and focus on what matters most
- Shift from quantity to quality issues, from endless acquisitions to internal satisfactions, from pleasing others to being their own person

During this period, many fortysomethings become more self-responsible, more entrepreneurial, more spiritual. Many report a profound spiritual stirring in their lives, helping them move beyond their ego needs to the broader issues around them. During individuation, fortysomethings experience significant body changes, changes in values, changes in rewards sought at work, caring for aging parents, caring for children. They realize that time is running out. Life balance is often a coachable issue.

Individuation often has its price. Alliances with careers, mates, children, and friends made during the twenties and thirties often get bruised, trashed, abandoned, or transformed. Coaches should coach for good judgment and for resisting impulsive, hurried decision making.

Fiftysomethings

So much has been written about the age forty transition that few people know much about the transition from forty to fifty, which for many is extremely important. This transition moves away from autonomy, take-charge themes in the direction of becoming more outgoing, light-hearted, and diffuse. People tend to leave the Hamlet-like personal heaviness of the forties and grow into a lifestyle with more sharing, optimism, caring, and fun.

Women who have spent their thirties and forties raising children and sustaining careers may use the decade of the fifties for completing the tasks of individuation begun in the forties. They may reenter educational programs, travel alone, take up hobbies, or begin new friendships. Assertiveness and self-directed behaviors increase, along with the caring connections that most women sustain as part of their core reality. In this decade, men and women who invested in individuation during their forties move in this decade into a broad celebration of life. The emphasis now is on living, not getting ready to live, and on realized expectations, not grandiose future ones. Friendships increase in number and quality, as do humor and leisure interests. The focus is on interdependence—sharing, working things out, and enjoying the journey.

Many researchers report that this decade receives the highest ratings of any adult decade for "life satisfaction" and "marital satisfaction." Fiftysomethings often report high self-esteem, comfort with life, and commitment to the art of living. They typically have money, and they demand time for *living*. Spiritually, fiftysomethings are experiencing what Carl Jung termed transcending "egos" and discovering "souls," as their spirituality blossoms as a dominant theme. Leisure is a vehicle for finding meaning in life and not merely changing pace away from work. Work continues to provide meaning, but fiftysomethings want to work smart, meaning two things: (1) balancing work with the other parts of their lives and (2) engaging in outer work that fits their inner sense of gifts and talent. Coaches might ask clients approaching their fifties to interview three people in their fifties and get the good news first hand. Of course aging is taking place, and some people are at increased risk from heart attacks, strokes, cancer, and degenerative diseases. But the overall picture shows the fifties to be some of the best years of the adult journey. (See Basic Library: Fiftysomethings.)

Sixtysomethings

People in their sixties redefine work, life, and meaning. Under the banner of "retirement," this shifting of gears has enormous social approval and resources to draw on. This transition often involves major changes: geographic relocation, marital renewal or change of partners, economic downsizing, and departure from social contexts that have provided meaning and validation while beginning new contexts of adventure and love.

The metaphor of "retirement" is no longer to disengage from work or life but to begin again, with all the old options (work, intimacy, family, leisure, travel, leadership roles) in addition to an increased drive toward living life to its fullest. I call this *protirement*, meaning to place yourself ahead into the activities and life style of your choice.

Most sixtysomethings spend this decade living their beliefs and seeking quality experiences. Assuming that finances and health are positive resources, the sixties often provide one of the best decades of the adult years. That's when you can do what you want to do and become who you want to be.

In the twenty-first century, few sixtysomethings sit around feeling old and impaired, waiting for the bell to toll for their departure. Rather, they seek vintage living and quality choices. Being sixty is just another time to begin again—with more life experience, money, and social resources for both enjoying the experience and deepening the journey ahead. If you live to be sixty, you should plan to live to one hundred. That will take coaching, just to break the stereotypes in your own head.

The single most important ability to impart is a capacity to vision and dream again, to imagine ways to add value to life as old overtakes young. Elderhood is, for many people their sixties, the beginning of the longest period of adulthood and often the most fulfilling.

Clients may seek help from coaches for

- *Their own desire to mentor.* Clients will probably experience a desire to mentor—to share their acquired competence as a professional and as a human being with others, particularly their progeny and younger persons in their specialized fields. Mentoring becomes a basic form of personal and social caring.
- *Reducing external necessities to a minimum.* Sixtysomethings launch a quest for simplicity, demonstrated by a reduction of things, possessions, and routine roles.
- *Deepening intimacy through friendships, hobbies, travel, and work.* Adventure traveling is a great choice.
- *Renewing their marriages or intimate lives,* which will probably become more important at this time in their lives.
- *Exploring personal spirituality,* another theme they often explore, with intense living and celebrating in the here and now.

Seventysomethings

By now transitions are quite familiar, but some issues make moving ahead into another decade difficult, including physical problems, from aches and pains to disease and accidents and other losses: old friends, a spouse, opportunities, social validation, global chaos. This age group often begins to suffer from the ageism of our society. They don't want to see people this old or to believe they can contribute to the future. They are seen as marginal, dependent, disappearing people. The secret to coaching this group is to remain focused on a proactive agenda that is future-oriented, possible, and engaging.

Eightysomethings, Ninetysomethings, Centenarians

At the present time, there are no explicit social expectations or roles for this age group. Most people would probably say this is the time to die. But life is pushing death further back as we live longer lives, and these decades can be positive times for attending to unfulfilled dreams, discovering new possibilities, blessing family members, and making forceful messages to the culture.

Eightysomethings and ninetysomethings (and those even older) are the elders of our society. Sometimes they get recognized and consulted for their wisdom, integrity, and cultural perspective. They often inspire others with their optimism and hope. They model the fullness of life. They are menschen, mentors, guides to the future. They are the consummate cultural reservoirs, resources, consultants, and symbols. Their blessings are the force that links generation after generation. They may be the most profound bearers of culture, consciousness, and spirit. If they are vital and awake, they have perspective because they link the past with the present and future. There is no greater time in adult life than this, however unheralded it is by our society. If seventysomethings and eightysomethings don't speak and act, and if we don't listen and learn, history itself is injured and deprived.

Our society offers little support for the notions of vital and full living in old age. We promote retirement, leisure life, and planned communities where the old can congregate and disengage from the mainstream of life. But in truth, few of these activities are based on the deep human capacities or dreams of the fullness of old age. We can do better by designing our own scripts for our seventies and eighties. Healthy adults do not disengage from life as they get older, until the betrayal of the body finally requires it.

People this age need

- To know how to assess their own lives as worthy, purposive, and important
- An ability to transcend ordinary problems with humor, perspective, and trust
- An ability to be grateful and appreciative
- To know how to endorse, sponsor, and bless others, particularly younger people
- To know how to sustain healthy social networks for support and expression
- New resources within the inner self to deepen spirituality
- Skill and advice for sustaining adequate levels of health, nutrition, leisure, and projects
- Ways to manage increasing levels of loss, pain, and suffering

Reading works that provide an overview of adult life is helpful preparation for working with older clients.

SPIRITUAL COACHING

At some point between forty and sixty—but possibly later—most people deepen their spirituality. They move beyond ego orientations into increased trust of a power or powers greater than themselves. As their physical bodies peak, they turn to their souls for a dependable bond for the years ahead. Some renew their traditional religious roots. Others embrace mysticism or increase their trust in others. Many find secular ways to express their sense of personal transcendence and reliance on a higher power. *Spirit* and *soul* refer to that place within a person that "speaks" and "cares" for all the other parts, and beyond the self as well. The developmental focus on autonomy shifts gradually to a focus on interdependence.

Spirituality is a theme that runs throughout the life cycle; it is not contained by the midlife years, and it almost always rises to its peak during elderhood. However, it is during the middle years that a shift from ego to self, from self-absorption to increased caring, and from getting ready to live to the deeper realities of living takes place.

Possible coaching goals include centering, deep inner work, personal transformation, awakening to a different path and future, enhancing solitude, enriching life as it is, spending time in nature, becoming self-transcendent, participating in rituals.

Some ways to reach those goals include inviting a client to consider taking a vision quest, spending time alone at a retreat center experiencing the wonder of nature, exploring the arts for ways to experience new wonder and awe, rededicating his or her coupling bond to include shared spiritual goals, engaging in community service or environmental cause as a volunteer, maintaining a personal journal, or engaging in study of the soul, spirit, and the history of religions. (See Basic Library: Spiritual Coaching.)

LATER-LIFE COACHING

The question of whether to retire or not comes up more and more frequently in midlife. Many companies are offering early-retirement buy-outs to make way for younger, less expensive workers. Many professional people, notably those in academe, are ending their thirty-year "tours of duty," drawing their pensions, and looking forward to new kinds of work. So coaches should keep this possibility in mind as they work with midlife clients. (See Basic Library: Coaching Elder Women; Coaching for Wisdom in Elderhood.)

RETIREMENT-PROTIREMENT CHOICES

Retirement is a concept that arose in the United States during the latter part of the nineteenth century. Until then, the elderly lived with their families; if they were poor, they lived in crudely maintained public institutions and kept working until it became physically impossible for them to do so.

Labor unions and corporate leaders were the forces behind the concept of retirement in the last part of the nineteenth and early twentieth centuries. The mean age of mortality was forty-seven at the turn of the century, and it seemed to workforce leaders that anyone older than fifty should be forced out of the workforce to make room for younger, more vigorous, and less expensive workers. All this had nothing to do with the best interests of those fifty or older. Retirement was invented to make elders into marginal human beings, not to fulfill them.

As the twentieth century proceeded, the federal government joined the forces shaping retirement policies. A fixed age was determined for retirement, and Social Security laws were passed to provide a modest income. But there was a catch. Seniors receiving Social Security were prohibited from working for money, or at least from working for very much money. As the life span of elders increased, the government permitted those over seventy to earn whatever they could. The government also added Medicare and Medicaid policies for elders who qualified.

During the twentieth century, insurance companies moved into the retirement myth, promoting retirement planning that would turn the elder years into the "golden years." Insurance companies promoted retirement planning, meaning financial planning, as if sufficient funds equaled a fulfilled life.

Now, more Americans than ever are entering the elder ranks. By the year 2030, there will be as many people over the age of fifty-five as there will be under the age of forty-five. This is an inversion of the youth-oriented American culture we have had for two hundred years. Except in pockets of rural poor, elders as a group are no longer a financially struggling group, the way they were at the beginning of the twentieth century. Today's elders are familiar with business success, and many of them do not see the value of retirement.

Life expectancy is rising each year. It is now about seventy-eight for men and eighty-two for women, although statistics compiled for those sixty-five and older show the life expectancy to be closer to eighty-seven for men and ninety-one for women. What are these people supposed to be about during their elder years from sixty-five on? What is their social importance?

Some of the reasons older people will continue to be socially and politically important are

- Elders today are much more informed about nutrition and exercise. Many are learning the principles of longevity and staying active.
- Careers have broken down into personal portfolios of skills, interests, and opportunities. Jobs are less and less contained by corporate offerings and more and more are short-term efforts of people wanting (and creating) meaningful work. It would be easy to generate meaningful work for elders if (1) elders wanted continued employment of some sort, (2) society embraced the value of having elders employed for as long as they wanted to work, and (3) the federal government removed all financial disincentives to elderly earnings.

- Many elders have traveled widely and become acquainted with the challenges and opportunities around the globe.

The society, however, is still woefully ageist, that is, prejudiced against old people. Elders themselves tend to view themselves as worth less than when they were younger. During the next few decades, new images of elders—sixtysomethings, seventysomethings, eightysomethings, ninetysomethings, and even centenarians—will evolve to reshape societal expectations of elders. The elder years will become an organic part of the rest of the life cycle. Life for elders contains the same basic elements as at any previous time in the life cycle, and the worst thing that can happen is to be sidelined at sixty-five when nothing is wrong except that the cultural myth has you becoming a marginal person for the rest of your life. As the twenty-first century begins, there are loud rumbles of dissatisfaction with the retirement myth.

This backdrop establishes an opportunity for coaches who are knowledgeable in life cycle realities to promote positive aging—lives that include work, leisure, sex, family, contributions, and legacy. Many, many people can be coached into making positive life plans for themselves and for the culture. Elder coaches need to understand networking; they must know how to promote positive aging, what the realities of death and dying are. And they must understand the crucial role of visioning for the future, no matter what a client's age. Protirement coaching explores work options, promotes engagement in leadership roles, and encourages decision making in community life and connecting to people of all ages. A healthy and socially inclusive view of elderhood would envision a continuation of the same renewal cycle that guided life in younger years, with several life chapters and life transitions throughout the elder years. Each life chapter would have varying combinations of work, travel, leisure, leadership, family contact, and social involvements. (See Basic Library: Coaching Around Retirement-Protirement Choices; Retirement-Protirement; Coaching Late Elderhood; Coaching Parents and Other Elders.)

DYING: COACHING THE FINAL TRANSITION

Coaching for a "good death" is a profound specialty. The demand for it is bound to increase over the next thirty or forty years. My advice here is more general: coaches should keep in mind that dying is part of the normal life cycle. Healthy people die a little each day; they let go of life that no longer belongs to them—life in themselves, in relationships, in careers, in the world. Every loss is a little death. Every transition is a dying. As adults get older they have many opportunities to learn how to die. Whether death is final or not no one knows, but our experiences of dying suggest that death is both an ending and a beginning of some sort.

Dying is managing all sorts of losses we experience and working through the grieving process. The way we face dying is partly shaped by the way we have managed "letting go" throughout our lives. If we have learned to trust the unknown, to find peace in resignation, and to search for new paths in darkness, then we do not have to rebel against dying. It can be perceived as a necessary adventure. People who know they are dying often rise to levels of clarity and boldness about their lives that they never before experienced. The experience of dying elicits honest, blunt words of personal truth.

Those who find dying meaningless and negative probably found old age meaningless and negative—and maybe all the adult years as well. If we are always seeking purpose and meaning at the cutting edge of our personal journeys, no matter what our age, dying will be a refinement of our spirituality, not a denial of life. If we live our dying fully and stay current with our life purpose, we are always ready to die. (See Basic Library: Dying: The Final Transition; Coaching for Dying; Death.)

QUESTIONS FOR COACHES: THE ASSETS OF AGING

A coach should consider these questions when working with an older client on issues related to aging:

- Does my client show any signs of ageism—negative expectations about getting older? How can I provide accurate information about the aging process and about ways my client can get further validation?
- Does my client have older friends, particularly same-gender friends? Is my client involved in caring for his or her parents? Does my client have positive images of being old?
- To what extent is my client familiar with the positive, developmental aspects of the life cycle in the second half of life? What can I do to enhance my client's learning from developmental information?
- How can I help my client obtain a realistic awareness of the trade-offs between the deficits of aging and the increments of development?
- How has my client managed previous transitions, and how does this translate into ways future transitions might be handled?
- Does my client have a sense of self that connects with all the roles and parts that he or she is? If not, how can I foster the development of self at this time?
- Is my client living out a version of "self" that is now false for the issues and life phase he or she is in? Does my client need help from me and during follow-up to shift from a false self to a real self?

- Does my client have a spiritual life? How does he or she describe it, and how can I explore ways to deepen it within my client's framework?
- Is it appropriate to talk about death and dying with my client at this time?

BASIC LIBRARY FOR COACHES

Midlife Development

*Belsky, J. K. *Here Tomorrow: Making the Most of Life After Fifty.* Baltimore, Md.: Johns Hopkins University Press, 1988. Projection of life issues from age fifty on, written by a New York City psychologist.

*Bergquist, W. H., and Associates. *In Our Fifties: Voices of Men and Women Reinventing Their Lives.* San Francisco: Jossey-Bass, 1993. Valuable for those worried about being over fifty.

Conway, J., and Conway, S. *Women in Midlife Crisis.* Wheaton, Ill.: Tyndale, 1998.

Farrell, M. P., and Rosenberg, S. D. *Men at Midlife.* Boston: Auburn House, 1981.

Galbraith, M. W., and Cohen, N. H. *Mentoring: New Strategies and Challenges.* San Francisco: Jossey-Bass, 1995.

*Gerzon, M. *Listening to Midlife: Turning Your Crisis into a Quest.* Boston: Shambhala, 1996. A warm, forthright conversation on midlife issues and how to deal with them.

Hagestad, G. O. "The Aging Society as a Context for Family Life." *Daedalus,* 1986, *115,* 119–139.

Hanin, I., Yoshida, M., and Fisher, A. (eds.). *Alzheimer's and Parkinson's Diseases: Recent Developments.* New York: Plenum, 1995.

*Helson, R. "Personality Change in Women from the Early 40s to the Early 50s." *Psychology and Aging,* 1992, *7,* 46–55.

Helson, R. "Women's Difficult Times and the Rewriting of the Life Story." *Psychology of Women Quarterly,* 1995, *16,* 331–347.

Helson, R., and Moane, G. "Personality Change in Women from College to Midlife." *Journal of Personality and Social Psychology,* 1987, *53,* 176–186.

*Helson, R., Steward, A. J., and Ostrove, J. "Identity in Three Cohorts of Midlife Women." *Journal of Personality and Social Psychology,* 1995, *69,* 554–557.

*Hollis, J. *The Middle Passage: From Misery to Meaning in Midlife.* Toronto: Inner City, 1993.

*Hudson, F. M. *LifeLaunch: A Passionate Guide to the Rest of Your Life.* Santa Barbara, Calif.: Hudson Institute Press, 1996. A workbook for composing chapters and life transitions of adult lives throughout the life cycle.

*Hudson, F. M. *The Adult Years: Mastering the Art of Self Renewal.* (rev. ed.) San Francisco: Jossey-Bass, 1999. Outlines the maturation process and human potential of adults and describes each adult decade.

Karp, D. A. "A Decade of Reminders: Changing Age Consciousness Between Fifty and Sixty Years Old." *The Gerontologist,* 1988, *28,* 727–738. Presents the voice of a cohort group reporting significant changes in their own outlook on life.

Landrum, G. N. *Profiles of Female Genius: Thirteen Creative Women Who Changed the World.* New York: Prometheus, 1995.

Landrum, G. N. *Profiles of Genius: Thirteen Creative Men Who Changed the World.* New York: Prometheus, 1995.

Landrum, G. N. *Profiles of Power and Success: Fourteen Geniuses Who Broke the Rules.* New York: Prometheus, 1996.

Landrum, G. N. *Profiles of Black Success: Thirteen Creative Geniuses Who Changed the World.* New York: Prometheus, 1997.

Lyell, R. (ed.). *Middle Age, Old Age: Short Stories, Poems, Plays, and Essays on Aging.* New York: Harcourt Brace Jovanovich, 1980. A brilliant way to convey the feelings of the ages.

McFarland, B., and Watson-Rouslin, V. *My Mother Was Right: How Today's Women Reconcile with Their Mothers.* San Francisco: Jossey-Bass, 1998. Describes how baby boomer women have made peace with their mothers.

Neugarten, B. L. "The Awareness of Middle Age." In *Middle Age and Aging.* Chicago: University of Chicago Press, 1968. A standard reference on middle age.

*Neugarten, B. L. (ed.). *Middle Age and Aging.* Chicago: University of Chicago Press, 1968. A book filled with articles by many top experts in adult studies.

Peterson, W. E., and Stewart, A. J. Antecedents and Contexts of Generativity Motivation at Midlife. *Psychology and Aging,* 1996, *11,* 21–33.

Ryff, C. D., Lee, Y. H., Essex, M. J., and Pamela, A. "My Children and Me: Midlife Evaluations of Grown Children and of Self." *Psychology and Aging,* 1994, *9,* 195–205.

*Schlossberg, N. K., and Entine, A. D. *Counseling Adults.* New York: Springer, 1995. One of the earliest applications of the adult development knowledge to the lives of adults outside the field of psychotherapy.

Schreiber, L. *Midstream.* New York: The Lyons Press, 1996.

Sharp, D. *The Survival Papers: Anatomy of a Midlife Crisis.* Toronto: Inner City, 1988. A Jungian perspective.

Sheehy, G. *The Silent Passage: Menopause.* New York: Pocket Books, 1998.

*Troll, L. E. *Early and Middle Adulthood.* Belmont, Calif.: Wadsworth, 1984. Concise, accurate information.

Fiftysomethings

Belsky, J. K. *Here Tomorrow: Making the Most of Life After Fifty.* Baltimore, Md.: Johns Hopkins University Press, 1988.

Bergquist, W. H., and Associates. *In Our Fifties: Voices of Men and Women Reinventing Their Lives.* San Francisco: Jossey-Bass, 1993.

*Hudson, F. M. *LifeLaunch: A Passionate Guide to the Rest of Your Life.* Santa Barbara, Calif.: Hudson Institute Press, 1996. A workbook for composing chapters and life transitions of adult lives throughout the life cycle.

*Hudson, F. M. *The Adult Years: Mastering the Art of Self Renewal.* (rev. ed.) San Francisco: Jossey-Bass, 1999.

Karp, D. A. "A Decade of Reminders: Changing Age Consciousness Between Fifty and Sixty Years Old." *The Gerontologist,* 1988, *28,* 727–738.

*Rubin, B. M. *Fifty on Fifty: Wisdom, Inspiration, and Reflections on Women's Lives Well Lived.* New York: Warner, 1998. Stories of fifty-year-old women.

Spiritual Coaching

Atthreya, N. H. *Spiritual Culture in the Corporate Drama.* Bombay, India: The Indian Centre for Encouraging Excellence, 1997. A book in the form of a long poem, seeking to evoke work role excellence from a spiritual place in each worker.

Berman, M. *The Reenchantment of the World.* Ithaca, NY: Cornell University Press, 1981.

*Bianchi, E. C. *Aging as a Spiritual Journey.* New York: Crossroad, 1987. Written by a respected authority on aging; helpful for spiritual coaching.

*Bly, R. (ed.). *The Soul Is Here for Its Own Joy: Sacred Poems from Many Cultures.* Hopewell, N.J.: Ecco, 1995. A collection of mostly unknown poems about the soul's function in human life and cultures.

*Bolman, L. G., and Deal, T. E. *Leading with Soul: An Uncommon Journey of Spirit.* San Francisco: Jossey-Bass, 1995.

*Brussat, F., and Brussat, M. A. *Spiritual Literacy: Reading the Sacred in Everyday Life.* New York: Scribner, 1996. Readings for finding sacredness in the ordinary experiences of our lives.

*Coles, R. *The Spiritual Life of Children.* Boston: Houghton Mifflin, 1990.

Cox, A. *Redefining Corporate Soul: Linking Purpose and People.* Chicago: Irwin, 1996.

Edwards, T. *Living Simply Through the Day: Spiritual Survival in a Complex Age.* New York: Paulist Press, 1998.

Fowler, J. *Stages of Faith: The Psychology of Human Development and the Quest for Meaning.* New York: Harper & Row, 1995. Proposes stages of development in faith throughout the life cycle.

*Frankl, V. E. *Man's Search for Meaning.* New York: Washington Square Press, 1998.

Greyson, B., and Flynn, C. P. *The Near-Death Experience.* Chicago: Thomas, 1984.

*Hammerschlag, C. A., and Silverman, H. D. *Healing Ceremonies: Creating Personal Rituals for Spiritual, Emotional, Physical, and Mental Health.* New York: Perigee, 1997. A practical book written by two physicians who discuss the social power of life's turning-points (rituals) throughout the life cycle.

Hillman, J. *The Soul's Code: In Search of Character and Calling.* New York: Random House, 1996. Describes the part of each of us that transcends definition and control.

Hope, J. *The Secret Language of the Soul.* San Francisco: Chronicle, 1997. Beautiful illustrations of soulful symbolism from many cultures, with narrations.

Hopkins, E., and Associates. *Working with Groups on Spiritual Themes: Structured Exercises in Healing,* Vol. 2. Duluth, Minn.: Whole Persons Associates, 1995. Useful exercises.

Inge, W. R. *Personal Religion and the Life of Devotion.* Kessinger Publishing, 1997. A basic reader in the field.

James, W. *The Varieties of Religious Experience.* New York: American Library, 1987 (originally published in 1902). A classic that remains crisp and insightful.

Johnston, W. *Silent Music: The Science of Meditation.* Fordham University Press, 1997.

*Moore, T. *Care of the Soul: A Guide for Cultivating Depth and Sacredness in Everyday Life.* New York: HarperCollins, 1994. A simple, straightforward book on everyday spirituality.

Morgan, F. E. *Living the Martial Way: A Manual for the Way a Modern Warrior Should Think.* Fort Lee, N.J.: Barricade Books, 1992. A unique book on being centered.

Murphy, J. S., and Hudson, F. M. *The Joy of Old: A Guide to Successful Elderhood.* Altadena, Calif.: Geode Press, 1998.

Neihardt, J. G. *Black Elk Speaks: Being the Life Story of a Holy Man of the Oglala Sioux.* Lincoln: University of Nebraska Press, 1988. An important book for understanding the beliefs of American Indians.

Ostow, M., and Scharfstein, B-A. *The Need to Believe.* Madison, Conn.: International Universities Press, 1991. An examination of spiritual beliefs in various cultures and how they keep hope and values alive.

*Owen, H. *SPIRIT: Transformation and Development in Organizations.* Potomac, Md.: Abbott Publishing, 1987.

*Peck, M. S. *The Road Less Traveled and Beyond: Spiritual Growth in an Age of Anxiety.* New York: Simon and Schuster, 1997. About consciousness, learning and growth, personal and organizational life choices, and the stages of spiritual growth.

*Pipher, M. *Another Country: Navigating the Emotional Terrain of our Elders.* New York: Riverhead, 1999.

*Prather, H., and Prather, G. *Spiritual Parenting: A Guide to Understanding and Nurturing the Heart of Your Child.* New York: Harmony Book, 1996.

Roof, W. C. *A Generation of Seekers: The Spiritual Journeys of the Baby Boom Generation.* New York: HarperCollins, 1993. Analyzes a survey of boomer attitudes.

Smart, N. *The Religious Experience of Mankind.* New York: Prentice Hall, 1997. A fine summary of the world's religions.

Stokes, K. *Faith is a Verb.* Mystic, Conn.: 23rd Publications, 1989. Proposes that faith is the unfolding tapestry of a person's life.

Thompson, F. *The Hound of Heaven.* Wilton, Conn.: Morehouse Press, 1986. A haunting poem of the voice in pursuit of us all.

*Thompson, P. *Finding Your Own Spiritual Path: An Everyday Guidebook.* New York: HarperCollins, 1994. A basic primer to spiritual development.

Coaching Elder Women

Armstrong, A., and Donahue, M. R. *On Your Own: A Widow's Passage.* Chicago: Dearborn, 1996.

Barusch, A. S. *Older Women in Poverty: Private Lives and Public Policies.* New York: Springer, 1994.

*Hayes, C. L., and Deren, J. M. (eds.). *Pre-retirement Planning for Women: Program Design and Research.* New York: Springer, 1990.

Lesnoff-Caravaglia, G. (ed.). *The World of the Older Woman: Conflicts and Resolutions.* New York: Human Sciences, 1984. A ground-breaking publication.

Pretat, J. R. *Coming to Age: The Croning Years and Late-Life Transformation.* Toronto: Inner City, 1994.

*Scott, L., with K. Schremp, B. Soldz, and B. Weiss. *Wise Choices Beyond Midlife: Women Mapping the Journey Ahead.* Watsonville, Calif.: Papier-Mache Press, 1997. A practical book for women over sixty who want to plan their lives proactively: relationships, money, health, and more.

*Stanford, B. *Gift of a Lifetime: A Woman's Guide to Triumphant Aging.* Cambria, Calif.: Lodge Hill Press, 1997. An original, autobiographical account of one person's experience of aging as a gigantic gift.

*Walker, B. G. *The Crone: Woman of Age, Wisdom, and Power.* New York: HarperCollins, 1988.

Coaching for Wisdom in Elderhood

Baltes, P. B., and Smith, J. "Toward a Psychology of Wisdom and Its Ontogenesis." In R. J. Sternberg (ed.), *Wisdom: Its Nature, Origins, and Development.* Cambridge, England: Cambridge University Press, 1990.

*Baltes, P. B., Smith, J., and Staudinger, U. M. "Wisdom and Successful Aging." In T. B. Sonderegger (ed.), *Nebraska Symposium on Motivation, 1991.* Lincoln: University of Nebraska Press, 1992.

Barkow, J. H., Cosmides, L., and Tooby, J. (eds.). *The Adapted Mind: Evolutionary Psychology and the Generation of Culture.* New York: Oxford University Press, 1992.

Bayley, N., and Oden, M. "The Maintenance of Intellectual Ability in Gifted Adults." *Journal of Gerontology,* 1955, *10,* Section B, 1, 133ff.

Walker, B. G. *The Crone: Woman of Age, Wisdom, and Power.* New York: HarperCollins, 1988.

Retirement-Protirement Choices

Bradford, L. P. *Preparing for Retirement: A Program for Survival.* San Diego, Calif.: University Associates, 1981.

Gibson, R. C. "The Black American Retirement Experience." In J. Jackson, L. M. Chatters, and R. J. Taylor (eds.), *Aging in Black America.* Newbury Park, Calif.: Sage, 1993.

Guillemard, A. M., and Rein, M. "Comparative Patterns of Retirement: Recent

Trends in Developed Societies." *Annual Review of Sociology*, 1993, *19*, 469–503.

Pifer, A., and Bronte, L. (eds.). *Our Aging Society: Paradox and Promise.* New York: Norton, 1986. Perhaps the best book available for understanding how the current society evolved its notions of aging and its social options.

*Pollan, S. M., and Levine, M. "The Rise and Fall of Retirement." *Worth Magazine,* Dec./Jan. 1995, 67–74.

Quinn, J. F., and Kozy, M. "The Role of Bridge Jobs in the Retirement Transition: Gender, Race, and Ethnicity." *Gerontologist,* 1996, *36,* 363–372.

Quirk, D. A. "The Aging Network: An Agenda for the Nineties and Beyond." *Generations,* 1991, *15*(3), 23–26.

Rabbitt, P. D., Donlan, C., McInnes, L., Watson, P., and Bent, N. "Unique and Interactive Effects of Depression, Age, Socioeconomic Advantage, and Gender on Cognitive Performance of Normal Healthy Older People." *Psychology and Aging,* 1995, *10,* 307–313.

Reitzes, D. C., Mutran, E. J., and Fernandez, M. E. "Does Retirement Hurt Well-Being? Factors Influencing Self-Esteem and Depression Among Retirees and Workers." *Gerontologist,* 1996, *26,* 649–656.

Rountree, C. *On Women Turning 60: Embracing the Age of Fulfillment.* New York: Three Rivers Press, 1997. Reports of successful sixty-year-old women.

*Wall, G., and V. F. Collins. *Your Next Fifty Years: A Completely New Way to Look at How, When and If You Should Retire.* New York: Henry Holt, 1997.

Coaching Around Retirement-Protirement Choices

*Ballard, J., and Ballard, P. *Beating the Age Game: Redefining Retirement.* New York: Mastermedia Limited, 1993. A source of good advice.

Bradford, L. P., and Bradford, M. I. *Retirement: Coping with Emotional Upheavals.* Chicago: Nelson-Hall, 1979. A unique book on retirement because it focuses upon emotional issues: losses, loneliness, marital adjustments, and transition management.

*Fetridge, G. A. *The Adventure of Retirement: It's About More Than Just Money.* New York: Prometheus, 1998. Looks at the life issues of the retirement years.

*Marsh, D. L. *Retirement Careers: Combining the Best of Work and Leisure.* Charlotte, Vt.: Williamson, 1991. Argues that having "work" is essential to life during retirement but that it can take many forms: part-time, hobbies, volunteering.

Monk, A. (ed.). *The Age of Aging: A Reader in Social Gerontology.* New York: Prometheus, 1993. A useful overview of the remarkable changes taking place in the meaning of "aging."

Murphy, J. S., and Hudson, F. M. *The Joy of Old: A Guide to Successful Elderhood.* Altadena Calif.: Geode Press, 1998.

Otterbourg, R. K. *Retire & Thrive.* Washington, D.C.: Kipplinger, 1995. A book of stories of people who have successfully retired, along with information on retirement planning.

*Pollan, S. M., and Levine, M. "The Rise and Fall of Retirement." *Worth Magazine,* Dec./Jan. 1995, 67–74. An excellent article on how the United States invented "retirement" and how little retirement relates to the human, developmental challenges and possibilities of persons over sixty-five.

Sonnenfeld, J. *The Hero's Farewell: What Happens When CEOs Retire.* New York: Oxford, 1988. A brilliant book on four styles CEOs have of leaving: the monarch, the general, the ambassador, and the governor.

*Wall, G., and Collins, V. F. *Your Next Fifty Years: A Completely New Way to Look at How, When, and If You Should Retire.* New York: Henry Holt, 1997.

Coaching Parents and Other Elders

Buckingham, R. W. (ed.). *When Living Alone Means Living at Risk: A Guide for Caregivers and Families.* New York: Prometheus, 1995.

Daly, E. J. *Thy Will Be Done: A Guide to Wills, Taxation, and Estate Planning for Older Persons.* (rev. ed.) New York: Prometheus, 1998.

Down, I. M., and Down, S. *Between Home and Nursing Home: The Board and Care Alternative.* New York: Prometheus, 1997.

Falk, U. A. *On Our Own: Independent Living for Older Persons.* New York: Prometheus, 1993.

*Greenbert, V. E. *Children of a Certain Age: Adults and Their Aging Parents.* Lexington, 1993. A well-researched study of how elderly parents can relate with genuine friendship while there is still time to heal old wounds.

*Hooyman, N. R., and Lustbader, W. *Taking Care of Your Aging Family Members: A Practical Guide.* New York: Free Press, 1993.

Kenny, J., and Spicer, S. *Eldercare: Coping with Late-Life Crisis.* New York: Prometheus, 1994.

*Morris, V. *How to Care for Aging Parents.* New York: Workman, 1996. By far the most comprehensive and informed book for caring for the parents who cared for you.

*Prather, H., and Prather, G. *Spiritual Parenting: A Guide to Understanding and Nurturing the Heart of Your Child.* New York: Harmony Books, 1996.

*Scott, L., with K. Schremp, B. Soldz, and B. Weiss. *Wise Choices Beyond Midlife: Women Mapping the Journey Ahead.* Watsonville, Calif.: Papier-Mache Press, 1997. A practical book for women over sixty who want to plan their lives proactively—relationships, money, health, and more.

*Waters, E. B., and Goodman, J. *Empowering Older Adults: Practical Strategies for Counselors.* San Francisco: Jossey-Bass, 1989. Offers strategies for helping older clients maintain a maximum of dignity and independence in their lives by designing a fulfilling life after retirement and learning to live with deficits.

Coaching Late Elderhood

Adler, L. P. *Centenarians: The Bonus Years.* Santa Fe: N.M.: Health Press, 1995.

*Hendricks, J. (ed.). *The Meaning of Reminiscence and Life Review.* Amityville, NY: Baywood 1995.

Pollock, G. H., and Greenspan, S. L. *The Course of Life, Vol. VI: Late Adulthood.* Madison, Conn.: International Universities Press, 1991.

Poon, L. W., Rubin, D. C., and Wilson, B. A. (eds.). *Everyday Cognition in Adulthood and Later Life.* Cambridge, England: Cambridge University Press, 1992.

Sarton, M. *Encore: Journal of the 80th Year.* New York: Norton, 1995.

*Troll, L. E., and Skaff, M. M. "Perceived Continuity of Self in Very Old Age." *Psychology and Aging,* 1997, *12,* 162–169.

Walker, B. G. *The Crone: Woman of Age, Wisdom, and Power.* New York: HarperCollins, 1988.

Wykle, M. L., Kahana, E., and Kowal, J. (eds.). *Stress and Health Among the Elderly.* New York: Springer, 1992.

Dying: The Final Transition

*Albom, M. *Tuesdays with Morrie: An Old Man, a Young Man, and Life's Greatest Lesson.* New York: Doubletree, 1997. A beautiful story of how a younger man attended to an older, dying man as they coached each other.

*Appleton, M., and Henschell, T. *At Home with Terminal Illness: A Family Guide to Hospice in the Home.* Englewood Cliffs, N.J.: Prentice Hall, 1995.

Baier, K. *Problems of Life & Death: A Humanist Perspective.* New York: Prometheus, 1996.

*Byock, I. *Dying Well: The Prospect for Growth at the End of Life.* New York: Riverhead, 1997. A practical book for coaching people who are dying, with chapters by experts in the field.

*Cason-Reiser, G., Demoratz, M., and Reiser, R. *Dying 101: A Short Course on Living for the Terminally Ill.* Laguna Beach, Calif.: Pushing the Envelope Publications, 1995.

Jamison, S. *Assisted Suicide: A Compassionate and Responsible Guide for Helping Professionals.* San Francisco: Jossey-Bass, 1998. Provides coaches with a range of ethical, emotional, and practical concerns surrounding assisted dying, along with suggestions, criteria, and techniques.

Kalish, R. A. *Death, Grief, and Caring Relationships.* Monterey, Calif.: Brooks/Cole, 1985. One of the finest books written about the meaning of death and the grieving process.

*Nuland, S. B. *How We Die: Reflections on Life's Final Chapter.* New York: Knopf, 1994. Provides detailed descriptions of the doors to death, and engages readers in thinking about this unthinkable final moment in life.

*Rando, T. A. *Grieving: How to Go on Living When Someone You Love Dies.* San Francisco: Jossey-Bass, 1994. Identifies what to do and how; provides tools, guidelines, and facts for coaches working with grieving clients.

*Rosen, E. J. *Families Facing Death: Family Dynamics of Terminal Illness, A Guide for Health-Care Professionals and Volunteers.* San Francisco: Jossey-Bass, 1996. A practical guide.

*Sanders, C. M. *Grief: The Mourning After.* New York: Wiley, 1998. A basic primer with stories and examples

Sankar, A. *Dying at Home.* Baltimore, Md.: Johns Hopkins University Press, 1991.

Schreiber, L. *Midstream.* New York: Lyons Ferry, 1996. A personal account of a man's own death.

Shirk, E. *After the Stroke: Coping with America's Third Leading Cause of Death.* New York: Prometheus, 1992.

*Tatelbaum, J. *The Courage to Grieve.* New York: Harper & Row, 1984. One of the best books on the grieving process ever written.

Coaching for Dying

Baird, R. M., and Rosenbaum, S. E. (eds.). *Euthanasia: The Moral Issues.* New York: Prometheus, 1996.

*Bianchi, E. C. *Aging as a Spiritual Journey.* New York: Crossroad, 1987. Helpful for spiritual coaching.

*Booth, W. *The Art of Growing Older.* Chicago: University of Chicago Press, 1996. A reader with many references about growing older.

Brubaker, T. H. *Later Life Families.* Newbury Park, Calif.: Sage, 1985.

*Carter, J. *The Virtues of Aging.* New York: Ballantine, 1998. A look at the "up" side of being old.

Cherlin, A., and Furstenberg, F. F., Jr. *The New American Grandparent: A Place in the Family, a Life Apart.* Cambridge, Mass.: Harvard University Press, 1992.

Deichman, E. S., and Kociecki, R. *Working with the Elderly.* New York: Prometheus, 1996.

Donnelly, J. (ed.) *Suicide: Right or Wrong?* (2nd ed.) New York: Prometheus, 1998.

*Downs, H. *Fifty to Forever.* Nashville, Tenn.: Nelson, 1994. Inspiring and accurate.

Erikson, E. H., Erikson, J. M., and Kivnick, H. Q. *Vital Involvement in Old Age.* New York: Norton, 1994.

*Friedan, B. *The Fountain of Age.* New York: Simon and Schuster, 1993. A powerful treatise on positive aging.

Guide to Choosing a Nursing Home. U.S. Department of Health and Human Services, Health Care Financing Administration, Pub. No. HCFA–02174.

*Hayflick, L. *How and Why We Age.* New York: Ballantine, 1996.

*Hess, B. B., and Markson, E. W. *Growing Old in America.* (4th ed.) New Brunswick, N.J.: Transaction, 1995. A book of readings by experts in their fields.

Karp, D. A. "A Decade of Reminders: Changing Age Consciousness Between Fifty and Sixty Years Old." *The Gerontologist,* 1988, 28, 727–738.

*Larue, G. A. *Gero-Ethics: A New Vision of Growing Old in America.* New York: Prometheus, 1992. A technical book on changing disengagement through ageism and retirement into active roles for elders.

*Mahoney, D., and Restak, R. *The Longevity Strategy.* New York: Wiley, 1998. Recommends ways adults can promote healthy and conscious living.

*Rowe, J. W., and Kahn, R. L. *Successful Aging.* New York: Pantheon, 1998. Current information on promoting learning and development throughout the aging process.

Sarton, M. *Encore: Journal of the 80th Year.* New York: Norton, 1995. A book about the experience of recovering from a stroke.

Schachter-Shalomi, Z., and Miller, R. S. *From Age-ing to Sage-ing: A Profound New Vision of Growing Older.* New York: Warner, 1997. An inspirational book on aging, without a rich database.

*Thau, R. D., and Heflin, J. S. (eds.). *Generations Apart: Xers vs. Boomers vs. the Elderly.* New York: Prometheus, 1997.

Toseland, R. W. *Group Work with Older Adults.* New York: Springer, 1995. Breaking new ground for coaches to work with older adults.

Turner, J. S., and Helms, D. B. *Lifespan Development.* Orlando, Fla.: Holt, Rinehart and Winston, 1997. A solid overview of the possibilities for human development.

Death

Aries, P. *The Hour of Our Death.* Oxford, England: Oxford University Press, 1991.

Baird, R. M., and Rosenbaum, S. E. (eds.). *Euthanasia: The Moral Issues.* New York: Prometheus, 1996.

*Becker, E. *The Denial of Death.* New York: Free Press, 1997. Offers the freedom and insight of a dying man.

*Buckingham, R. W. *The Handbook of Hospice Care.* New York: Prometheus, 1997. Details the role of each member of the hospice team in providing care based on the needs of patients and families.

*Byock, I. *Dying Well: The Prospect for Growth at the End of Life.* New York: Riverhead, 1997. A study of human growth in the dying process.

Callahan, D. *The Troubled Dream of Life: In Search of a Peaceful Death.* New York: Touchstone, 1996. An ethical exploration of ways to live with mortality, both personally and as a society.

de Beauvoir, S. *A Very Easy Death.* New York: Pantheon, 1984.

DeSpelder, L. A., and Strickland, A. L. *The Last Dance. Encountering Death and Dying.* Palo Alto, Calif.: Mayfield, 1998.

Dickenson, D., and Johnson, M. (eds.). *Death, Dying, & Bereavement.* London: Sage, 1993.

Firth, S. "Approaches to Death in Hindu and Sikh Communities in Britain." In D. Dickenson and M. Johnson (eds.), *Death, Dying, & Bereavement.* London: Sage, 1993.

Fulton, R. "The Contemporary Funeral: Functional or Dysfunctional?" In H. Wass and R. A. Neimeyer (eds.), *Dying: Facing the Facts.* Washington, D.C.: Taylor & Francis, 1995.

Jacobs, S. C., Kosten, T. R., Stanislav, V., Ostfeld, A. M., and Berkman, L. "Attachment Theory and Multiple Expressions of Grief." *Omega,* 1987–1988, *18,* 41–52.

Jamison, S. *Assisted Suicide: A Compassionate and Responsible Guide for Helping Professionals.* San Francisco: Jossey-Bass, 1998.

*Kalish, R. A. *Death, Grief, and Caring Relationships.* Monterey, Calif.: Brooks/Cole, 1985. A well-written book on the meaning of death, the process of dying, grief and bereavement, and caring relationships.

*Kübler-Ross, E. *Death: The Final Stage of Growth.* Englewood Cliffs, N.J.: Prentice Hall, 1975. A standard reference.

Kübler-Ross, E. *On Death and Dying.* New York: Simon and Schuster, 1997. Her original treatise on the stages of grieving and letting go.

Leenaars, A. (ed.). *Lifespan Perspectives on Suicide.* New York: Plenum, 1991.

Lentzner, H. R., Pamuk, E. R., Rhodenhiser, R. R., and Powell-Griner, E. "The Quality of Life in the Year before Death." *American Journal of Public Health,* 1992, *82,* 1093–1098.

McIntosh, J. L., and Associates. *Elder Suicide: Research, Theory, and Treatment.* San Antonio, Tex.: The Psychological Corporation, 1994.

*Mor, V. *Hospice Care Systems. Structure, Process, Costs, and Outcome.* New York: Springer, 1987.

Osgood, N. J. *Suicide in Later Life.* Lexington, Mass.: Lexington Books, 1992.

*Rando, T. A. *Grieving: How to Go on Living When Someone You Love Dies.* San Francisco: Jossey-Bass, 1994.

*Sanders, C. M. *Grief: The Mourning After.* New York: Wiley, 1998. A laymen's guide with examples and straightforward language.

*Stroebe, M. S., Stroebe, W., and Hansson, R. O. (eds.). *Handbook of Bereavement: Theory, Research, and Intervention.* Cambridge, England: Cambridge University Press, 1993. Has chapters by most of the experts on bereavement.

*Tatelbaum, J. *The Courage to Grieve: Creative Living, Recovery, and Growth Through Grief.* New York: Harper & Row, 1984.

*Viorst, J. *Necessary Losses.* New York: Fireside, 1998. Tough talk about a difficult subject.

Wass, H., and Neimeyer, R. A. (eds.). *Dying: Facing the Facts.* Washington, D.C.: Taylor & Francis, 1995.

APPENDIX A: COACHING TOOLS—ASSESSMENTS, INVENTORIES, AND TRAINING RESOURCES

Adventure Center—The Adventure Travel Specialists—has a brochure on vacations that challenge clients to learn and grow. Write: Adventure Center, 1311 63rd Street, Suite 200, Emeryville, CA 94608. Call 800-227-8747.

American Demographics Books issues lists of helpful books for understanding the social trends: leisure, baby boomers, lifestyle marketing, working with Generation X, targeting transitions, and such. Write to them at American Demographic Books, PO Box 68, Ithaca, NY 14851. Call 800-828-1133 or access their website [www.demographics.com].

Other Sources

Andrulis, R. S. *Adult Assessment: A Source Book of Tests and Measures of Human Behavior.* (rev. ed.) Springfield, Ill.: Charles C. Thomas, 1991.

Barbazette, J. *Successful New-Employee Orientation.* San Francisco: Jossey-Bass, 1994. Helps groups assess, plan, conduct, and evaluate their programs. 128 pages. Call 800-274-4434.

Beels, C., Hopson, B., and Scally, M. *Assertiveness, A Positive Process.* San Francisco: Jossey-Bass, 1993. A self-development workbook. 85 pages. Call 800-274-4434.

Bellman, G. M. *Getting Things Done When You Are Not in Charge.* San Francisco: Jossey-Bass. 1993. 278 pages. Call 800-323-7445.

Bernstein, B., and Kaye, B. *Invest in Your Values: A Self-Assessment Instrument.* Career Systems, Inc., PO Box 34744, Washington, DC 20043. Call 800-283-8839.

Birkman Method, a profile evaluation of a client's behavior and their career matches. Developed by Roger W. Birkman, Ph.D., Houston, Texas.

Bolton, R. *People Skills.* New York: Touchstone, 1979. An elementary list of people skills.

Borchard, D. *The Passion Revealer and the Skill Profiler.* An assessment that identifies the energy sources of a client and what they relate to for life/career planning.

Burn, B. E. *Flip Chart Power: Secrets of the Masters.* San Francisco: Jossey-Bass, 1996. How to use a flip chart to support the results you are after.

Caldwell, C M. *Performance Appraisal: The Human Touch.* 100 pages.

Canfield, J., and Hansen, M. V. *Chicken Soup for the Soul.* Deerfield Beach, Fla.: Health Communications, Inc., 1993. Stories that touch the human spirit, and can be used as illustrations in your public speaking. This was the first of many Chicken Soup books.

CAPS (Career Ability Placement Survey). San Diego, Calif.: EDITS. Identifies abilities clients need for career planning.

CareerTrack Video & Audio Training Resources. More than 90 performance-boosting programs, including Sexual Harassment, Performance Appraisal, Project Management, Making Change Work, Focused Listening Skills, Dealing with Conflict and Confrontation, Conquering Team Conflict, Presentation Skills, Self-Discipline and Emotional Control, and CareerTrack. MS20-13, 3085 Center Green Drive, Boulder, CO 80301. Call 800-334-1018.

Consalvo, C. *Workplay: Playing to Learn and Learning to Play.* King of Prussia, Penn.: HRDQ, 1992. Call 800-633-4533.

COPS (Career Occupational Preference System). San Diego, Calif.: EDITS. Identifies key areas of career interests of clients.

Counseling Psychologist, 1981, *9*(3), on Leisure Counseling.

Creative Education Foundation, 1050 Union Road, Buffalo, NY 14224. Call 800-447-2774. Excellent resource for materials on and training opportunities in creative problem solving, using group techniques.

Creative Training Institute. *INSIGHT Inventory.* Helps with team building, personal effectiveness, and stress management. Call 816-931-5606.

D'Andrea, V., and Salovey, P. *Peer Counseling: Skills and Perspectives.* Palo Alto, Calif.: Science and Behavior Books, 1983. A sound presentation of peer counseling skills along with special application perspectives.

Deems, R. S. *Interviewing: More Than a Gut Feeling.* San Francisco: Jossey-Bass, 1995. 100 pages. Call 800-274-4434.

Deems, R. S. *Termination: I Have to Fire Someone.* San Francisco: Jossey-Bass, 1994. 100 pages. Call 800-274-4434.

*Dyer, W. G. *Team Building: Issues and Alternatives.* (2nd ed.) Reading, Mass.: Addison-Wesley, 1987. A simple and straightforward book on small groups, teams, and corporate applications.

Edwards Personal Preference Schedule. San Antonio, Tex.: The Psychological Corporation, 1959. Helps the coach understand motives and preferences of client in relation to future choices. Call 800-211-8378.

Fordyce, J. K., and Weil, R. *Managing with People: A Manager's Handbook of Organization Development Methods.* (2nd ed.) Reading, Mass.: Addison-Wesley, 1971. Concentrates on the management of change and how organization development fits into that change. Covers how to conduct meetings to bring about change, methods for finding out what's going on, methods for better meetings, and methods for changing the quality of relationships.

Gendlin, E. T. *Focusing.* New York: Everest House, 1978. A step-by-step technique that puts clients in touch with their feelings, enabling them to solve their problems.

Glaser, R., Russo, E., and Eckler, M. *Force Field Problem Solving Model.* King of Prussia, Penn.: HRDQ, 1995. Call 800-633-4533.

Gough, H. G. *California Psychological Inventory.* (rev. ed.) Palo Alto, Calif.: Consulting Psychologists Press. Predicts performance and can be used for selecting managers or leaders, advising high school or college students, assessing high-level talent, and identifying creative potential. Highly reliable.

Gutterman, M. *Career Coaching for Parents of Adolescent and Young Adult Children.* Union City: Calif.: G and G Associates, 4741 Michelle Way, Union City, CA 94587.

Hagberg, J., and Leider, R. *The Inventurers—Excursions in Life and Career Renewal.* (3rd ed.) Reading, Mass.: Addison-Wesley, 1988. A 235-page workbook in which clients plan what they want for their lives, inside and out.

Hanks, K. *The Change Navigator: Preparing a New Kind of Leader for an Uncharted Tomorrow.* Menlo Park, Calif.: Crisp, 1994. This is 151 pages about a trip through corporate America preparing leaders for the future. Easy read.

Harper, A., and Harper, R. *Skill-Building for Self-Directed Team Members: A Complete Course.* MW Corporation, 3150 Lexington Ave., Mohegan Lake, NY 10547. 1992. Call 914-962-2933. 200 pages. Training guide.

Hogan, R. Craig, and Champagne, D. W. *Personal Style Inventory.* Bryn Mawr, Penn.: Organization Design and Development. Applies the Myers-Briggs Type categories to different corporate tasks to find congruence of personal style and work style. Call 215-525-9505.

Holland, J. L. *The Self Directed Search: A Guide to Educational and Vocational Planning.* Palo Alto, Calif.: Consulting Psychologists Press.

Hollister, P., and Hollister, R. *The PEOPLE process.* San Francisco: Jossey-Bass, 1992. A training tool for interpersonal communication and team-building, based on Myers-Briggs types. You get a process wheel, profile sheets, and a 63-page booklet filled with tips for using the principles of The PEOPLE process. Call 800-274-4434.

Honey, P., and Mumford, A. *Learning Styles Questionnaire.* King of Prussia, Penn.: HRDQ, 1995. Call 800-633-4533.

Hudson, F. M. *Purpose Cards.* 1997. Useful for helping clients identify their current core values. Attractively formatted and boxed. Call 800-582-4401. E-mail: Hudson@silcom.com; Web site: www.Hudsoninstitute.com

Hudson, F. M. *Life Review: Evaluating Eleven Dimensions of Your Life.* 1998. A resource for coaches to gain information on a client's personal history, nutrition and health, spiritual development, current family and friendships, hobbies and leisure preferences, career development, financial planning, internal obstacles, external threats, stress indicators, and possible future scenarios. 17 pages. Pack of ten Life Reviews, with instructions for using them. Call 800-582-4401.

Independent Living Scales. San Antonio, Tex.: The Psychological Corporation, 1996. Indicate the degree to which adults are capable of caring for themselves and their property. Call 800-211-8378.

International Training Corporation. *Effective Presentation Skills.* Video Training Package. Call 800-274-4434.

Jerome, P. J. *Re-Creating Teams During Transitions.* San Francisco: Jossey-Bass, 1995. 100 pages. Call 800-274-4434.

Jolles, R. L. *How to Run Seminars and Workshops: Presentation Skills for Consultants, Trainers, and Teachers.* San Francisco: Jossey-Bass, 1994. 240 pages. Call 800-274-4434.

Jones, J. E., and Bearley, W. L. *Burnout Assessment Inventory,* with a Trainer Guide. Organization Design and Development, Inc., 101 Bryn Mawr Ave., Ste. 310, Bryn Mawr, PA 19010. Call 215-525-9505.

Jones, J. E., and Bearley, W. L. *Group Development Assessment.* King of Prussia, Penn.: HRDQ, 1988. With facilitator guide. Call 800-633-4533.

Jones, J. E. *The Empowerment Profile.* King of Prussia, Penn.: HRDQ, 1988. Call 800-633-4533.

Jones, J. E. *Group Development Assessment.* King of Prussia, Penn.: HRDQ, 1993. Call 800-633-4533.

Jones, K. *Icebreakers, A Sourcebook of 50 Games, Exercises and Simulations.* Gulf Publishing, Houston, TX 77252. 238 pages. Call 800-231-6275.

Kapes, J. T., Mastie, M., and Moran, C. (eds.). *A Counselor's Guide to Career Guidance Instruments.* Alexandria, Va.: National Career Development Association, 1994. Includes multiple aptitude batteries, interest inventories, measures of work values, career development maturity instruments, card sorts, and instruments for special populations. If you join NCDA (5999 Stevenson Ave., Alexandria, VA 22304) you can get training in the use of these instruments.

Karp, H. B. *The Change Leader: Using a Gestalt Approach with Work Groups.* San Francisco: Jossey-Bass, 1995. 224 pages. Call 800-274-4434.

Kaye, B., and Kaye, N., with Harway, M., Leibowitz, Z., and Farren, C. *Career Leverage Inventory: A Tool for Goal Identification.* Career Systems, Scranton, Pa. 18505. Designed to help employees identify and assess their realistic career options. Call 800-283-8839.

Kilburg, R. R. *Hay/McBer Executive 360.* Boston, Mass. A summative evaluation of executive performance.

Longino, C. F., Jr. *Retirement Migration in America: An Analysis of the Size, Trends, and Economic Impact of the Country's Newest Growth Industry.* Ithaca, N.Y.: American Demographics, 1995.

Management Style Diagnosis Test. Organizational Tests, Ltd., Box 324, Fredericton, N.B. Canada.

MacDonald, I. *Presentation Skills Profile.* King of Prussia, Penn.: HRDQ, 1997. Call 800-633-4533.

Mergenhagen, P. *Targeting Transitions—Marketing to Consumers During Life Changes.* Ithaca, N.Y.: American Demographics, 1994.

Mescon Group. *Planning and Goal Setting for Improved Performance.* San Francisco: Jossey-Bass, 1995. Leader's Guide and Participant's Guide. Call 800-274-4434.

Mink, O., and Owen, K. *Work Values Inventory.* Helps clients determine career choices, motivation, commitment to goals, and job satisfaction. Somerset Consulting Group, Inc, 1208A Somerset Ave., Austin, TX 78753.

Murphy, J. *Conflict Management: Managing Conflict at Work.* 100 pages.

Myers-Briggs Type Indicator. (rev. ed.) Palo Alto, Calif.: Consulting Psychologists Press, 1998. Call 800-624-1765.

New Strategist Editors. *American Women: Who They Are and How They Live.* Ithaca, N.Y.: American Demographics, 1997.

Parenting Stress Index. Helps identify parent-child problem areas. San Antonio, Tex.: 1995. The Psychological Corporation. Call 800-211-8378.

Personal Coaching Styles Inventory: A Self Assessment Tool. CoachWorks Development Group, 5050 Quorum Drive, Ste. 700, Dallas, TX 75240. Call 972-663-0301.

Personal Profile System: A Plan to Understand Self and Others. Performax Systems.

Personal Skills Map: Adult Growth and Development Personal Skills Assessment. People Builders International, Inc., 110 North Lake Drive, Lexington, SC 29072. Call 803-359-1390.

Phillips, K. R. *Coaching Skills Inventory.* King of Prussia, Penn.: HRDQ, 1991. Call 800-633-4533.

Phillips, K. R. *Problem Solving Style Inventory.* King of Prussia, Penn.: HRDQ, 1986. Call 800-633-4533.

Pope, B. "The Initial Interview." In C. E. Walker (ed.), *The Handbook of Clinical Psychology* (pp. 344–390). Homewood, Ill.: Dorsey, 1983.

Porter, E. H. *Job Interactions Inventory.* 1996. Helps people assess the kinds of rewards a given job or position has to offer. Self-administered. Order from Personal Strengths Publishing, Inc., PO Box 2605, Carlsbad, CA 92018. Call 800-624-7347.

Porter, E. H. *Strength Deployment Inventory.* 1996. A self-administered test to identify best ways to use personal strengths in relating to others. Order from Personal Strengths Publishing, Inc., PO Box 2605, Carlsbad, CA 92018. Call 800-624-7347.

Positive Partnering: Building Bridges with Customers. San Francisco: Jossey-Bass, 1994. Video, participant guide, facilitator's guide. Call 800-274-4434.

Prometheus Books has many books relevant to the coaching field, such as *The Adventure of Retirement, The Art of Becoming Human, Live Now, The Total Success Book,* and many more. Order their free catalogue: Prometheus Books, 59 John Glenn Drive, Amherst, NY 14228. Call 800-421-0351.

Psychological Assessment Resources, Inc., has may testing resources for career development and planning, human development, learning, etc. Order their catalogue from PAR, PO Box 998, Odessa, FL 33556. Call 800-331-TEST.

Richey, T. *The Marketer's Visual Tool Kit Using Charts, Graphs, and Models for Strategic Planning and Problem Solving.* Ithaca, N.Y.: American Demographics, 1994.

Rubin, I. M. *The ABC's of Effective Feedback—A Guide for Caring Professionals.* San Francisco: Jossey-Bass, 1998. An essential tool for coaches.

Russo, E. M., and Eckler, M. *Conflict Strategies Inventory.* King of Prussia, Penn.: HRDQ, 1995. Call 800-633-4533.

Russo, E. M., and Eckler, M. *Mastering Conflict.* King of Prussia, Penn.: HRDQ, 1995. Call 800-633-4533.

Schutz, W. *Firo-B, A Test for Emotional Resilience.* Palo Alto, Calif.: Consulting Psychologists Press, 1978. Call 800-624-1765.

Self-Directed Search. Lutz, Fla.: Psychological Assessment Resources, 1994. An easy way for clients to evaluate career preferences. Call 800-331-TEST.

**Skills for Success: The Experts Show the Way.* Bristol, Vt.: Soundview, 1989. A book on how you can be successful, creative, organized, communicative, and able to lead and motivate others. Tells how to, writing on getting the right skills to reach your goals.

Snow, H. *The Power of Team Building Using Ropes Techniques.* San Francisco: Jossey-Bass, 1992. 206 pages. $34.95. Call 800-274-4434.

Sork, T. J. (ed.). *Designing and Implementing Effective Workshops.* San Francisco: Jossey-Bass, 1984. How to create participatory learning environments, workshops, work-oriented learning, evaluating workshops, and such.

Strong-Campbell Interest Inventory of the Strong Vocational Interest Blank Interpretive Report. (rev. ed.) Palo Alto, Calif.: Consulting Psychologists Press, 1994. Interprets client themes and correlates them with occupational areas. Call 800-624-1765.

Super, D. E., and Nevill, D. D. *The Salience Inventory.* Palo Alto, Calif.: Consulting Psychologists Press, 1985. An inventory of activities, attitudes, and values so you can better understand how to coach your clients. Call 800-624-1765.

Suzuki, L. A., Meller, P. J., Ponterotto, J. G. (eds.). *Handbook of Multicultural Assessment—Clinical, Psychological, and Educational Applications.* San Francisco: Jossey-Bass, 1988. Useful for coaches working in multicultural settings.

Taeuber, C. M. *Statistical Handbook on Women in America.* (2nd ed.) Ithaca, N.Y.: American Demographics, 1996.

Target Training International in Scottsdale, AZ, is an excellent producer of DISC-based instruments and other assessments measuring: behavioral style, attitudes and values, sales/customer service performance, team performance, organizational alignment, career strategy, communication fit. The reports are highly personalized (385 + variations) and speak clear, constructive English, not just "graphs." Agnes Mura, a California coach at 310-450-5035 (e-mail: mura@earthlink.net), would be delighted to train coaches or others in how to work with these instruments and also become distributors.

TeamView/360: Evaluating Team Performance. 1994. Using 360-degree feedback, this software provides data that reveal a person's behavioral strengths and areas for growth as a team member. Lead Guide and two IBM diskettes, $49.00. Participant Profile and additional reports, $29.95. Call 808-707-0779.

Tepper, B. B. *Managing Conflict at Work.* 100 pages. Call 800-274-4434.

Tepper, R. *The Consultant's Proposal, Fee, and Contract Problem-Solver.* Ithaca, N.Y.: American Demographics, 1993.

University Associates, Inc. Order their catalogue for descriptions of professional development materials. Includes training techniques, team building, management development, and much more. University Associates, Inc., 8517 Production Ave., San Diego, CA 92121. Call 619-578-5900.

Whole Work Catalog. A reliable source of career books, videos, and software. Order from: The New Careers Center, Inc., 1515 23rd Street, PO Box 339-SK, Boulder, CO 80306. Call 800-634-9024.

Wilder, C., and Fine, D. *Point, Click, and Wow! A Quick Guide to Brilliant Laptop Presentations.* San Francisco: Jossey-Bass, 1996. 144 pages. Call 800-274-4434.

Wilderness Survival. San Francisco: Jossey-Bass, 1990. Simulation text with 12 scenarios and leader's manual. Call 800-274-4434.

Zins, J. E., Kratochwill, T. R., Elliott, S. N. (eds.). *Handbook of Consultation Services for Children.* San Francisco: Jossey-Bass, 1995. A good reference book for coaches working with families and/or children. Call 800-274-4434.

APPENDIX B: TRAINING PROGRAMS FOR COACHES

Academy of Executive Coaching, 1304 DeSoto Ave., Tampa, FL 33606.

Coach for Life, 6343 El Cajon Blvd., Ste. 138, San Diego, CA 92115. Call 888-262-2446. E-mail [Coaching@coachforlife.com].

Coach University, 1971 W. Lumsden Rd., Ste. 331, Brandon, FL 33511. Call 800-482-6224. E-mail [www@coachu.com], website [http://www.coachu.com].

The Coaches Training Institute, 1879 Second Street, San Rafael, CA 94901. Call 415-274-7551. E-mail [coachtraining@aol.com], website [http://www.thecoaches.com].

Entrepreneurship Centre Mentoring Program, 111 Lisgar St., Ottawa, Ontario CANADA, K2P 2L7. One-on-one mentoring by business owners and senior managers.

The Hudson Institute of Santa Barbara, 3463 State St., Ste. 520, Santa Barbara, CA 93105. Call 800-582-4401. E-mail [Hudson@silcom.com] for the coaching seminar. The Professional Coaching Certification Program website is [Hudsoninstitute.com].

Integritas, Inc., 400 Cote Lane #5, Missoula, MT 59802. Programs for exploring spiritual consciousness, $2,100 per year.

Living Your Vision, LYV Enterprises, 1620 184th Ave., N.E., Bellevue, WA 98008. Call 800-897-8707. Program for clarity of vision, purpose, and alignment. E-mail [lyvcoach@aol.com].

Menttium Corporation, 8009 34th Ave. S., Ste. 1350, Bloomington, MN. Call 612-814-2600. Internal corporate programs as well as a one-year executive development program for midlevel women executives.

New Ventures West, PO Box 591525, San Francisco, CA 94159. Call 800-332-4618.

Newfield Network, 9304 Glenville Rd., Silver Spring, MD 20901. Call 301-439-1662. E-mail [Coaching@coachingforlife.com].

Straightline Coaching, 21 Bellair Drive, Dobbs Ferry, NY 10522. Call 914-693-1758.

Strategic Life Planning, 18105 Brittany Drive, SW Seattle, WA 98166. Call 206-444-0590.

Success Unlimited Network, 2016 Lakebreeze Way, Reston, VA 20191. Call 703-716-8374.

AN INVITATION TO THE READER

This book is a living document. To be useful it will need frequent updating, with new resources and additional topics of concern to coaches. Please send any suggestions for improving *The Handbook of Coaching* to Frederic M. Hudson, The Hudson Institute of Santa Barbara, 3463 State Street, Suite 520, Santa Barbara, CA 93105. Send e-mail to Frederic@silcom.com or access the website [Hudsoninstitute.com]; telephone 805-682-3883 or fax 805-569-0025.

OTHER BOOKS BY FREDERIC M. HUDSON

The Adult Years: Mastering the Art of Self-Renewal

Revised Edition. San Francisco: Jossey-Bass, 1999.
This is the basic text of theory for the Hudson Model of Adult Development and Organizational Change; footnotes and reading list contain references for understanding adult renewal.

LifeLaunch—A Passionate Guide to the Rest of Your Life

Revised Edition (coauthored with Pamela D. McLean).
Santa Barbara: Hudson Institute Press, 1996.
This book applies the theory of *The Adult Years* to the lives of adults of all ages and justifies the importance of establishing a profession of coaches and mentors—a how-to-guide-adults book.

The Joy of Old—A Guide to Successful Elderhood

(coauthored with John Murphy).
Altadena, Calif.: Geode Press, 1995.
An original book on the challenges of life after sixty.

INDEX